ECONOMIC AND SOCIAL HISTORY
OF MEDIEVAL EUROPE

Henri Pirenne was born in Verviers, Belgium, in 1862, and was for many years a professor of medieval history at the University of Ghent. His first book to appear in translation was the seven-volume *History of Belgium*, which completely revolutionized the current conceptions of Belgian history. This was followed by *Belgian Democracy: Its Early History, Medieval Cities: Their Origins and the Revival of Trade, Economic and Social History of Medieval Europe*, and *Mohammed and Charlemagne*, which appeared in this country four years after his death in 1935. During his lifetime he received honorary degrees from the universities of Brussels, Oxford, Paris, Leipzig, Tübingen, Manchester, Groningen, Strasbourg, and Bordeaux.

Henri Pirenne

ECONOMIC AND SOCIAL HISTORY OF MEDIEVAL EUROPE

A HARVEST/HBJ BOOK
HARCOURT BRACE JOVANOVICH
NEW YORK AND LONDON

TRANSLATED FROM THE FRENCH BY

I. E. CLEGG

First appeared in 1933 in volume 8 by HENRI PIRENNE,
GUSTAVE COHEN, *and* HENRI FOCILLON *of "Histoire du
Moyen Age"*

First published in England in 1936
First published in the United States in 1937

AA

ISBN 0-15-627533-3

PRINTED IN THE UNITED STATES OF AMERICA

PREFACE TO THE
ENGLISH TRANSLATION

In the following pages I have tried to sketch the character
and general movement of the economic and social evolution of Western Europe from the end of the Roman Empire
to the middle of the fifteenth century. I have tried to en-
visage this great area as a single whole, of which the parts
were in constant communication with each other; in other
words I have adopted an international standpoint and
have been concerned above all to set forth the essential
character of the phenomena described, reducing to a subordinate place the particular forms which they assumed,
not only in different countries but in different parts of
the same country. Thus I have naturally been obliged to
give special prominence to those countries in which economic activity developed most rapidly and most completely during the Middle Ages, such, for instance, as
Italy and the Low Countries, whose direct or indirect
influence may so often be traced in the rest of Europe.

There are still so many gaps in our knowledge that I
have in many cases been obliged to resort to probability
or to conjecture, in order to explain events or to trace
their interconnection. But I have been careful not to resort
to theories, lest I should do violence to the facts. My own
object has been to be guided by the latter, though of course
I cannot flatter myself that I have succeeded. Finally, I
have throughout tried to give as clear an account as possible, even of the most controversial problems.

The necessary references to books, which will enable
the reader to supplement my account or to criticise my
opinions, will be found in the bibliographies attached to

each chapter (which have been specially revised for the English edition). In these I have aimed at including only works which are really valuable, either for the wealth of their contents or for the importance of their conclusions; this explains why I have included a large number of articles in periodicals. I must apologise in advance for the omissions which will easily be found; some are due to my own ignorance, others to the fact that all select bibliographies must necessarily reflect the predilections of their compiler.

HENRI PIRENNE

CONTENTS

TWO. THE TOWNS

THREE. LAND AND THE RURAL CLASSES

FOUR. COMMERCE TO THE END OF THE THIRTEENTH CENTURY

SIX. URBAN ECONOMY AND THE REGULATION OF INDUSTRY

SEVEN. THE ECONOMIC CHANGES OF THE FOURTEENTH AND FIFTEENTH CENTURIES

ECONOMIC AND SOCIAL HISTORY
OF MEDIEVAL EUROPE

INTRODUCTION

In order to understand the economic revival which took place in Western Europe from the eleventh century onwards, it is necessary first of all to glance at the preceding period.

From the point of view which we must here adopt, it is at once apparent that the barbarian kingdoms, founded in the fifth century on the soil of Western Europe, still preserved the most striking and essential characteristic of ancient civilisation, to wit, its Mediterranean character.[1] Round this great land-locked sea all the civilisations of the ancient world had been born; by it they had communicated with one another, and spread far and wide their ideas and their commerce, until at last it had become in a real sense the centre of the Roman Empire, towards which converged the activity of all her provinces from Britain to the Euphrates. But the great sea continued to play its traditional rôle after the Germanic invasions. For the barbarians established in Italy, Africa, Spain and Gaul, it remained the highway of communication with the Byzantine Empire and the relations thus maintained enabled it to foster an economic life, which was simply a

[1] This truth is generally recognised to-day even by historians who consider that the invasions of the fifth century overthrew and transformed western civilisation. See F. Lot in t. I of *Histoire du Moyen Age* (*Histoire Générale*, ed. G. Glotz), p. 347. A. Dopsch, *Wirtschaftliche und soziale Grundlagen der Europäischen Kulturentwickelung aus der Zeit von Caesar bis auf Karl den Grossen*, 2nd ed. (Vienna, 1923–4, 2 vols.), has the merit of having shown that there is no breach in economic history between the period before and after the establishment of the Germans in the Empire.

continuation of that of the ancient world. It will suffice here to recall the activity of Syrian navigation from the fifth to the eighth century between the ports of the West and those of Egypt and Asia Minor, the preservation by the German kings of the Roman gold *solidus*, at once the instrument and the symbol of the economic unity of the Mediterranean basin, and, finally, the general direction of commerce towards the coasts of this sea, which men might still have called, with as much right as the Romans, *Mare nostrum*.

It was only the abrupt entry of Islam on the scene, in the course of the seventh century, and the conquest of the eastern, southern and western shores of the great European lake, which altered the position, with consequences which were to influence the whole course of subsequent history.[2] Henceforth, instead of the age-old link which it had hitherto been between the East and the West, the Mediterranean became a barrier. Though the Byzantine Empire, thanks to its navy, succeeded in repulsing the Moslem offensive from the Aegean Sea, the Adriatic and the southern shores of Italy, the Tyrrhenian Sea fell completely under the domination of the Saracens. They encircled it to the south and the west through Africa and Spain, while the possession of the Balearic Isles, Corsica, Sardinia and Sicily gave them naval bases which completed their mastery over it. From the beginning of the eighth century European commerce in this great maritime quadrilateral was doomed, and the whole economic movement was now directed towards Baghdad. The Christians, says Ibn

[2] H. Pirenne, *Mahomet et Charlemagne*, and *Un contraste économique: Mérovingiens et Carolingiens*, in *Revue belge de philologie et d'histoire*, t. I (1922) and II (1923). *Id.*, *Les villes du Moyen Age*, p. 7 *et seq.* (Brussels, 1927). This opinion has raised objections which it is not possible to meet here. An account of them will be found in H. Laurent, *Les travaux de M. Henri Pirenne sur la fin du monde antique et les débuts du Moyen Age*, in *Byzantion*, t. VII (1932), p. 495 *et seq.*

Kaldun picturesquely, "can no longer float a plank on it."[3] On these coasts, which had once maintained an intercourse based on community of manners, needs and ideas, two civilisations, or rather two foreign and hostile worlds, now faced one another, the worlds of the Crescent and the Cross. The economic equilibrium of antiquity, which had survived the Germanic invasions, collapsed under the invasion of Islam. The Carolingians prevented the Arabs from expanding north of the Pyrenees, but they could not, and, conscious of their impotence, did not even try to recover the sea. The empire of Charlemagne, in striking contrast to Roman and Merovingian Gaul, was essentially a land empire, or (as some would prefer to express it) a continental empire. And from this fundamental fact there necessarily sprang a new economic order, which is peculiar to the early Middle Ages.[4]

Later history, which shows us the Christians borrowing so much from the higher civilisations of the Moslems, should not be allowed to foster illusions about their early relations. It is true that in the ninth century, the Byzantines and their outlying ports on the Italian coast, Naples, Amalfi, Bari, and above all Venice, traded more or less actively with the Arabs of Sicily, Africa, Egypt and Asia Minor. But it was quite otherwise with Western Europe. Here, the antagonism of two faiths face to face kept them in a state of war with each other. The Saracen pirates never ceased to infest the littoral of the Gulf of Lyons, the estuary of Genoa, and the shores of Tuscany and Catalonia. They pillaged Pisa in 935 and 1004, and destroyed Barcelona in 985. Before the beginning of the

---

[3] As Georges Marcais, *Histoire et historiens de l'Algérie,* p. 212 (Paris, 1931), says: "From the moment that Barbary fell under the rule of Islam, for the whole of the Middle Ages, with occasional exceptions, the bridges between it and Christian Europe were almost cut. . . . It became like a province of the Oriental world." I owe the knowledge of Ibn Kaldun's text to a kind communication from M. Marcais.

[4] H. Pirenne, *Un contraste économique.* See above, n. 2.

eleventh century, there is not the slightest trace of any communication between these regions and the Saracen ports of Spain and Africa. The insecurity was so great along the coast that the bishopric of Maguelonne had to be transferred to Montpellier. Nor was the mainland itself safe from attack. We know that in the tenth century the Moslems established a military outpost in the Alps, at Garde-Frainet, whence they held to ransom or massacred the pilgrims and travellers passing from France into Italy. Roussillon in the same period lived in terror of the raids which they carried beyond the Pyrenees. In 846, the Saracen bands had advanced as far as Rome and laid siege to the castle of Saint Angelo. In such conditions the proximity of the Saracens could bring nothing but un-alloyed disaster to the Christians of the West. Too weak to think of taking the offensive, they shrank back upon themselves and abandoned the sea, upon which they dared no longer venture, to their adversaries. In fact, from the ninth to the eleventh century the West was bottled up. Though ambassadors, at long intervals, were still sent to Constantinople, and though pilgrims in fairly large num-bers directed their steps to Jerusalem, they reached their goal only by a long and difficult journey through Illyrium and Thrace, or by crossing the Adriatic to the south of Italy, in Greek boats from Bari. There is thus no justifica-tion for citing their voyages, as is sometimes done, as proof of the persistence of navigation in the Western Mediterranean after the Islamic expansion. It was com-pletely at an end.

Nor did commercial activity survive it, for the Mediter-ranean had been the great artery of commerce. It is easy to show that as long as it remained active it was this navigation which kept up the trade of the ports of Italy, Africa, Spain and Gaul and of their hinterland. The docu-ments, unfortunately all too rare, which we have at our disposal, show beyond a doubt that in all these countries, down to the Arab conquest, a class of professional mer-chants had carried on an export and import trade, the existence of which is incontestable though its importance may perhaps be questioned. Through it, the Roman towns remained the business centres and concentration points of a traffic which extended from the sea-coast to the north, at least as far as the Rhine valley, to which were imported papyrus, spices, eastern wines and oil unloaded on the shores of the Mediterranean.[5]

The closing of the latter through the expansion of Islam in the seventh century necessarily resulted in the very rapid decline of this activity. In the course of the eighth century the interruption of commerce brought about the disappearance of the merchants,[6] and urban life, which had been maintained by them, collapsed at the same time. The Roman cities certainly continued to exist, because they were the centres of diocesan administration, and therefore the bishops resided there and gathered a numerous body of clergy round them, but they lost both their economic significance and their municipal administration. A general impoverishment was manifest. Gold currency disappeared to give place to the silver coinage which the Carolingians were forced to substitute for it. The new monetary system, which they instituted in place of the old Roman gold *solidus,* is clear proof of their rupture with the ancient economy, or, rather, with the Mediterranean economy.

It is manifestly erroneous to consider the reign of Charlemagne, as it almost always is considered, as an era of economic advancement. This is nothing but a delusion.

[5] P. Scheffer-Boichorst, *Die Syrer im Abendlande,* in *Mitteilungen des Instituts für Oesterreichische Geschichtsforschung,* t. VI (1885), p. 521 *et seq.*; L. Bréhier, *Les colonies des Orientaux en Occident au commencement du Moyen Age,* in *Byzantinische Zeitschrift,* t. XII (1903), p. 11 *et seq.* J. Ebersolt, *Orient et Occident,* p. 26 *et seq.* (Paris, 1929): H. Pirenne, *Le commerce du papyrus dans la Gaule Mérovingienne,* in *Comptes rendus des séances de l'Acad. des Inscriptions et Belles-Lettres,* 1928, p. 178 *et seq.*; Id., *Le cellarium fisci,* in *Bull. de la Classe des Lettres de l'Acad. Royale de Belgique,* 1930, p. 201 *et seq.*

[6] But on this point see two articles by E. Sabbé in *Revue belg. de philol. et d'hist.,* 1934–5.

In reality, compared with the Merovingian, the Carolingian period is an era of decadence or even of regression from the commercial point of view.[7] Even had he tried, Charles would have been unable to prevent the inevitable consequences of the disappearance of maritime traffic and the closing of the sea. It is true enough that these consequences did not affect the North with the same intensity as they did the South. During the first half of the ninth century, the ports of Quentovic (to-day Etaples-sur-la-Canche) and Duurstede (on the Rhine, above Utrecht) were fairly frequented, and Frisian boats continued to cross the Scheldt, the Meuse and the Rhine, and to carry on a coasting trade along the shores of the North Sea.[8] But we must beware of envisaging these facts as symptoms of renaissance. They are nothing more than the prolongation of an activity which dated back to the Roman Empire and which persisted during Merovingian times.[9] It is possible, and even probable, that the habitual presence of the imperial court at Aix-la-Chapelle and the necessity of provisioning its very numerous personnel, contributed not only to the maintenance, but even to the development of trade in the neighbouring territories, and made them the only part of the Empire where some commercial activity is still to be observed. But, however that may be, the Northmen soon put an end to this last survival of the past. Before the end of the ninth century Quentovic and Duurstede were plundered and destroyed by them so thoroughly that they were never to rise again from their ruins.

[7] L. Halphen, *Études critiques sur l'histoire de Charlemagne*, p. 239 *et seq.* (Paris, 1921); H. Pirenne, *loc. cit.*, n. 1.

[8] O. Fengler, *Quentowic, seine maritime Bedeutung unter Merowingern und Karolingern*, in *Hansische Geschichtsblätter*, 1907, p. 91 *et seq.*; H. Pirenne, *Draps de Frise ou draps de Flandre?*, in *Vierteljahrschrift für Social-und Wirtschaftsgeschichte*, VII (1909), p. 308 *et seq.*; H. Poelman, *Geschiedenis van den handel van Noordnederland gedurende het Merowingische en Karolingische tijdperk* (Amsterdam, 1908).

[9] F. Cumont, *Comment la Belgique fut romanisée*, 2nd ed. (Brussels), 1919.

It might be, and indeed it has sometimes been, thought, that the valley of the Danube took the place of the Mediterranean as the great route of communication between the East and the West. This might indeed have happened, had it not been rendered inaccessible from the very first by the Avars, and, soon afterwards, by the Magyars. The sources show us no more than the traffic of a few boats loaded with salt from the salt-mines of Strasburg. As for the so-called commerce with the pagan Slavs on the banks of the Elbe and the Saale, it was limited to the interloping operations of adventurers, seeking to supply arms to the barbarians, or buying prisoners of war taken by the Carolingian troops among these dangerous neighbours of the Empire, in order to sell them again as slaves. The capitularies show very clearly that there was no normal and regular traffic on these military frontiers, which were in a state of permanent insecurity.

It is quite plain, from such evidence as we possess, that from the end of the eighth century Western Europe had sunk back into a purely agricultural state. Land was the sole source of subsistence and the sole condition of wealth. All classes of the population, from the Emperor, who had no other revenues than those derived from his landed property, down to the humblest serf, lived directly or indirectly on the products of the soil, whether they raised them by their labour, or confined themselves to collecting and consuming them. Movable wealth no longer played any part in economic life. All social existence was founded on property or on the possession of land. Hence it was impossible for the State to keep up a military system and an administration which were not based on it. The army was now recruited only from among the holders of fiefs and the officials from among the great landowners. In these circumstances, it became impossible to safeguard the sovereignty of the head of the State. If it existed in principle, it disappeared in practice. The feudal system simply represents the disintegration of public authority in the hands of its agents, who, by reason of the very fact that each one of them held a portion of the soil, had become independent and considered the authority with which they were invested as a part of their patrimony. In fact, the appearance of feudalism in Western Europe in the course of the ninth century was nothing but the repercussion in the political sphere of the return of society to a purely rural civilisation.

From the economic point of view the most striking and characteristic institution of this civilisation is the great estate. Its origin is, of course, much more ancient and it is easy to establish its affiliation with a very remote past. There were great landowners in Gaul long before Caesar, just as there were in Germany long before the invasions. The Roman Empire allowed the great Gallic estates to stand and they very rapidly adapted themselves to the organisation which prevailed on the estates of the conquerors. The Gallic *villa* of the imperial era, with its reserve set apart for the proprietor and numerous holdings of *coloni*, represents the same type of exploitation as that described by the Italian agronomists in the time of Cato. It went through the period of the Germanic invasions with hardly a change, Merovingian France preserved it and the Church introduced it beyond the Rhine, step by step as the lands there were converted to Christianity.[10]

Thus the organisation of the great estate was not, in any respect, a new fact. But what was new was the way in which it functioned from the moment of the disappearance of commerce and the towns. So long as the former had been capable of transporting its products and the latter of furnishing it with a market, the great estate had commanded and consequently profited by a regular sale outside. It participated in the general economic activity as a producer of foodstuffs and a consumer of manufactured articles. In other words, it carried on a reciprocal exchange with the outside world. But now it ceased to do

[10] For all this I am content to refer the reader to the excellent account by M. Bloch, *Les caractères originaux de l'histoire rurale française,* p. 67 *et seq.*

this, because there were no more merchants and townsmen. To whom could it sell, when there were no longer any buyers, and where was it to dispose of a produce for which there was no demand, because it was no longer needed? Now that everyone lived off his own land, no one bothered to buy food from outside, and for sheer want of demand, the landowner was obliged to consume his own produce. Thus, each estate devoted itself to the kind of economy which has been described rather inexactly as the "closed estate economy," and which was really simply an economy without markets. It did so not from choice but from necessity, not because it did not want to sell, but because buyers no longer came within its range. The lord made arrangements not only to live on his demesne and the dues of his peasants, but also to produce at home, since he could not procure them elsewhere, the tools and garments which he needed for the cultivation of his lands and the clothing of his servants. Hence the establishment of those workshops or "gynaeceas," so characteristic of the estate organisation of the early Middle Ages, which were simply designed to make up for the absence of commerce and industry.

It is obvious that such a state of things inevitably exposed men to all the hazards of climate. If the harvest chanced to fail, the supplies laid up against a scarcity were soon exhausted and it was necessary to tax all one's wits to get the indispensable grain. Then serfs were sent round the countryside to get it from some more fortunate neighbour, or in some region where abundance reigned. In order to provide them with money the lord caused his plate to be melted down at the nearest mint, or ran into debt with the abbot of a neighbouring monastery. Thus, under the influence of atmospheric phenomena, a spasmodic and occasional commerce existed and kept up an intermittent traffic on the roads and waterways. Similarly, in years of prosperity people sought to sell the surplus of their vintage or their harvest in the same way. Finally salt, a condiment necessary to life, was found only in certain regions, where they had perforce to go and get it. But there is nothing in all this that can be regarded as commercial activity, in the specific and professional sense. The merchant was, so to speak, improvised at the will of circumstances. Sale and purchase were not the normal occupation of anyone; they were expedients to which people had recourse when obliged by necessity. Commerce had so completely ceased to be one of the branches of social activity that each estate aimed at supplying all its own needs. This is why we see abbeys situated in regions without vineyards, such as the Low Countries, leaving no stone unturned in their efforts to obtain the gift of estates in the Seine basin, or in the valleys of the Rhine and the Moselle, so as to be sure each year of replenishing their wine-cellars.[11]

The large number of markets might seem at first sight to contradict the commercial paralysis of the age, for from the beginning of the ninth century they increased rapidly and new ones were continually being founded. But their number is itself proof of their insignificance. Only the fair of St. Denys, near Paris (the fair of Lendit), attracted once a year, among its pilgrims, occasional sellers and buyers from a distance. Apart from it there were only innumerable small weekly markets, where the peasants of the district offered for sale a few eggs, chickens, pounds of wool, or ells of coarse cloth woven at home. The nature of the business transacted appears quite clearly from the fact that people sold *per deneratas,* that is to say, by quantities not exceeding a few pence in value.[12] In short, the utility of these small assemblies was limited to satisfying the household needs of the surrounding population, and also, no doubt, as among the Kabyles to-day, to satisfying that instinct of sociability which is inherent in all men. They constituted the sole distraction offered by a

[11] H. Van Werveke, *Comment les établissements religieux belges se procuraient-ils du vin au haut Moyen Age?* in *Revue belge de philol. et d'hist.*, t. II (1923), p. 643 *et seq.*

[12] *Edictum Pistense,* 20. Boretius, *Capitularia,* t. II, p. 318.

society settled in work on the land. Charlemagne's order to the serfs on his estates not to "run about to markets" shows that they were attracted much more by the desire to enjoy themselves than by considerations of trade.[13]

Thus we seek in vain for professional merchants. None existed, or rather none but the Jews, who alone, from the beginning of the Carolingian era, carried on a regular commerce, so much so that the words *Judaeus* and *mercator* appear almost synonymous. A certain number of them were settled in the south, but the majority came from the Moslem countries of the Mediterranean and reached Western and Northern Europe through Spain. They were the Radanites, perpetual travellers who still kept up a superficial contact with Oriental countries.[14] The commerce in which they engaged was, moreover, exclusively that of spices and precious stuffs, which they laboriously transported from Syria, Egypt and Byzantium to the Carolingian Empire. Through them, a church could procure the incense indispensable to the celebration of the divine offices, and, at long intervals, those rich fabrics of which cathedral treasuries have preserved occasional specimens down to our own day. They imported pepper, a condiment which had become so rare and dear that it was sometimes used instead of money, and enamels or ivories of oriental manufacture, which formed the luxuries of the aristocracy. Thus the Jewish merchants addressed themselves to a very limited clientèle. The profits which they realised must have been substantial, but when full allowance is made for this, their economic rôle cannot be considered as anything but that of accessories. Society lost nothing essential by their disappearance.

Thus, from every point of view, Western Europe, from the ninth century onwards, appears in the light of an essentially rural society, in which exchange and the move-

[13] *Capitulaire de Villis*, 54. *Ibid.*, t. I, p. 88.
[14] On the Jews see the *Livre des routes et des pays* of Ibn Khordadbeh (about 850), translated by Barbier de Maynard, *Journal asiatique*, 1865.

ment of goods had sunk to the lowest possible ebb. The merchant class had disappeared. A man's condition was now determined by his relation to the land, which was owned by a minority of lay and ecclesiastical proprietors, below whom a multitude of tenants were distributed within the framework of the great estates. To possess land was at the same time to possess freedom and power; thus the landowner was also a lord. To be deprived of it, was to be reduced to serfdom; thus the word *vilain* was used both for the peasant living on a domain (*villa*) and for the serf. It is of no importance that here and there among the rural population a few individuals happened to preserve their land and consequently their personal liberty. As a general rule serfdom was the normal condition of the agricultural masses, that is to say, of all the masses. There were, of course, many gradations in this serfdom, for, side by side with men who were still not far removed from the slavery of antiquity, there were to be found descendants of small dispossessed proprietors who had voluntarily commended themselves to the protection of the great. The essential fact was not their legal but their social condition, and socially all who lived on seigneurial soil were now dependents, at once exploited and protected.

In this strictly hierarchical society, the first place, and the most important, belonged to the Church, which possessed at once economic and moral ascendancy. Its innumerable estates were as superior in extent to those of the nobility, as it was itself superior to them in learning. The Church alone, moreover, thanks to the gifts of the faithful and the alms of pilgrims, had at its disposal financial resources which allowed it, in times of scarcity, to lend to necessitous laymen. Furthermore, in a society which had relapsed into general ignorance, it alone still retained those two indispensable instruments of culture, reading and writing, and it was from churchmen that kings and princes had necessarily to recruit their chancellors, their secretaries, their "notaries," in short, the whole lettered personnel without which it was impossible for them to function. From the ninth to the eleventh century the whole business of government was, in fact, in the hands of the Church, which was supreme here, as in the arts. The organisation of its estates was a model which the estates of the nobility sought in vain to equal, for only in the Church were there men capable of drawing up *polyptycha,* keeping registers of accounts, reckoning up receipts and expenditure, and, consequently, balancing them. Thus, the Church was not only the great moral authority of the age, but also the great financial power.

Moreover, the Church's conception of the world was admirably adapted to the economic conditions of an age in which land was the sole foundation of the social order. Land had been given by God to men in order to enable them to live here below with a view to their eternal salvation. The object of labour was not to grow wealthy but to maintain oneself in the position in which one was born, until mortal life should pass into life eternal. The monk's renunciation was the ideal on which the whole of society should fix its gaze. To seek riches was to fall into the sin of avarice. Poverty was of divine origin and ordained by Providence, but it behoved the rich to relieve it by charity, of which the monasteries gave them an example. Let the surplus of their harvests, then, be garnered and distributed freely, just as the abbeys themselves advanced freely sums borrowed from them in cases of need.

"Mutuum date nihil inde sperantes." Lending at interest, or "usury" (to employ the technical term used for it, which now took on the derogatory meaning which it has retained down to our own day), was an abomination. It had been forbidden from the very beginning to the clergy, and from the ninth century the Church succeeded in prohibiting it also to the laity and in reserving it for the jurisdiction of ecclesiastical courts. Moreover, commerce in general was hardly less disreputable than commerce in money, for it too was dangerous to the soul, which it turned away from the contemplation of its latter

end. *"Homo mercator vix aut nunquam potest Deo placere."* [15]

It is easy to see how well these principles harmonised with the facts and how easily the ecclesiastical ideal adapted itself to reality. It provided the justification for a state of things by which the Church itself was the first to benefit. What was more natural than the reprobation of usury, commerce, and profit for profit's sake, in those centuries when each estate was self-supporting and normally constituted a little world of its own? And what could have been more beneficent, when we remember that famine alone compelled men to borrow from their neighbours and hence would at once have opened the door to every abuse of speculation, usury and monopoly, to the irresistible temptation to exploit necessity, if these very abuses had not been condemned by religious morality? Of course, theory and practice are miles apart and the monasteries themselves very often transgressed the Church's order. But, for all that, so deeply did it impress its spirit upon the world, that it took men centuries to grow used to the new practices demanded by the economic revival of the future and to learn to accept as legitimate, without too great a mental reservation, commercial profits, the employment of capital, and loans at interest.

[15] L. Goldschmidt, *Universalgeschichte des Handelsrechts,* t. I, p. 139 (Stuttgart, 1891).

One

THE REVIVAL OF COMMERCE

I. THE MEDITERRANEAN[1]

The irruption of Islam into the basin of the Mediterranean in the seventh century closed that sea to the Christians of the West, but not to all Christians. The Tyrrhenian Sea, it is true, became a Moslem lake, but this was not the fate of the waters which bathed Southern Italy, or of the Adriatic or the Aegean Sea. We have already seen that in these latitudes the Byzantine fleets succeeded in repulsing the Arab invasion, and after the check which it experienced at the siege of Constantinople in 719, the Crescent reappeared no more in the Bosphorus. But the struggle between the two warring faiths continued, with alternations of success and reverse. Masters of Africa, the Arabs were bent on seizing Sicily, which they completely dominated after the capture of Syracuse in 878; but that was the limit of their advance. The south Italian towns, Naples, Gaeta, Amalfi, and Salerno in the west, and Bari in the east, continued to recognise the Emperor at Con-

[1] BIBLIOGRAPHY.—See the works of W. Heyd and A. Schaube, quoted below in the general bibliography, p. 221—H. Kretschmayr, *Geschichte von Venedig*, Gotha, 1905–34, 3 vols.—R. Heynen, *Zur Entstehung des Kapitalismus in Venedig*, Stuttgart-Berlin, 1905.—L. Brentano, *Die byzantinische Volkswirtschaft*, in *Jahrbuch für Gesetzgebung, Verwaltung*, etc., t. XLI, 1917.—H. Pirenne, *Medieval Cities: Their Origins and the Revival of Trade*, translated by Frank D. Halsey, Princeton, 1925.—French edition, *Les villes du Moyen Age*. Brussels, 1927.

stantinople, and so also did Venice, which, at the head of the Adriatic, never had anything seriously to fear from the Saracen expansion.

The tie which continued to unite these ports to the Byzantine Empire was, it is true, not very strong, and it grew steadily weaker. The establishment of the Normans in Italy and Sicily (1029–91) definitely broke it as regards this region. Venice, over which the Carolingians had been unable to establish their control in the ninth century, had been all the more willing to continue under the authority of the Basileus, because he prudently refrained from exerting it, and allowed the town to be gradually transformed into an independent republic. For the rest, if the political relations of the Empire with its distant Italian annexations were not very active, it made amends by carrying on a very lively trade with them. In this respect, they moved in its orbit and, so to speak, turned their backs on the West and looked towards the East. The business of provisioning Constantinople, whose population numbered about a million inhabitants, kept up their exports, and in return the factories and bazaars of the capital furnished them with silks and spices which they could not do without.

For urban life, with all the luxury demands which it made, had not disappeared in the Byzantine Empire as it had done in that of the Carolingians. To pass from the latter to the former, was to pass into another world. Here, economic evolution had not been rudely interrupted by the advance of Islam, and an important maritime commerce continued to supply towns peopled with artisans and professional merchants. No more striking contrast could be imagined than that between Western Europe, where land was everything and commerce nothing, and Venice, a landless city, living only by trade.

Constantinople and the Christian ports of the East soon ceased to be the sole objective of the navigation of the Byzantine towns of Italy and Venice. The spirit of enterprise and the search for gain were too powerful and too necessary to allow religious scruples to prevent them for very long from renewing their former business relations with Africa and Syria, although these were now in the power of the infidels. From the end of the ninth century connections were formed which grew steadily more active. The religion of their customers mattered little to the Italians, provided that they paid. The love of gain, which the Church condemned and stigmatised by the name of avarice, was manifest here in its most brutal form. The Venetians exported to the harems of Egypt and Syria young Slavs, whom they carried off or bought on the Dalmatian coast, and this traffic in "slaves" [2] unquestionably contributed quite as largely to their growing prosperity as did the slave trade of the eighteenth century to that of so many French and English shippers. To this was added the transport of timber and iron, with which the countries of Islam were unprovided, although there was no room for doubt that the timber would be used to build vessels and the iron to forge weapons which would be employed against Christians, perhaps even against the mariners of Venice. The merchant, here as always, could see nothing beyond his immediate profit, and bringing off a good business deal. It was in vain that the Pope threatened to excommunicate the sellers of Christian slaves, or that the Emperor prohibited the supply to infidels of articles capable of being employed in warfare. Venice, whither merchants in the ninth century had brought back from Alexandria the relics of St. Mark, went her own way, secure in their protection, and considered the steady progress of her wealth as the just reward of the veneration in which she held them.

That progress was, indeed, uninterrupted. By any and every means, the city of the lagoons devoted itself with astonishing energy and activity to advancing that maritime trade, which was the very condition of its existence.

[2] The word *slave* is, of course, simply the word *slav.*

The entire population practised and depended on it, as on the Continent men depended on the land. So serfdom, the inevitable consequence of the rural civilisation of the peasants of this time, was unknown in the city of sailors, artisans and merchants. The hazards of fortune alone established between them social differences independent of legal status. From very early times, commercial profits had created a class of rich traders, whose operations already present an incontestably capitalistic character. The *commenda* appeared in the tenth century, obviously borrowed from the practices of Byzantine customary law.

The use of writing, indispensable to every business movement of any importance, bears indisputable witness to economic progress. A "clerk" formed part of the equipment of every merchant ship sailing abroad and from this we can infer that shipowners themselves had quickly learned to keep accounts and to despatch letters to their correspondents.[3] No reproach, it should be mentioned, was here attached to the business of large-scale commerce. The most important families engaged in it. The doges themselves set the example and were doing so as early as the middle of the ninth century, which seems almost incredible in contemporaries of Lewis the Pious. In 1007, Peter II Orseolo set apart for charitable institutions the profits from a sum of 1,250 livres which he had invested in business. At the end of the eleventh century, the city was full of wealthy patricians, owners of a quantity of shares in ships (*sortes*), whose shops and landing-places (*stationes*) stood close together along the rivo-alto and the quays, which stretched further and further along the isles of the lagoon.

Venice was then already a great maritime power. She had succeeded before 1100 in ridding the Adriatic of the Dalmatian pirates who infested it and in establishing her hegemony firmly on the whole of the east coast of that sea, which she considered as her domain and which re-

[3] Heynen, *op. cit.*, p. 82. The earliest example of this practice which can be quoted is in 1110. But it was obviously older.

mained hers for centuries. In order to preserve control
over its entrance to the Mediterranean, she had helped the
Byzantine fleet in 1002 to expel the Saracens from Bari.
Seventy years later, when the Norman State, set up by
Robert Guiscard in southern Italy, threatened her with a
maritime competition as dangerous to herself as to the
Greek Empire, she allied herself once more with the latter
to fight and overcome the peril. After the death of Robert
(1076) the dream of Mediterranean expansion conceived
by this prince of genius was doomed. The war turned
out to the advantage of Venice and with the same stroke
she rid herself of the rivalry of Naples, Gaeta, Salerno,
and, above all, Amalfi. These cities, which had been
absorbed by the Norman State, were dragged down with
it, and henceforth abandoned the markets of Constantinople and the East to the Venetians.

For that matter they had already enjoyed an indisputable superiority there for a long time. In 992 the doge,
Pietro II Orseolo, had obtained a chrysobull from the
Emperors Basil and Constantine freeing the Venetian
boats from the customs which they had hitherto had to
pay at Abydos. Relations were so active between the port
of the lagoons and that of the Bosphorus that a Venetian
colony was established in the latter, with judicial privileges ratified by the emperors. In the following years,
other establishments were founded at Laodicea, Antioch,
Mamistra, Adana, Tarsus, Satalia, Ephesus, Chios, Pho-
caea, Selembria, Heraclea, Rodosto, Andrinople, Salonica,
Demetrias, Athens, Thebes, Coron, Modon, and Corfu.
At all points of the Empire Venice possessed bases of
supplies and penetration, which secured her commercial
domination. From the end of the eleventh century she
may be said to have held a practical monopoly of transport in all the provinces of Europe and Asia still possessed
by the rulers of Constantinople.

Nor did the emperors try to oppose a situation with
which it was to their own disadvantage to quarrel. The
privilege accorded to the doge in May 1082 by Alexis

Comnenus may be regarded as the final consecration of Venetian superiority in the Byzantine empire. Henceforth the Venetians were exempt, throughout the Empire, from every kind of commercial tax, and were thus favoured above the Emperor's own subjects. The stipulation that they should continue to pay duties on foreign merchandise is final proof that thenceforth the whole of the maritime trade of the eastern end of the Mediterranean was in their hands. For, though we are rather badly informed in regard to the progress of their trade with the Moslem lands from the tenth century, everything indicates that it developed in the same way, if not entirely with the same vigour.

II. THE NORTH SEA AND THE BALTIC SEA[4]

The two inland seas, the North Sea and the Baltic, which bathe the coasts of Northern Europe, as the Mediterranean, to which they form a pendant, bathes its southern coasts, presented, from the middle of the ninth century to the end of the eleventh, a spectacle which, profoundly as it differs from that which we have been describing, resembles it nevertheless in one essential character. For here, too, on the coast and, so to speak, on the very edge of Europe, we find a maritime and commercial activity which is in striking contrast with the agricultural economy of the Continent.

[4] BIBLIOGRAPHY.—A. Bugge, *Die nordeuropäischen Verkehr-swege im frühen Mittelalter und die Bedeutung der Wikinger für die Entwickelung des europäischen Handels und der europäischen Schiffahrt*, in *Vierteljahrschrift für Social-und Wirtschaftsgeschichte*, t. IV, 1906.—W. Vogel, *Geschichte der deutschen Seeschiffahrt*, Berlin, 1925.—J. Kulischer, *Russische Wirtschaftsgeschichte*, t. I, Berlin, 1915.—E. Babelon, *Du commerce des Arabes dans le nord de l'Europe avant des croisades*, in *Athénée oriental*, Paris, 1882.—O. Montelius, *Kulturgeschichte Schewedens*, Leipzig, 1906.—K. T. Strasser, *Wikinger und Normannen*, Hamburg, 1928.

We have already seen that the activity of the ports of Quentovic and Duurstede did not survive the Viking invasion of the ninth century. Lacking a fleet, the Carolingian Empire was unable to defend itself against the Northern barbarians as the Byzantine Empire had defended itself against the Moslems. Its weakness had been only too well exploited by the energetic Scandinavians who, for more than half a century, subjected it to annual raids, not only by way of the estuaries of the northern rivers but also by those of the Atlantic. But the Northmen must not be represented as mere pillagers. Masters of the sea, they could and did combine their aggressions. Their object was not and could not be conquest; though they won a few settlements on the Continent and in the British Isles, that was the most they could do. But the incursions which they pushed so deeply into the mainland were essentially great razzias. Their organisation was obviously carefully planned; they all set off from a fortified camp as centre, where booty collected from neighbouring regions was piled up while awaiting transport to Denmark or Norway. The Vikings, in fact, were pirates, and piracy is the first stage of commerce. So true is this that from the end of the ninth century, when their raids ceased, they simply became merchants.

To understand Scandinavian expansion, however, it must also be remembered that it was not directed exclusively towards the West. While the Danes and the Norwegians threw themselves on the Carolingian Empire, England, Scotland and Ireland, their neighbours, the Swedes, turned to Russia. From our point of view it is immaterial whether they had been asked for assistance by the Slav princes in the valley of the Dnieper in their struggle with the Patzinaks, or whether, in search of gain, they made a spontaneous thrust towards the Byzantine shores of the Black Sea, by the great natural route which from remotest times had been followed by Greek merchants from the Chersonese and the Sea of Azov seeking Baltic amber. It is enough to state that from the middle of the ninth century they established entrenched camps along the Dnieper and its tributaries, similar to those that their Danish and Norwegian brothers were establishing at the same date in the basins of the Scheldt, the Meuse and the Seine. Constructed at so great a distance from their mother country, these *enceintes* or, to use the Slavonic word, *gorods,* became permanent fortresses, from which the invaders dominated and exploited the not very warlike people who surrounded them. It was there that they amassed the tribute imposed on the vanquished and the slaves taken from among them, as well as the honey and furs which they obtained from the virgin forests. But before long, the position which they occupied inevitably led them to engage in trade.

Southern Russia, where they had installed themselves, lay, in fact, between two areas of superior civilisation. To the east, beyond the Caspian Sea, stretched the caliphate of Baghdad, to the south, the Black Sea bathed the shores of the Byzantine Empire and led to Constantinople. The Scandinavians in the basin of the Dnieper at once felt this double attraction. The Arab, Jewish and Byzantine merchants, who were already frequenting this region before their arrival, showed them a road which they were more than ready to follow. The country conquered by them put at their disposal products particularly suited for trade with rich empires leading a life of refinement: honey, furs and above all slaves, the demand for whom from Moslem harems, as well as from the great estates, promised the same high profits which tempted the Venetians.

Constantine Porphyrogenitus, in the tenth century, has left us a picture of the Scandinavians, or rather the Russians (to give them the name by which the Slavs knew them), assembling their boats each year at Kiev, after the melting of the ice. The flotilla slowly descended the Dnieper, whose innumerable rapids presented obstacles which

had to be got round by towing the barks along the bank.[5]
Having reached the sea, it sailed along the coast to Constantinople, the goal of the long and perilous voyage.
There the Russians possessed a special quarter, and their
trade with the great city was regulated by treaties, of
which the oldest dated back to the ninth century. The
influence which she soon came to exercise over them is
well known. It was from her that they received Christianity (957–1015); it was from her that they borrowed their
art, their writing, the use of money and a good part of
their organisation. There can be no more striking witness
to the importance of the trade they kept up with the Bosphorus. At the same time they were making their way,
through the valley of the Volga, to the Caspian Sea and
trafficking with the Jewish and Arab merchants who frequented its ports.

But their activity was not confined to this. They exported merchandise of all sorts to the north, spices, wines,
silks, goldsmiths' work, etc., which they obtained in exchange for their honey, furs and slaves. The astonishing
number of Arab and Byzantine coins discovered in Russia
mark, as with the silver point of a compass, the trade
routes which crossed it, converging either from the course
of the Volga, or from that of the Dnieper to the Dvina
and the lakes which are attached to the Gulf of Bothnia.
There, the commerce from the Caspian and Black Seas
joined the Baltic and continued through it. Across the
immense stretches of continental Russia Scandinavian
navigation was thus linked with the oriental world.[6] The
island of Gothland, in which there have been dug up even

[5] W. Thomson, *Der Ursprung des russischen Staates*, p. 55
et seq. (Gotha, 1879). *Cf.* E. J. Arne, *La Suède et l'Orient*
(Upsala, Paris, Leipzig, 1914, in the *Archives d'études orien-
tales,* ed. by J. A. Lundell).

[6] For the finds of Arab and Byzantine coins in Russia, see
E. J. Arne, *op. cit.,* and R. Vasmer, *Ein im Dorfe Staryi Dedin
in Weissrussland gemachter Fund Kufischer Münzen* (*Forn-
vännen* of the Academy of History of Stockholm, 1929).

more hoards of Islamic and Greek coins than have been found in Russia, appears to have been the great entrepôt of this traffic and its point of contact with Northern Europe. It is tempting to believe that the booty gathered by the Northmen in England and France was there exchanged for the precious goods brought from Russia.

In any case, it is impossible to doubt the part played by Scandinavia as a middleman, when we consider the astonishing progress of its navigation in the tenth and eleventh centuries, that is to say, during the period which succeeded the invasion of the Danes and Norwegians in the West. It is quite clear that they ceased to be pirates and became merchants after the example of their Swedish brothers; barbarian merchants, perhaps, who were always ready to become pirates again on the slightest occasion, but merchants all the same, and what is more, merchants navigating the high seas.[7] Their deckless ships now carried the articles of trade which came to Gothland far and wide. Trading posts were founded on the Swedish coast and on the shores, still Slavonic at this period, of the extensive littoral which lay between the Elbe and the Vistula; in the south of Denmark, excavations made quite recently at Haithabu (north of Kiel) have revealed the existence of an emporium, whose ruins bear witness to its importance during the course of the eleventh century.[8] This commercial activity naturally extended to the harbours of the North Sea, well known to the northern navigators who had devastated its hinterland for so long. Hamburg on the Elbe and Tiel on the Waal became, in the tenth century, ports actively frequented by the Northmen's ships. England received a still greater number of them and the trade carried on by the Danes conferred

---

[7] Interesting details on Swedish commerce in the ninth century are to be found in E. de Moreau, *Saint Anschaire*, Louvain, 1930.

[8] O. Scheel and P. Paulsen, *Quellen zur Frage Schleswig-Haithabu im Rahmen der fränkischen, sächsischen und nordischen Beziehungen* (Kiel, 1930).

on them a superiority which the Anglo-Saxons could not resist and which reached its height when Canute the Great (1017–35) united England, Denmark and Norway in an ephemeral empire. The trade which was thus carried on from the mouths of the Thames and the Rhine to that of the Dvina and the Gulf of Bothnia is attested by the discovery of English, Flemish and German coins in the basins of the Baltic and North Sea. The Scandinavian sagas, in spite of the late date at which they were written down, still preserve the memory of the risks run by the intrepid seamen, who ventured to far-away Iceland and Greenland. Daring young men went to join their fellow-countrymen in Southern Russia; Anglo-Saxons and Scandinavians are found at Constantinople in the bodyguard of the emperors. In short, the Nordic people gave proof at this time of an energy and a spirit of enterprise which reminds us of the Greeks in the Homeric era. Their art was characterised by a barbarous originality, which nevertheless betrays the influence of that East with which their commerce brought them into communication. But the energy which they displayed could have no future. Too few numerically to retain the mastery over the immense expanses where their ships had sailed, they had to yield place to more powerful rivals, when the extension of commerce to the Continent brought about a revival of navigation to compete with their own.

III. THE REVIVAL OF COMMERCE [9]

Continental Europe was bound soon to feel the force of the two great commercial movements which appeared on its borders, the one in the Western Mediterranean and the Adriatic, the other in the Baltic and the North Sea. Re-

[9] BIBLIOGRAPHY.—See the works of W. Heyd, A. Schaube, H. Kretschmayr, H. Pirenne cited in Bib., p. 15.—C. Manfroni, *Storia della marina italiana dalle invasione barbariche al trattato di Ninteo,* t. I, Livourne, 1899.—G. Caro, *Genua und die Mächte am Mittelmeer,* Halle, 1895–9, 2 vols.—G. J.

sponding as it does to the craving for adventure and the love of gain which are inherent in human nature, commerce is essentially contagious. Moreover, it is by nature so all-pervasive that it necessarily imposes itself on the very people whom it exploits. Indeed it depends on them by reason of the relationship of exchange which it sets up and the needs which it creates, while it is impossible to conceive of commerce without agriculture, since it is sterile itself and needs agriculture to supply food for those whom it employs and enriches.

This ineluctable necessity was imposed on Venice from its very foundation on the sandy islets of a lagoon, on which nothing would grow. In order to procure a livelihood its first inhabitants had been forced to exchange salt and fish with their continental neighbours for the corn, wine and meat which they could not have obtained otherwise. But this primitive exchange inevitably developed, as commerce made the town richer and more populous,

Bratianu, Recherches sur le commerce génois dans la mer Noire au XIII⁰ siècle, Paris, 1929.—A. E. Sayous, Le rôle du capital dans la vie locale et le commerce extérieur de Venise entre 1050 et 1150, in the Revue belge de philol. et d'histoire, t. XIII, 1934.—E. H. Byrne, Genoese Shipping in the Twelfth and Thirteenth Centuries, Cambridge (Mass.), 1930.—R. Davidsohn, Geschichte von Florenz, t. I, Berlin, 1896.—A. Sayous, Le commerce des Européens à Tunis depuis le XII⁰ siècle, Paris, 1929.—E. H. Byrne, Genoese Colonies in Syria, in The Crusades and other Historical Essays presented to D. C. Munro, New York, 1928.—L. de Mas-Latrie, Traités de paix et de commerce . . . concernant les relations des chrétiens avec les Arabes de l'Afrique septentrionale au Moyen Age, Paris, 1866.—H. Pirenne, Histoire de Belgique, t. I, 5th ed., Brussels, 1929.—R. Häpke, Brügges Entwickelung zum mittel-alterlichen Weltmarkt, Berlin, 1908.—H. Pirenne, Draps de Frise ou draps de Flandre?, see above, p. 6, n. 8.—R. L. Reynolds, Merchants of Arras and the Overland Trade with Genoa, in Revue Belge de philol. et d'histoire, t. IX, 1930.—Id., The Market for Northern Textiles in Genoa, 1179–1200, ibid., t. VIII, 1929.—F. Rousseau, La Meuse et le pays mosan en Belgique, in Annales de la société archéologique de Namur, t. XXXIX, 1930.

and at the same time increased its demands and sharp-
ened its enterprise. At the end of the ninth century, it was
already commandeering the territory of Verona and above
all the valley of the Po, which provided an easy avenue
for penetration into Italy. A century later its relations had
extended to a number of points on the coast and mainland: Pavia, Treviso, Vicenza, Ravenna, Cesena, Ancona,
and many others.

It is clear that the Venetians, taking the practice of
trade with them, acclimatised it, so to speak, wherever
they went. Their merchants gradually found imitators. It
is impossible, in the absence of evidence, to trace the
growth of the seeds sown by commerce in the midst of the
agricultural population. That growth was no doubt opposed by the Church, which was hostile to commerce, and
nowhere were bishoprics more numerous and more powerful than south of the Alps. A curious epsiode in the life
of St. Gerald of Aurillac (d. 909) bears striking witness
to the incompatibility of the moral standards of the
Church with the spirit of gain, that is to say, the business
spirit. As the pious lord was returning from a pilgrimage
to Rome, he met in Pavia some Venetian merchants, who
asked him to buy oriental stuffs and spices. Now, he had
himself purchased in Rome a magnificent pallium which
he took the opportunity of showing to them, mentioning
how much he had paid for it. But when they congratu-
lated him on his good bargain, since according to them
the pallium would have cost considerably more in Constantinople, Gerald, reproaching himself for having defrauded the vendor, hastened to forward him the difference, considering that he could not take advantage of
it without falling into the sin of avarice.[10]

This anecdote admirably illustrates the moral conflict
which the revival of commerce was to provoke every-

[10] S. *Geraldi comitis, Aureliaci fundatoris Vita* (written by
Odo of Cluny, c. 925), in Migne, *Patrologia latina*, t. CXXX-
III, col. 658, on which see F. L. Ganshof in *Mélanges Iorga*,
p. 295 (Paris, 1933).

where, and which indeed never ceased during the whole of the Middle Ages. From the beginning to the end the Church continued to regard commercial profits as a danger to salvation. Its ascetic ideal, which was perfectly suited to an agricultural civilisation, made it always suspicious of social changes, which it could not prevent and to which necessity even compelled it to submit, but to which it was never openly reconciled. Its prohibition of interest was to weigh heavily on the economic life of later centuries. It prevented the merchants from growing rich with a free conscience and from reconciling the practice of business with the prescripts of religion. For proof of this we need only read the many wills of bankers and speculators, directing that the poor whom they had defrauded should be repaid and bequeathing to the clergy a part of the property which at the bottom of their hearts they felt to be ill-gotten. If they could not refrain from sin, at least their faith remained unshaken and they counted on it to obtain absolution for them on the day of judgment.

It must, however, be recognised that this ardent faith contributed largely all the same to economic expansion in the West. It played a great part when the Pisans and Genoese took the offensive against Islam at the beginning of the eleventh century. Unlike the Venetians, in whom the spirit of gain ruled supreme, these cities were impelled by hatred of the infidel and by enterprise alike to wrest the mastery of the Tyrrhenian Sea from the Saracens. An unending struggle was waged between the two religions face to face there. In the beginning it had constantly turned to the advantage of the Mohammedans; in 935, and again in 1004, they had pillaged Pisa, doubtless with the intention of suppressing the first feeble efforts at maritime expansion there. But the Pisans were determined to expand, and the following year they defeated a Saracen fleet in the Straits of Messina. The enemy had their revenge by invading and destroying their bold competitors' port, but the Pisans, exhorted by the popes and lured by their adversary's wealth, resolved to continue a war which was at once religious and commercial. With the Genoese, they attacked Sardinia and succeeded in establishing themselves there in 1015. In 1034, emboldened by success, they ventured as far as the coast of Africa and for a time made themselves masters of Bona. A little later, their merchants began to frequent Sicily and it was to protect them that in 1052 a Pisan fleet forced the entrance of the port of Palermo and destroyed its arsenal.

From that time fortune turned in favour of the Christians. An expedition, to which the presence of the Bishop of Modena added all the prestige of the Church, was directed against Mehdia in 1087. The sailors saw in the sky the archangel Michael and St. Peter leading them into battle. They took the town, massacred "the priests of Mohammed," pillaged the mosque and imposed an advantageous commercial treaty on the vanquished. The Cathedral of Pisa, built after this triumph, symbolises to perfection both the faith of the Pisans and the wealth which their victories were beginning to bring them. Pillars, precious marbles, gold and silver ornaments, curtains of purple and gold carried away from Palermo and Mehdia adorned it. It is as though they wished to symbolise by its splendour the revenge of the Christians upon the Saracens, whose wealth was a thing of scandal and of envy.[11]

Islam fell back before the Christian counter-attack and lost its hold over the Tyrrhenian Sea, which had been a Moslem lake. The launching of the first crusade in 1096 was to mark its definite overthrow. In 1097, the Genoese sent a fleet with reinforcements and supplies to the Crusaders besieging Antioch, and the following year obtained from Bohemond of Tarento a *fondaco* with commercial privileges, which was the first of a long series to be obtained in due course by the maritime towns on the coast

---

[11] A spirited contemporary poem published by E. Du Méril, *Poésies populaires latines du Moyen Age*, p. 251 (Paris, 1847), enables us to appreciate the large part played by religious enthusiasm in Pisan expansion.

of the Holy Land. After the capture of Jerusalem the relations of Genoa with the Eastern Mediterranean increased
rapidly. In 1104, she possessed a colony at St. John of
Acre to which King Baldwin ceded a third of the town, a
street by the sea and the rent of six hundred gold bezants
out of the customs. Venice set up counting-houses at Tyre,
Sidon, St. John of Acre and Kaffa. Pisa devoted herself
with growing energy to provisioning the states founded
in Syria by the Crusaders. Moreover, the commercial revival which had begun on the coast of Italy soon reached
that of Provence. In 1136, Marseilles already occupied an
important place, her citizens having founded a settlement
at St. John of Acre. From the other side of the Gulf of
Lyons, Barcelona was already ushering in her future prosperity, and, just as in former times the Moslems had engaged in the Christian slave trade, so Moorish slaves cap-
tured in Spain furnished her with one article of her
traffic.

Thus the whole Mediterranean was opened, or rather
re-opened, to western navigation. As in the time of Rome,
communications were established from one end to the
other of this essentially European sea. The exploitation
of its waters by Islam was at an end. The Christians had
recaptured the islands whose possession guaranteed its
mastery, Sardinia in 1022, Corsica in 1091, Sicily in 1058–
90. It matters little that the Turks soon destroyed the
ephemeral principalities founded by the Crusaders, that
the country of Edessa was reconquered by the Crescent
in 1144 and Damascus in 1154, that Saladin took Aleppo
in 1183, then, in 1187, Acre, Nazareth, Caesarea, Sidon,
Beyrout, Ascalon, and finally Jerusalem, and that in spite
of all their efforts the Christians never recovered until
our own day the domination of Syria which they had won
in the first crusade. However important it may be in
general history, and however heavily it has weighed since
on the destinies of the world, the Turkish thrust did not
shake the position that the Italian towns had gained in
the Levant. The new offensive of Islam extended only to

the mainland. The Turks had no fleet and did not attempt to create one. Far from harming them, Italian trade on the coasts of Asia Minor was to their advantage, for by it the spices brought by the caravans of China and India to Syria continued to be carried to the West by Italian ships. Nothing could have been more profitable than the persistence of a navigation which served to maintain the economic activity of the Turkish and Mongolian lands.

Undoubtedly the Italian fleets continued to lend an increasingly active co-operation to the crusades down to the day when the defeat of St. Louis at Tunis (1270) brought them to an end and marked a definite check both in the political and in the religious sphere. It would not be untrue to say that without the support of Venice, Pisa and Genoa, it would have been impossible to persist so long in these fruitless enterprises. Only the first crusade was carried out by the land route, the transport by sea of masses of men going to Jerusalem being at that time still unfeasible. The Italian ships contributed nothing beyond supplies for the armies. But almost immediately the demands of the crusaders upon their navigation galvanised it into incredible life and vigour. The profits realised by army contractors have been immense in all ages, and it cannot be doubted that the Venetians, Pisans, Genoese and Provençals, finding themselves suddenly rich, hastened to put new ships on their stocks. The establishment of the crusading states in Syria ensured the regular use of these means of transport, without which the Franks would have been unable to maintain themselves in the East. Thus they were prodigal of privileges to the towns whose services were indispensable to them, and from the end of the eleventh century helped them to set up their *fondaci* and *échelles* all along the coasts of Palestine and Asia Minor, and of the Aegean islands. Before long, indeed, they began to make use of them for military operations. During the second crusade the Italian boats carried the troops of Louis VII and Conrad III along the coast of Anatolia, to the Holy Land. The third crusade furnishes

a characteristic proof of the growth of Italian and Provençal tonnage, which was considerable enough to transport
the troops of Richard Coeur de Lion and Philip Augustus.
From then onwards, all subsequent expeditions were carried out exclusively by the sea route. It is well known
how the Venetians exploited the situation by diverting to
Constantinople the fleet equipped for the fourth crusade,
whose commanders, unable to pay the agreed price for
the passage, were compelled to abandon the direction of
the whole enterprise to them and how they finally used
the fleet for the siege and capture of Constantinople. The
ephemeral Latin empire then set up on the shores of the
Bosphorus was largely a creation of Venetian policy, and
when it disappeared (1261), Venice had to resign herself
to allowing the Genoese, who, in order to outwit her, had
worked for the restoration of Michael Palaeologus, to dis-
pute with her the economic supremacy of the Levant.

Thus the one lasting and essential result of the crusades
was to give the Italian towns, and in a less degree, those
of Provence and Catalonia, the mastery of the Mediterranean. Though they did not succeed in wresting the holy
places from Islam, and though no more than a few places
on the coast of Asia Minor and in the islands remained
of their early conquests, at least they enabled Western
Europe not only to monopolise the whole trade from the
Bosphorus and Syria to the Straits of Gibraltar, but to
develop there an economic and strictly capitalistic activity
which was gradually to communicate itself to all the lands
north of the Alps.

Islam did not react against this triumphant advance
until the fifteenth century and the helpless Byzantine Empire was forced to submit to it. From the beginning of
the twelfth century its supremacy in the eastern Mediterranean was at an end. It rapidly fell under the influence
of the maritime towns, which now monopolised its import
and export trade. Sometimes in an endeavour to shake
off their yoke, the emperor tried to play off the Pisans and
Genoese against the Venetians, or allowed the populace to

massacre the detestable foreigners indiscriminately, as, for example, in 1182. But he could not do without them, and willy-nilly had to abandon Byzantine commerce to them, even more completely than Spain in the seventeenth century was to abandon hers to the Dutch, the English and the French.

The revival of maritime commerce was accompanied by its rapid penetration inland. Not only was agriculture stimulated by the demand for its produce and transformed by the exchange economy of which it now became a part, but a new export industry was born. In both directions the lead was taken by the Lombard plain, admirably situated as it was between the powerful commercial centres of Venice, Pisa and Genoa. Country and towns shared equally in production, the former with its grain and wines, the latter with their linen and woollen stuffs. As early as the twelfth century Lucca was manufacturing silk fabrics, the raw material for which came to her by sea. In Tuscany, Sienna and Florence communicated with Pisa by the valley of the Arno and shared in her prosperity. Behind Genoa the movement spread to the coast of the Gulf of Lyons and reached the basin of the Rhône. The ports of Marseilles, Montpellier and Narbonne traded all over Provence as did Barcelona over Catalonia. So vigorous was the trade of the maritime countries that in the eleventh century it began to spread northwards through the Alpine passes, which the Saracens of Garde-Frainet had blocked so dangerously in the tenth century. From Venice it reached Germany by the Brenner, the Saône and Rhine valleys by the Septimer and St. Bernard, and the Rhône valley by Mont Cenis. The St. Gothard was long impassable, but eventually a suspension bridge was slung from rock to rock across the gorge and it too became a route of transit.[12] In the second half of the eleventh century we hear of Italians in France. It is more

[12] This is the first suspension bridge of whose existence we know. It probably dates from the beginning of the thirteenth century.

than probable that they were already frequenting the fairs of Champagne at this period and met there the flow of commerce from the coast of Flanders.[13]

Indeed, the economic revival which was in process of achievement in the Mediterranean, was matched on the shores of the North Sea by a revival which, if it differed from it in extent and character, proceeded from the same causes and produced the same result. As we have seen above, the Northmen had established, in the estuary formed by the arms of the Rhine, the Meuse and the Scheldt, a mart which soon attracted trade from far and wide along these rivers. In the eleventh century Tiel already appears as a commercial centre frequented by many merchants and in communication by way of the Rhine valley with Cologne and Mainz, which now show signs of considerable activity. No other proof is needed than the six hundred *mercatores opulentissimi* mentioned in 1074 in the first of those towns by Lampert of Hersfeld, although we may doubt the figure quoted and it is impossible to know what was the chronicler's standard of wealth.[14] At the same period, a trade developed in the Meuse valley, extending as far as Verdun by way of Maastricht, Liége, Huy and Dinant. The Scheldt enabled Cambrai, Valenciennes, Tournai, Ghent and Antwerp to communicate with the sea and the large rivers which

[13] See the letter written by Gregory VII to the archbishops and bishops of France, on Sept. 10th, 1074, condemning the conduct of King Philip I, accusing him of having robbed the "mercatoribus qui de multis terrarum partibus ad forum quoddam in Francia nuper convenerant . . . more praedonis infinitam pecuniam" (E. Caspar, *Das Register Gregors VII, M.M.G.G.,* p. 131). In a second letter the Pope calls the merchants "Italiae negociatores" (*ibid.,* p. 150); in a third, he speaks of "Italis et aliarum provinciarum mercatoribus" (*ibid,* p. 168). His insistence may be considered as proof of the development of international commerce at that period. If, as A. Schaube, *op. cit.,* p. 91, thinks, the incident occurred at the unimportant fair of Lendit, it is difficult to explain the magnitude of the losses suffered by the merchants.

[14] *Lamperti Hersfeldensis opera,* ed. O. Holder-Egger, p. 192.

emptied their waters among the Zealand Islands. The harbour of Bruges at the end of the Gulf of Zwyn, now silted up, was so convenient that from the end of the eleventh century ships began to put in there in preference to other ports, and the future glory of the city was thus ensured.

It is certain that at the end of the tenth century Scandinavian trade kept Flanders in close relations with the North Sea and Baltic countries. Coins struck by Counts Arnold II and Baldwin IV (965–1035) have been discovered in Denmark, Prussia and even Russia. Her trade was naturally still more active with England. The tariff of London tolls, between 991 and 1002, mentions the Flemings as being among the foreigners who traded in the city.[15] The Channel was less frequented than the North Sea, but there was a regular trade between the Norman and English coasts, by way of Rouen and the estuary of the Seine, and thence along the river to Paris and to the confines of Champagne and Burgundy. The Loire and the Garonne, by reason of their distance, did not experience until later the effects of the commercial revival in the northern seas.

Flanders soon came to occupy a privileged position, which it was to keep until the end of the Middle Ages. Here we meet with a new factor, industry, which was nowhere else in operation at so early a date and with such remarkable results. Already in the Celtic era, the Morini and Menapii in the valleys of the Lys and the Scheldt had been manufacturing the wool from the large flocks of sheep which they kept in that country of lush meadows. Their primitive cloth manufacture was perfected during the long Roman occupation, when their conquerors introduced them to the technical methods of the Mediterranean. So rapid was its progress that in the second century Flanders was exporting cloth as far as Italy.[16] The Franks, who invaded the region in the fifth century, con-

[15] F. Liebermann, *Die Gesetze der Angelsachsen*, t. I, p. 232.
[16] Camille Julian, *Histoire de la Gaule*, t. II, p. 282 ff.

tinued the tradition of their predecessors. Until the coming of the Northmen in the ninth century, Frisian boatmen regularly carried cloths woven in Flanders along the rivers of the Low Countries; under the name of *pallia fresonica,* their beautiful colours made them so popular that Charlemagne could find nothing better to send as a gift to the Caliph Haroun-al-Raschid.[17] The destruction of commerce by the Scandinavian invasions naturally interrupted this export. But when, in the course of the tenth century, the pillagers became traders whose boats reappeared on the Meuse and the Scheldt in quest of merchandise, the cloth manufacture found a market once again. The fineness of the cloths soon caused a demand for them along all the coasts frequented by the Northern seamen and, to meet that demand, their manufacture increased to proportions hitherto unattained. It was already so considerable that at the end of the tenth century native wool was insufficient for its needs, and wool had to be imported from England. The superior quality of English wool naturally improved that of the cloth, the sale of which increased as its fame grew. In the course of the twelfth century the whole of Flanders became a country of weavers and fullers. Cloth-making, which up till then had been carried on in the country, was concentrated in the merchant towns, which were founded on all sides and supplied an ever-growing commerce. It was cloth which created the nascent wealth of Ghent, Bruges, Ypres, Lille, Douai and Arras. Already an essential article of maritime trade, it now brought into existence an extremely important trade by the land routes. From the beginning of the twelfth century Flemish cloth was being taken by sea to the fair of Novgorod,[18] while the Italians were coming to Flanders to buy it in exchange for the spices, silks, and

[17] H. Pirenne, *Draps de Frise ou draps de Flandre?,* see Introduction, n. 8.

[18] H. Pirenne, *Draps d'Ypres à Novgorod au commencement du XII° siècle,* in *Revue belge de philol. et d'histoire,* t. IX (1930), p. 563.

goldsmiths' work which they imported from south of the Alps. But the Flemings themselves frequented the famous fairs of Champagne, where, midway between the North Sea and the Alps, they met buyers from Lombardy and Tuscany. These carried Flemish cloth in enormous quantities to the port of Genoa, whence under the name of *panni francesi* they were taken by sea as far as the ports of the Levant.

Of course, Flanders was not the only place where cloth was manufactured. Weaving is by nature a domestic occupation, which is known to have existed from prehistoric times and is met with wherever there is wool, i.e., in all countries. It was only necessary to stimulate its production and perfect its technique for it to become a real industry. This was not neglected. In the thirteenth century, Genoese notarial instruments mention the names of a number of towns which were sending cloth to that port: Amiens, Beauvais, Cambrai, Liége, Montreuil, Provins, Tournai, Châlons, etc. Nevertheless, Flanders and soon afterwards its neighbour, Brabant, occupied an unrivalled place among their competitors. The proximity of England enabled them to obtain excellent wool on the best terms and in much larger quantities than the latter. In the thirteenth century the overwhelming superiority of the Flemish industry is reflected in the admiration which it inspired in foreigners. Throughout the history of medieval Europe no other region presented this character of an industrial country which distinguished the basin of the Scheldt. It offers, in this respect, a contrast to the rest of Europe which brings to mind England in the eighteenth and nineteenth centuries. Nowhere else was it possible to equal the finish, the flexibility, the softness and the colours of these fabrics. Flemish and Brabantine cloth was, indeed, a cloth *de luxe*, and it was this which made its success and assured its world-wide expansion. In an age when the means of transport were not sufficiently developed to be adaptable to the circulation of cheap and heavy goods, the first place in international commerce belonged to merchandise of **great** value and medium weight. In short, the success of Flemish cloths is to be explained, like that of spices, by their high price and the ease with which they could be exported.

In striking contrast to the Italian towns, Flanders and Brabant, as they became more industrialised, became also less interested in the maritime commerce for which their geographical situation seemed to have destined them. They abandoned it to the foreigners whom their industry attracted in ever-increasing numbers to the port of Bruges, Scandinavians in the eleventh century, and, later, Hansards. In this respect it is tempting to compare them with modern Belgium, in so far as it is permissible to compare the Middle Ages with our own times, taking into account their relative economic development. In the same territory once occupied by them, does not the Belgium of to-day present the same paradoxical spectacle of extraordinary industrial productivity combined with a relatively insignificant marine?

𝔗𝔴𝔬

THE TOWNS

I. THE REVIVAL OF URBAN LIFE[1]

As long as Mediterranean commerce continued to draw
Western Europe into its orbit, urban life went on in Gaul

[1] BIBLIOGRAPHY.—H. Pirenne, *Les villes du Moyen Age*, see
Introduction, n. 2.—G. von Below, *Der Ursprung der deutschen
Stadtverfassung*, Dusseldorf, 1892.—K. Hegel, *Städte und
Gilden der Germanischen Völker im Mittelalter*, Leipzig, 1891,
2 vols.—*Id.*, *Die Entstehung des deutschen Städtewesens*,
Leipzig, 1898.—F. Keutgen, *Untersuchungen über den Urs-
prung der deutschen Stadtverfassung*, Leipzig, 1895.—S.
Rietschel, *Die civitas auf deutschem Boden*, Leipzig, 1894.
—*Id.*, *Markt und Stadt in ihrem rechtlichen Verhältniss*, Leip-
zig, 1897.—F. Beyerle, *Zur Typenfrage in der Stadtverfassung*,
in *Zeitschrift für Rechtsgeschichte*, Germ. Abt., 1930.—G.
Espinas, *La vie urbaine de Douai au Moyen Age*, Paris, 1913,
4 vols.—C. Gross, *The Gild Merchant*, Oxford, 1890, 2 vols.—
F. W. Maitland, *Township and Borough*, Cambridge, 1898.
—C. Petit-Dutaillis, *The Origin of the Towns in England*, in
Studies Supplementary to Stubbs' Constitutional History, vol.
I, Manchester, 1908.—C. Stephenson, *The Origin of the Eng-
lish Towns*, in *Amer. Hist. Rev.*, t. XXXII, 1926.—*Id.*, *The
Anglo-Saxon Borough*, in *Eng. Hist. Rev.*, 1930.—*Id.*, *Borough
and Town, a study of urban origins in England*, Cambridge
(Mass.), 1933.—H. Pirenne, *Les villes flamandes avant le XII*ᵉ
siècle*, in *Annales de l'Est et du Nord*, t. I, 1905.—*Id.*, *Les
anciennes démocraties des Pays-Bas*, Paris, 1910.—G. Des
Marez, *Étude sur la propriété foncière dans les villes du
Moyen Age et spécialement en Flandre*, Ghent, 1898.—F.
Vercanteren, *Étude sur les civitates de la Belgique Seconde*,
Brussels, 1934.—L. von Heinemann, *Zur Entstehung der Stadtverfassung in Italien*, Leipzig, 1896.—G. Mengozzi, *La città
italiana nell'alto medio evo*, 2nd ed., Florence, 1931.

as well as in Italy, Spain and Africa. But when the Islamic invasion had bottled up the ports of the Tyrrhenian Sea after bringing the coasts of Africa and Spain under its control, municipal activity rapidly died out. Save in southern Italy and in Venice, where it was maintained thanks to Byzantine trade, it disappeared everywhere. The towns continued in existence, but they lost their population of artisans and merchants and with it all that had survived of the municipal organisation of the Roman Empire.

The "cities," in each of which there resided a bishop, now became no more than centres of the ecclesiastical administration of their dioceses. Thus they preserved considerable importance, no doubt, from the religious point of view, but from the economic point of view none. At most, a small local market, supplied by the peasants round about, provided for the daily needs of the numerous clergy of the cathedral and of the churches or monasteries grouped around it and those of the serfs employed in their service. At the big annual festivals the diocesan population and pilgrims flocking into the city kept up a certain activity, but in none of this are any signs of a revival visible. In reality these episcopal cities were merely living on the country. The bishops and abbots within their walls lived on the rents and dues which they obtained from their estates, and their existence thus rested essentially on agriculture. The cities were the centres not only of religious but also of manorial administration.

In time of war their old walls furnished a refuge to the surrounding population. But during the period of insecurity which set in with the dissolution of the Carolingian Empire, the need for protection became the first necessity of a people threatened in the South by the Saracen incursions and in the North and West by those of the Normans, to which were added, at the beginning of the tenth century, the terrible cavalry raids of the Hungarians. These invasions led on all sides to the construction of new places of refuge. In this period Western Europe became covered with fortified castles, erected by the feudal princes to serve as a shelter for their men. These castles, or, to use the term by which they were customarily designated, these *bourgs* or *burgs*, were usually composed of a rampart of earth or stones, surrounded by a moat and pierced with gates. The *vilains* from round about were requisitioned to construct and maintain them. A garrison of knights resided inside; a donjon served as the lord's dwelling-place; a church of canons looked after the needs of religion; and barns and granaries were set up to receive the grain, smoked meats and dues of all kinds levied on the manorial peasants, which served to feed the garrison and the people who, in times of peril, came huddling into the fortress with their cattle. Thus the lay burg, like the ecclesiastical city, lived on the land. Neither had any real economic life of its own. They were perfectly compatible with an agricultural civilisation, for, far from opposing it, they may be said to have served in its defence.

But the revival of commerce soon completely altered their character. The first symptoms of its action are observable in the course of the second half of the tenth century. The wandering life of the merchants, the risks of every sort to which they were exposed, in an age when pillage formed one of the means of existence of the smaller nobility, caused them from the very beginning to seek the protection of the walled towns and burgs, which stood at intervals along the rivers or natural routes by which they travelled. During the summer these served as halting-places, during the bad season as wintering-places. The most favourably situated, whether at the foot of an estuary or in a creek, at the confluence of two rivers, or at a spot where the river ceased to be navigable and cargoes had to be unloaded before they could proceed farther, thus became places of passage and of sojourn for merchants and merchandise.

Soon the space that cities and burgs had to offer these new-comers, who became more and more numerous and embarrassing in proportion as trade increased, was no longer sufficient. They were driven to settle outside the walls and to build beside the old burg a new burg, or, to use the term which exactly describes it, a *faubourg* (*foris-burgus*), i.e., an outside burg. Thus, close to ecclesiastical towns or feudal fortresses there sprang up mercantile agglomerations, whose denizens devoted themselves to a kind of life which was in complete contrast to that led by the people of the inside town. The word *portus*, often applied in documents of the tenth and eleventh centuries to these settlements, exactly describes their nature.[2] It did not, in fact, signify a port in the modern sense, but a place through which merchandise was carried, and thus a particularly active place of transit. It was from it that in England and in Flanders the inhabitants of the *port* themselves received the name of *poorters* or *portmen,* which was long synonymous with *bourgeois* or *burgess* and indeed described them rather better than the latter, for the primitive bourgeoisie was exclusively composed of men living by trade. The reason why they came, before the end of the eleventh century, to be known by the word *bourgeois,* which was really much better suited to the inhabitants of the old burgs, at the foot of which they settled, is to be found in the fact that very early the mercantile group too surrounded itself by a wall or palisade for the sake of security, and thus became a burg in its turn. This extension of meaning is all the more easily comprehensible, since the new burg very soon overshadowed the old. In the most active centres of commercial life, such as Bruges, it was already at the beginning of the twelfth century surrounding the fortress, which had been its nucleus, on all sides. The accessory ·had become the essential, the new-comers had triumphed over the old inhabitants. In this sense it is strictly true to say that the medieval town, and consequently the modern town, had its birth in the faubourg of the city, or of the bourg which determined its site.

The collection of merchants in favourable spots soon

[2] H. Pirenne, *Les villes flamandes avant le XIIe siècle,* in *Annales de l'Est et du Nord,* t. I (1905).

caused artisans also to collect there. Industrial concentration is as old as commercial concentration. We can observe it with particular plainness in Flanders. Cloth-making, which had at first been carried on in the country, emigrated of itself to places which offered a sale for its products. There weavers found wool imported by the merchants, fullers' and dyers' soap and dye-stuffs. A real industrial revolution, of which we do not, unfortunately, know the details, accompanied this transformation of a rural industry into an urban one. Weaving, which had up to then been an occupation carried on by women, passed into the hands of men, and at the same time the old small *pallia* were replaced by pieces of cloth of great length, which were better suited for export and have remained the stock size used in the cloth manufacture up to the present day. There is good reason also for supposing that a change took place at this time in the looms used by the weavers, if only to allow a warp measuring from twenty to sixty ells to be fitted to the beam.

In the metallurgical industry of the Meuse valley an evolution analogous to that which took place in the Flemish cloth industry may also be observed. Copper-working, which perhaps dates back to the bronze-working which was actively developed there at the time of the Roman occupation, received a powerful impetus when the revival of navigation on the river gave it the chance to produce for export. At the same time, it became concentrated at Namur, Huy, and above all at Dinant, towns whose *marchands batteurs* went to the mines of Saxony for their copper in the eleventh century.[3] Similarly, the excellent stone in which the region of Tournai abounded was worked in that town, and the manufacture of baptismal fonts became so active that we meet with them as far away as Southampton and Winchester.[4] In Italy, the story is the

[3] See F. Rousseau, *op. cit.*, p. 89 *et seq.*

[4] P. Rolland, *L'expansion tournaisienne aux XI° et XII° siècles. Art et commerce de la pierre* in *Annales de l'Académie royale d'archéologie de Belgique*, 1924.

same. Silk-weaving, introduced by sea from the East, became concentrated at Lucca, while Milan and the Lombard towns, soon imitated by Tuscany, devoted themselves to the manufacture of fustians.

II. THE MERCHANTS AND THE BOURGEOISIE[5]

The essential difference between the merchants and artisans of the nascent towns and the agricultural society in the midst of which they appeared, was that their kind of life was no longer determined by their relations with the land. In this respect they formed, in every sense of the word, a class of *déracinés*. Commerce and industry, which up till then had been merely the adventitious or intermittent occupations of manorial agents, whose existence was assured by the great landowners who employed them, now became independent professions. Those who practised them were incontestably "new men." Attempts have often been made to derive them from the servile personnel attached to the domestic workshops of the manor, or the serfs who were charged with feeding the household in times of scarcity and in time of plenty disposed of their surplus production outside.[6] But such an evolution is neither supported by the sources nor probable. There is no doubt that territorial lords here and there preserved economic prerogatives in the nascent towns for a fairly long time, such prerogatives, for instance, as the obligation of the burgesses to use the lord's oven and mill, the monopoly of sale enjoyed by his wine for several days

[5] BIBLIOGRAPHY.—See above, n. 1. Add: W. Vogel, *Ein seefahrender Kaufmann um 1100*, in *Hansische Geschichtsblätter*, t. XVIII, 1912.—H. Pirenne, *Les périodes de l'histoire sociale du capitalisme*, in *Bull. de l'Acad. royale de Belgique*, Cl. des Lettres, 1914.

[6] R. Eberstadt, *Der Ursprung des Zunftwesens und die älteren Handwerksverbände des Mittelalters*, Leipzig, 1915, and in a modified form, F. Keutgen, *Ämter und Zünfte*, Jena, 1903.

after the vintage, or even certain dues levied from the craft gilds. But the local survival of these rights is no proof of the manorial origin of urban economy. On the contrary, what we note everywhere is that from the moment that it appears, it appears in a condition of freedom.

But the question immediately occurs, how are we to explain the formation of a class of free merchants and artisans in the midst of an exclusively rural society, where serfdom was the normal condition of the people? Scarcity of information prevents us from replying with that precision which the importance of the problem demands, but it is at least possible to indicate the chief factors. First, it is incontestable that commerce and industry were originally recruited from among landless men, who lived, so to speak, on the margin of a society where land alone was the basis of existence. Now these men were very numerous. Apart altogether from those, who in times of famine or war left their native soil to seek a livelihood elsewhere and returned no more, we have to remember all the individuals whom the manorial organisation itself was unable to support. The peasants' holdings were of such a size as to secure the regular payment of the dues assessed upon them. Thus the younger sons of a man overburdened with children were often forced to leave their father in order to enable him to make his payments to the lord. Thenceforth they swelled the crowd of vagabonds who roamed through the country, going from abbey to abbey taking their share of alms reserved for the poor, hiring themselves out to the peastants at harvest time or at the vintage, and enlisting as mercenaries in the feudal troops in times of war.

These men were quick to profit by the new means of livelihood offered them by the arrival of ships and merchants along the coasts and in the river estuaries. Many of the more adventurous certainly hired themselves to the Venetian and Scandinavian boats as sailors; others joined the merchant caravans which took their way more and more frequently to the "ports." With luck, the best among them could not fail to seize the many opportunities of making a fortune, which commercial life offered to the vagabonds and adventurers who threw themselves into it with energy and intelligence. Strong probability would suffice to support such a reconstruction of the facts, even if we did not possess, in the story of St. Godric of Finchale, a valuable example of the way in which the *nouveaux riches* were then formed.[7] Godric was born towards the end of the eleventh century in Lincolnshire of poor peasant stock and, forced, no doubt, to leave his parents' holding, he must have had to use all his wits to get a living. Like many other unfortunates in every age he became a beach-comber, on the look-out for wreckage thrown up by the waves. Shipwrecks were numerous and one fine day a lucky chance furnished him with a windfall which enabled him to get together a pedlar's pack. He had amassed a little store of money, when he met with and joined a band of merchants. Their business prospered and he soon made enough profit to enable him to form a partnership with others, in common with whom he loaded a ship and engaged in coastal trade along the shores of England, Scotland, Flanders and Denmark. The partnership prospered. Its operations consisted in taking abroad goods which were known to be scarce there and bringing back a return cargo, which was then exported to places where the demand was greatest and where, in consequence, the largest profits could be realised.

The story of Godric was certainly that of many others. In an age when local famines were continual, one had only to buy a very small quantity of grain cheaply in regions where it was abundant, to realise fabulous profits, which could then be increased by the same methods. Thus speculation, which is the starting-point in this kind of

[7] For St. Godric see the article of Vogel mentioned in n. 5. The *Libellus de vita et miraculis S. Godrici, heremitae de Finchale, auctore Reginaldo monacho dunelmensi,* was edited in London in 1847 by Stevenson for the Surtees Society.

business, largely contributed to the foundation of the first commercial fortunes. The savings of a little pedlar, a sailor, a boatman, or a docker, furnished him with quite enough capital, if only he knew how to use it.[8] It might also happen that a landowner would invest a part of his income in maritime commerce. It is almost certain that the nobles on the Ligurian coast advanced the necessary funds to build the Genoese ships and shared in the profits from the sale of cargoes in the Mediterranean ports. The same thing must have happened in other Italian cities; at least we are tempted to assume so when we observe that in Italy a large proportion of the nobility always lived in the cities, in contrast to their brothers north of the Alps. It is only natural to suppose that a certain number of them were in some way interested in the economic revival which was developing around them. In these cases landed capital unquestionably contributed to the formation of liquid capital. However, their share was secondary, and though they profited by the recovery of trade, it was certainly not they who revived it.

The first impetus started from outside, in the South with Venetian and in the North with Scandinavian navigation. Western Europe, crystallised in its agricultural civilisation, could not of itself have become so rapidly acquainted with a new sort of life, in the absence of external stimulus and example. The attitude of the Church, the most powerful landowner of the time, towards commerce, an attitude not merely passive but actively hostile, is quite enough proof of that. If the first beginnings of commercial capitalism partly evade our notice, it is much easier to follow its evolution during the course of the twelfth century. In the vigour and relative rapidity of its development it may, without exaggeration, be compared with the industrial revolution of the nineteenth century. The new kind of

[8] For a few examples, which could easily be multiplied, see my work, *Les périodes de l'histoire sociale du capitalism,* in the *Bulletin de la Classe des Lettres de l'Académie royale de Belgique,* 1914.

life which offered itself to the roving masses of landless
men had an irresistible attraction for them, by reason of
the promise of gain which it offered. The result was a real
emigration from the country to the nascent towns. Soon,
it was not only vagabonds of the type of Godric who bent
their steps thither. The temptation was too great not to
cause a number of serfs to run away from the manors
where they were born and settle in the towns, either as
artisans or as employees of the rich merchants whose reputation spread through the land. The lords pursued them
and brought them back to their holdings, when they succeeded in laying hands on them. But many eluded their
search, and as the city population increased, it became
dangerous to try to seize the fugitives under its protection.

By concentrating in the towns industry was able to
supply their export trade more and more largely. Thus the
number of merchants steadily increased and with it the
importance and the profits of their business. At that time
of commercial growth, it was not difficult for young men
to find employment as assistants to some rich master, to
share in his business and in the end to make their own
fortunes. The *Gesta* of the bishops of Cambrai relate in
detail the story of a certain Werimbold, who, in the time
of Bishop Burchard (1114–30), entered the service of a
wealthy merchant, married his daughter and developed
his business to such a degree that he himself became rich.
He purchased a great deal of land in the town, built a
magnificent house, bought off the toll collected at one of
the gates, constructed a bridge at his own expense and in
the end left the greater part of his property to the Church.[9]

The foundation of large fortunes was certainly at this
period a common phenomenon in all centres where an
export trade was developing. Just as landowners had in
the past showered gifts of land on the monasteries, so now
merchants used their fortunes to found parish churches,
hospitals, almshouses, in short, to spend themselves in

[9] *Gesta episcoporum cameracensium continuata*, ed. G.
Waitz, *M.M.G.G.*, t. XIV, p. 214 *et seq.*

religious or charitable works for the benefit of their fellow-citizens and the good of their own souls. Indeed, religion may well have spurred many of them on to win a fortune, which they intended to dedicate to the service of God. It should not be forgotten that Peter Waldo, the founder in 1173 of the Poor Men of Lyons, which shortly gave rise to the sect of the Waldenses, was a merchant and that, almost at the same date, St. Francis was born at Assisi in the house of another merchant.[10] Other *nouveaux riches*, more bitten with worldly ambition, sought to raise themselves in the social hierarchy by giving their daughters in marriage to knights; and their fortune must have been very large to have stifled the aristocratic reluctance of the latter.

These great merchants, or rather *nouveaux riches*, were naturally the leaders of the bourgeoisie, since the bourgeoisie itself was a creation of the commercial revival and in the beginning the words *mercator* and *burgensis* were synonymous. But while it developed as a social class this bourgeoisie was also forming itself into a legal class of a highly original nature, which we must now consider.

III. URBAN INSTITUTIONS AND LAW

The needs and tendencies of the bourgeoisie were so incompatible with the traditional organisation of Western Europe that they immediately aroused violent opposition. They ran counter to all the interests and ideas of a society dominated materially by the owners of large landed property and spiritually by the Church, whose aversion to trade was unconquerable.[11] It would be unfair to attribute to "feudal tryranny" or "sacerdotal arrogance" an opposition which explains itself, although the attribution

[10] The Life of St. Guy (eleventh century) relates that he applied himself to business in order that he might have more money to bestow in alms. *Acta Sanct. Boll.*, Sept., t. IV, p. 42.

[11] The author of the Life of St. Guy cited above, n. 10, calls the merchant who advised the saint to go into business *diaboli minister*.

has often been made. As always, those who were the beneficiaries of the established order defended it obstinately, not only because it guaranteed their interests, but because it seemed to them indispensable to the preservation of society. Moreover, the bourgeois themselves were far from taking up a revolutionary attitude towards this society. They took for granted the authority of the territorial princes, the privileges of the nobility and, above all, those of the Church. They even professed an ascetic morality, which was plainly contradicted by their mode of life. They merely desired a place in the sun, and their claims were confined to their most indispensable needs.

Of the latter, the most indispensable was personal liberty. Without liberty, that is to say, without the power to come and go, to do business, to sell goods, a power not enjoyed by serfdom, trade would be impossible. Thus they claimed it, simply for the advantages which it conferred, and nothing was further from the mind of the bourgeoisie than any idea of freedom as a natural right; in their eyes it was merely a useful one. Besides, many of them possessed it *de facto;* they were immigrants, who had come from too far off for their lord to be traced and who, since their serfdom could not be presumed, necessarily passed for free, although born of unfree parents. But the fact had to be transformed into a right. It was essential that the villeins, who came to settle in the towns to seek a new livelihood, should feel safe and should not have to fear being taken back by force to the manors from which they had escaped. They must be delivered from labour services and from all the hated dues by which the servile population was burdened, such as the obligation to marry only a woman of their own class and to leave to the lord part of their inheritance. Willy-nilly, in the course of the twelfth century these claims, backed up as they often were by dangerous revolts, had to be granted. The most obstinate conservatives, such as Guibert de Nogent, in 1115, were reduced to a wordy revenge, speaking of those "detestable communes" which the serfs had set up to escape from

their lord's authority and to do away with his most lawful
rights.[12] Freedom became the legal status of the bourgeoisie, so much so that it was no longer a personal privilege only, but a territorial one, inherent in urban soil just
as serfdom was in manorial soil. In order to obtain it, it
was enough to have resided for a year and a day within the
walls of the town. "City air makes a man free" (*Stadtluft
macht frei*), says the German proverb.

But if liberty was the first need of the burgess, there
were many others besides. Traditional law with its narrow,
formal procedure, its ordeals, its judicial duels, its judges
recruited from among the rural population, and knowing
no other custom than that which had been gradually
elaborated to regulate the relations of men living by the
cultivation or the ownership of the land, was inadequate
for a population whose existence was based on commerce
and industry. A more expeditious law was necessary,
means of proof more rapid and more independent of
chance, and judges who were themselves acquainted with
the professional occupations of those who came under their
jurisdiction, and could cut short their arguments by a
knowledge of the case at issue. Very early, and at latest
at the beginning of the eleventh century, the pressure of
circumstances led to the creation of a *jus mercatorum*, i.e.,
an embryonic commercial code. It was a collection of
usages born of business experience, a sort of international
custom, which the merchants used among themselves in
their transactions. Devoid of all legal validity, it was
impossible to invoke it in the existing law courts, so the
merchants agreed to choose among themselves arbitrators
who had the necessary competence to understand their

[12] Guibert de Nogent, *Histoire de sa vie*, ed. G. Bourgin, p.
156 (Paris, 1907). At the beginning of the thirteenth century
again Jacques de Vitry preaches against the "violent and
pestiferous *communitates*." A. Giry, *Documents sur les relations
de la royauté avec les villes en France*, p. 59 (Paris, 1885).
Similarly, in England, Richard de Devizes says, "Communia
est tumor plebis, timor regni tepor sacerdotii." W. Stubbs,
Select Charters, p. 252 (Oxford, 1890).

disputes and to settle them promptly. It is here undoubt-edly that we must seek the origin of those law courts, which in England received the picturesque name of courts of *piepowder* (*pied poudré*), because the feet of the mer-chants who resorted to them were still dusty from the roads.[13] Soon this *ad hoc* jurisdiction became permanent and was recognised by public authority. At Ypres, in 1116, the Count of Flanders abolished the judicial duel, and it is certain that about the same date he instituted in most of his towns local courts of *échevins,* chosen from among the burgesses and alone competent to judge them. Sooner or later the same thing happened in all countries. In Italy, France, Germany and England the towns ob-tained judicial autonomy, which made them islands of in-dependent jurisdiction, lying outside the territorial custom.

This jurisdictional autonomy was accompanied by ad-ministrative autonomy. The formation of urban agglomera-tions entailed a number of arrangements for convenience of defence, which they had to provide for themselves in the absence of the traditional authorities, who had neither the means nor the wish to help them. It is a strong testi-mony to the energy and the initiative of the bourgeoisie that it succeeded by its own efforts in setting on foot the municipal organisation, of which the first outlines appear in the eleventh century, and which was already in posses-sion of all its essential organs in the twelfth. The work thus accomplished is all the more admirable because it was an original creation. There was nothing in the existing order of things to serve it as a model, since the needs it was designed to meet were new.

The most pressing was the need for defence. The mer-chants and their merchandise were, indeed, such a tempt-

---

[13] "Extraneus mercator vel aliquis transiens per regnum, non habens certam mansionem infra vicecomitatum sed vagans, qui vocatur piepowdrous" (1124–53). Ch. Gross, *The Court of Piepowder,* in *The Quarterly Journal of Economics,* t. XX (1906), p. 231, n. 4.

ing prey that it was essential to protect them from pillagers by a strong wall. The construction of ramparts was thus the first public work undertaken by the towns and one which, down to the end of the Middle Ages, was their heaviest financial burden. Indeed, it may be truly said to have been the starting-point of their financial organisation, whence, for example, the name of *firmitas,* by which the communal tax was always known at Liége, and the appropriation in a number of cities *ad opus castri* (i.e., for the improvement of the fortifications) of a part of the fines imposed by the borough court. The fact that to-day municipal coats of arms are surrounded by a walled crown shows the importance accorded to the ramparts. There were no unfortified towns in the Middle Ages.

Money had to be raised to provide for the expenses occasioned by the permanent need for fortifications, and it could be raised most easily from the burgesses themselves. All were interested in the common defence and all were obliged to meet the cost. The quota payable by each was calculated on the basis of his fortune. This was a great innovation. For the arbitrary seigneurial tallage, collected in the sole interest of the lord, it substituted a payment proportionate to the means of the taxpayer and set apart for an object of general utility. Thus taxation recovered its public character, which had disappeared during the feudal era. To assess and collect this tax, as well as to provide for the ordinary necessities whose numbers grew with the constant increase of the town population, the establishment of quays and markets, the building of bridges and parish churches, the regulation of crafts and the supervision of food supplies, it soon became necessary to elect or allow the setting up of a council of magistrates, consuls in Italy and Provence, *jurés* in France and aldermen in England. In the eleventh century they appeared in the Lombard cities, where the consuls of Lucca are mentioned as early as 1080. In the following century, they became everywhere an institution ratified by public authority and inherent in every municipal constitution. In many towns, as in those of the Low Countries, the *échevins* were at once the judges and administrators of the townsfolk.

The lay princes soon discovered how advantageous the growth of the cities was to themselves. For in proportion as their trade grew on road and river and their increasing business transactions required a corresponding increase of currency, the revenues from every kind of toll and from the mints likewise flowed in increasing quantities into the lord's treasury. Thus it is not surprising that the lords assumed on the whole a benevolent attitude towards the townsfolk. Moreover, living as a rule in their country castles, they did not come in contact with the town population and thus many causes of conflict were avoided. It was quite otherwise with the ecclesiastical princes. Almost to a man they offered a resistance to the municipal movement, which at times developed into an open struggle. The fact that the bishops were obliged to reside in their cities, the centres of diocesan administration, necessarily impelled them to preserve their authority and to oppose the ambitions of the bourgeoisie all the more resolutely because they were roused and directed by the merchants, ever suspect in the eyes of the Church. In the second half of the eleventh century the quarrel of the Empire and the Papacy gave the city populations of Lombardy a chance to rise against their simoniacal prelates. Thence the movement spread through the Rhine valley to Cologne. In 1077, the town of Cambrai rose in revolt against Bishop Gerard II and formed the oldest of the "communes" that we meet with north of the Alps. In the diocese of Liége the same thing happened. In 1066 Bishop Théoduin was forced to grant the burgesses of Huy a charter of liberties which is several years earlier than those whose text has been preserved in the rest of the Empire. In France, municipal insurrections are mentioned at Beauvais about 1099, at Noyon in 1108–9, and at Laon in 1115.

Thus, by fair means or foul, the towns gained peaceably or by force, some at the beginning, others in the course of

the twelfth century, municipal constitutions suitable to the
life of their inhabitants. Originating in the "new burgs,"
in the *portus,* where the merchants and artisans were
grouped, they were soon developed to include the population of the "old burgs" and the "cities," whose ancient
walls, surrounded on all sides by the new quarters, were
falling into ruin like the old law itself. Henceforth, all
who resided within the city wall, with the sole exception
of the clergy, shared the privileges of the burgesses.

The essential characteristic of the bourgeoisie was,
indeed, the fact that it formed a privileged class in the
midst of the rest of the population. From this point of
view the medieval town offers a striking contrast both to
the ancient town and to the town of to-day, which are
differentiated only by the density of their population and
their complex administration; apart from this, neither in
public nor in private law do their inhabitants occupy a
peculiar position in the State. The medieval burgess, on
the contrary, was a different kind of person from all who
lived outside the town walls. Once outside the gates and
the moat we are in another world, or more exactly, in the
domain of another law. The acquisition of citizenship
brought with it results analogous to those which followed
when a man was dubbed knight or a clerk tonsured, in
the sense that they conferred a peculiar legal status. Like
the clerk or the noble, the burgess escaped from the common law; like them, he belonged to a particular estate
(*status*), which was later to be known as the "third estate."

The territory of the town was as privileged as its inhabitants. It was a sanctuary, an "immunity," which protected the man who took refuge there from exterior authority, as if he had sought sanctuary in a church. In short,
the bourgeoisie was in every sense an exceptional class.
Each town formed, so to speak, a little state to itself,
jealous of its prerogatives and hostile to all its neighbours.
Very rarely was a common danger or a common end able
to impose on its municipal particularism the need for
alliances or leagues such, for example, as the German

Hanse. In general, urban politics were determined by the same sacred egoism which was later to inspire State politics. For the burgesses the country population existed only to be exploited. Far from allowing it to enjoy their franchises, they always obstinately refused it all share in them. Nothing could be further removed from the spirit of modern democracy than the exclusiveness with which the medieval towns continued to defend their privileges, even, and indeed above all, in those periods when they were governed by the crafts.

Three

THE LAND AND THE RURAL CLASSES

I. MANORIAL ORGANISATION AND SERFDOM [1]

The influence of the bourgeoisie in every period of the Middle Ages, is all the more surprising because it is in strong contrast with its numerical importance. The towns

[1] BIBLIOGRAPHY.—To the works by Inama-Sternegg, Lamprecht, H. Sée and M. Bloch, mentioned in the general bibliography, should be added K. Lamprecht, *Étude sur l'état économique de la France pendant la première partie du Moyen Age*, trans. Marignan, Paris, 1889.—L. Delisle, *Études sur la condition de la classe agricole et l'état de l'agriculture en Normandie au Moyen Age*, Paris, 2nd ed., 1903.—A. Hansay, *Étude sur la formation et l'organisation économique du domaine de Saint-Trond jusqu'à la fin du XIIIe siècle*, Gand, 1899.— L. Verriest, *Le servage dans la comté de Hainaut. Les sainteurs. Le meilleur catel*, Brussels, 1910 (Mém. de l'Académie de Belgique).—G. des Marez, *Note sur le manse brabançon au Moyen Age*, in *Mélanges Pirenne*, Brussels, 1926.—F. Seebohm, *The English Village Community*, London, 1883.—P. Vinogradoff, *The Growth of the Manor*, London, 1905.— *Id., English Society in the Eleventh Century*, Oxford, 1908.—G. G. Coulton, *The Medieval Village*, Cambridge, 1925.—G. F. Knapp, *Grundherrschaft und Rittergut*, Leipzig, 1897.—W. Wittich, *Die Grundherrschaft in Nordwestdeutschland*, Leipzig, 1896.—O. Siebeck, *Der Frondienst als Arbeitssystem*, Tübingen, 1904.— R. Gaggese, *Classi e communi rurali nel medio evo italiano*, Florence, 1906-9, 2 vols.—H. Blink, *Geschiedenis van den boerenstand en den landbouw in Nederland*, Groningen, 1902-4, 2 vols.—G. Roupnel, *Histoire de la campagne française*, Paris, 1932.—M. Bloch, *Liberté et servitude personnelles*

contained a minority, sometimes even a very small minority of the population. In the absence of statistical data prior to the fifteenth century no precise numerical estimate can, of course, be formed, but we shall probably not be far wrong in supposing that in the whole of Europe between the twelfth and the fifteenth centuries the urban population never comprised more than a tenth part of the total number of inhabitants.[2] It was only in a few districts, such as the Low Countries, Lombardy or Tuscany, that this proportion was exceeded to any large extent. In any case, it is an undoubted fact that from the demographic point of view, medieval society was essentially agricultural.

Upon this rural society the great estate set so deep a mark that in many countries its traces did not disappear until the first half of the nineteenth century. We need not here go back to the origin of this institution, which the Middle Ages inherited from antiquity. All that is necessary is to describe it as it existed at its height in the course of the twelfth century, that is to say, at a time when it had not yet begun to change owing to the influence of the towns.[3] It is, perhaps, unnecessary to add that the manorial organisation was not imposed on all the rural population. It spared a certain number of small free proprietors, and in isolated districts we meet with villages which more or less escaped its control. But those are

---

au Moyen Age, particulièrement en France, in Annario de Historia del Derecho Español, 1933.—C. E. Perrin, Recherches sur la seigneurie rurale en Lorraine, Paris, 1935.

[2] F. Lot, L'État des paroisses et des feux de 1328, in the Bibliothèque de l'École des Chartes, t. XC (1929), p. 301, holds that at the beginning of the fourteenth century the urban population of France constituted between one-tenth and one-seventh of the total population. But, for Brabant, J. Cuvelier, Les dénombrements de foyers en Brabant, p. cxxxv, states that in 1437 two-thirds of the houses in the whole duchy were to be found in the countryside.

[3] It is hardly necessary to call attention to the fact that since manorial organisation differed in different parts of Europe, it can only be described here in a very general way, only the main and typical features being outlined.

only exceptions which need not be considered in a broad outline of the general evolution of Western Europe.

From the point of view of size, the great medieval estates amply justified the name. They seem to have contained on an average three hundred farms (*mansi*), or about 10,000 acres, and many of them were undoubtedly considerably larger. But their lands were never all together. They were always scattered. The "villas" of the same landowner were separated by greater and greater distances, the further they lay from the manorial centre. The monastery of Saint-Trond, for example, was the lord of a vast property, the bulk of which was grouped around it, but which had distant annexes, as far north as the environs of Nimwegen and as far south as those of Trier.[4] This scattering naturally resulted in a considerable interweaving of manors, to such an extent that the same village often owed allegiance to two or three lords. The situation was still further complicated when an estate extended, as frequently happened, to regions under the rule of several princes, or to territories speaking different languages. This situation was the result of the building up of territorial agglomerations by means of successive gifts from a multitude of benefactors, in the case of the Church, or by the accident of matrimonial alliances or of inheritance, in that of the nobility. No uniform design had brought about the formation of the large estate; it was what history had made it, independent of all economic considerations.

Scattered though it was, it nevertheless possessed a powerful organisation, which in essentials seems to have been the same in all countries. The centre of the estate was the customary residence of the landowner, whether it was cathedral, church, abbey or fortified castle. The whole of the land was parcelled out into a number of divisions,

---

[4] See the map of this estate in the thirteenth century in H. Pirenne, *Le Livre de l'abbé Guillaume de Ryckel, polyptyque et comptes de l'abbaye de Saint-Trond au milieu du XIII° siècle* (Brussels, 1896).

each of which contained one or more villages (*villae*) and was under the jurisdiction of a *curtis* (*cour* in the countries of the Romance tongue, *hof* in those of the German, and *manor* in England). Here were grouped the farm buildings, barns, cattle-sheds, stables, etc., as well as the domestic serfs (*servi quotidiani, dagescalci*) employed in looking after them. Here also lived the agent in charge of the administration, the *villicus* or *major* (*maire, mayeur* on the Continent; *seneschal, steward,* or *bailiff* in England), chosen from among the *ministeriales*, that is to say, the serfs attached as confidential men to the house of the lord. By virtue of the general evolution peculiar to the agricultural period of the Middle Ages, this agent, who in the beginning was liable to dismissal, soon came to have an hereditary right to his office.

The whole of the soil under the jurisdiction of a *cour* or manor was divided into three parts: the demesne, the tenants' holdings and the commons. The *demesne* (*terra indominicata, mansus indominicatus*) constituted the seigneurial reserve, and consisted of all the lands set apart for the exclusive use of the lord. It is impossible to determine exactly their proportional importance, which varied considerably in the different manors. As a general rule, they consisted of scattered strips lying among those of the tenants. The size of the tenants' holdings, on the other hand, showed a remarkable fixity in each *villa,* though they often differed very considerably in different regions. They comprised, in fact, the amount of land sufficient for the support of a family, with the result that they varied in size with the fertility of the soil.[5] They were known by the name of *mancus* (*manse, mas*), in Latin, *hufe* in German and *virgate* or *yardland* in English.

[5] According to the work of Des Marez, cited in the bibliography (n. 1), the *manse* in Brabant consisted ordinarily of 10 to 12 *bonniers*, which, given the varying size of the *bonniers*, was equivalent to about 8 to 15 hectares (i.e., about 20 to 37½ acres). According to Marc Bloch, *op. cit.,* p. 159, the area of the farms in France fluctuated between 5 and 30 hectares, the average being about 13 hectares.

All were burdened with labour services and dues (usually in kind) for the profit of the lord. All gave their occupant common rights of usage over the natural meadows, marshes, heath or forest which surrounded the cultivated soil and which are called *communia* or *warescapia* in the documents. Efforts have been made without success to find traces of so-called collective ownership in these common lands. In reality their ownership was vested in the lord.

With the exception of the lord, all who lived on the territory of a manor were either serfs or, so to speak, quasi-serfs. Though the slavery of the ancient world had disappeared, traces of it still remained in the status of the *servi quotidiani* and *mancipia*, whose very persons belonged to the lord, and who were attached to his service and kept by him. It was from among them that he recruited the labourers on his demesne, herdsmen, shepherds and the workpeople of both sexes whom he employed in the "gynecea," under which name were indiscriminately grouped the workshops of the manorial *curtis*, where the flax and wool produced on the estate were woven, and where wheelwrights, blacksmiths, ale brewers and other artisans were also set to work. Personal serfdom was less marked among the tenants established, or (to use an expression general down to the twelfth century) *casati*, on the holdings, though there were still a large number of nuances. But in reality all in the end had acquired hereditary possession of the land they cultivated, although many had held it in the beginning by a very precarious title. Among them were even to be found former freemen, whose liberty was very much curtailed by the obligation to pay the labour services and dues which weighed heavily on their holdings. On the monastic manors a privileged class had grown up in the midst of the manorial population, *cerocensuales,* the descendants for the most part of widowed women of free origin who had placed themselves under the protection of an abbey, granting it the ownership of their estates on condition that they themselves enjoyed the revenues, in return for a payment of wax at the big annual church festivals.[6] Slightly different from the tenants, properly so-called, where the cotters or bordars (*cotarii, bordarii*), serfs holding a mere patch of ground, who were employed as agricultural labourers in the service of the lord or of the virgaters.

The dependence of the manorial population upon the lord was still further increased by the fact that the latter exercised jurisdiction over them. All serfs were, without exception, amenable to it, while the other tenants were not infrequently subject to the common law courts, in the matter of crimes and misdemeanours. The competence of seigneurial jurisdiction varied in the different countries according to the extent of feudal encroachments on the sovereignty of the king. It attained its maximum in France and its minimum in England. But everywhere it extended at least to all questions concerning holdings, labour services, dues and the cultivation of the soil. Each manor had its court, composed of peasants, presided over by the bailiff or *villicus* and giving judgment according to "the custom of the manor," that is to say, the traditional usages which at long intervals the population, consulted by the lord, declared and set down in the custumals or *Weistümer*.

Just as each manor formed a jurisdictional unity, so also it formed a religious one. The lords had built near their principal seat a chapel or a church, endowed with land, the incumbent of which they themselves nominated. This was the origin of a very large number of rural parishes, so that ecclesiastical organisation, whose dioceses have preserved for so long the boundaries of Roman "cities," sometimes still perpetuates to-day in the outline of its parishes, that of many a lordship of the early Middle Ages.

Thus the manor was not only an economic but a social institution. It imposed itself upon the whole life of its

---

[6] In Hainault and the neighbouring regions they were called *sainteurs*.

inhabitants. They were a good deal more than merely tenants of their lord; they were his men in every sense of the word, and it has been justly observed that seigneurial authority rested more on the attributes of chieftainship which it conferred on its possessor than on his attributes as a landed proprietor. The manorial organisation was essentially patriarchal. Language itself bears testimony to this. What was the *seigneur* (senior) if not the elder, whose authority extended over the *familia* whom he protected? For, unquestionably, he did protect them. In times of war he defended them against the énemy and sheltered them within the walls of his fortress, and it was clearly to his own advantage to do so, since he lived by their labour. The idea we are accustomed to form of seigneurial exploitation is perhaps a little summary. The exploitation of man implies the wish to make use of him as a tool to obtain the maximum of production. The rural slavery of the ancient world, that of the Negroes in the colonies in the seventeenth and eighteenth centuries, or the condition of the workers in the great industry in the first half of the nineteenth century, furnish us with familiar examples. But all this is very different from the medieval manors, where all-powerful custom determined every man's rights and obligations. This fact alone was enough to prevent the pitiless severity to which the free exercise of economic supremacy gives rise under the spur of profit. Moreover, the whole idea of profit, and indeed the possibility of profit, was incompatible with the position occupied by the great medieval landowner. Unable to produce for sale owing to the want of a market, he had no need to tax his ingenuity in order to wring from his men and his land a surplus which would merely be an encumbrance, and as he was forced to consume his own produce, he was content to limit it to his needs. His means of existence was assured by the traditional functioning of an organisation which he did not try to improve. Before the middle of the twelfth century, the greater part of the soil belonging to him was given over to heaths, forests and marshes.

Nowhere do we perceive the least effort to break with the age-old system of rotation, to suit the crops cultivated to the properties of the soil, or to improve agricultural implements. Considering its potential capacity, the enormous landed capital at the disposal of the Church and the nobility produced in the main no more than an insignificant return.

It would be interesting, though it is impossible, to discover how much the peasants made on these manors which their holders did not farm for profit, after working for a whole year from one to three days a week on the lord's demesne and after paying on the customary dates the dues in kind which burdened their land. It must have been little, if anything. But this little sufficed for men whose sole object, like that of their lord, was to produce enough for their own needs. Free from all fear of expulsion, since his land was hereditary, the *vilain* enjoyed the advantage of security, but on the other hand the agrarian system gave him neither the opportunity nor the desire for individual exploitation. The system, indeed, of necessity entailed work in common. This was the case with the two great methods of cultivation whose origin undoubtedly dates back to prehistoric times, long strips or irregular fields. In both the rotation of cultivation, whether the two-field or the three-field system was in use (that is to say, whether one-half or one-third of the cultivable surface lay fallow each year), imposed collective cultivation on all alike. The same patches of the same *shot,* or *quartier,* or *gewann* had to be ploughed together, sown, or given over to common of shack after the harvest. The fact that they were intermingled meant that they had to remain open up to the moment the corn began to come up, when they were enclosed by a temporary fence. After the harvest, the community did not lose its rights. All the animals in the village were driven in a single herd to pasture on the stubble of the ploughed fields, from which the corn had been garnered and the fences removed.

In such a state of things, the activity of each depended

upon the activity of all and as long as it lasted economic equality must have been the general rule among the peasant-farmers. In case of illness or invalidism, neighbours would come to the rescue. Certainly, the taste for saving, which was later to become characteristic of the peasant, had no opportunity of manifesting itself. If a family were too numerous, the younger sons entered the group of cotters (*cotarii*), or went to increase the crowds of vagrants who drifted through the country.

Again, the rights of the lord fettered individual activity, in divers degrees, according to persons. The serfs, properly so-called, could not marry without paying a tax, nor *formarier*, i.e., marry a woman outside the manor, without permission. At their death, the lord received all or part of their inheritance (*corimedis, mort-main, heriot*). Labour services and dues in kind weighed heavily on all tenants, or, rather, on all holdings, for in the course of time they had been transformed from personal into real charges. In this connection there were various distinct categories of *mansi;* some were *ingenuiles,* some *serviles,* some *lidiles,* and their obligations differed according to whether they had originally been occupied by a "body serf," a *lite* (half-free) or a freeman. The tallage which the lord also required from his men in case of need was unquestionably the heaviest and the most odious burden to which they were submitted. It subjected them to a levy which was not only gratuitous, but arbitrary, and was thus capable of grave abuse. It was otherwise with the "banalities" which obliged the *vilains* to grind their grain in the lord's mill, to brew their ale in his brewery, or to press their grapes in his wine-press. The taxes which had to be paid for all this were at least compensated for by the use of plant which had been set up at the lord's expense.

In conclusion it should be observed that the lord did not profit by all the dues collected on the manor. It frequently happened that his lands were encumbered by "justiciary" rights, that is to say, rights emanating not from property but from sovereignty. This was very often the case, for instance, with the *champart* or *medem,* which may be considered as a remote survival, incorporated in the land, of the Roman public tax. Many landowners had confiscated it for their own benefit, but sometimes also it was collected for the benefit of the territorial prince, or for someone else entitled thereto. Very different in kind, the tithe constituted a much severer and, above all, a much more general charge. Theoretically, it should have been collected by the Church; actually, many lords had possessed themselves of it. In any case, the origin of all these dues mattered little to the peasant, since, whatever their nature, it was on him that all alike were piled.

II.   CHANGES IN AGRICULTURE FROM THE BEGINNING OF THE TWELFTH CENTURY [7]

From the middle of the tenth century the population of Western Europe, delivered at last from the pillages of the Saracens, the Northmen and the Hungarians, began an upward movement concerning which we have no precise details, but the results of which appear clearly in the following century. It is plain that manorial organisation no longer harmonised with the excess of births over deaths,

[7] BIBLIOGRAPHY.—See above, n. 1.—Add: Ed. Bonvalot, *Le tiers-état d'après la charte de Beaumont et ses filiales,* Paris, 1884.—M. Prou, *Les coutumes de Lorris et leur propagation au XIIe et au XIIIe siècle,* in the *Nouv. Rev. hist. du droit français,* t. VIII, 1884.—L. Vanderkindere, *La loi de Prisches,* in *Mélanges P. Fredericq,* Brussels, 1904.—M. Bateson, *The Laws of Breteuil,* in *English Hist. Review,* vol. XV, 1900.—F. Goblet d'Alviella, *Histoire des bois et forêts en Belgique,* t. I, Brussels, 1927.—A. Schwappach, *Grundriss des Forst-und Jagdwesens Deutschlands,* Berlin, 1892.—E. de Borchgrave. *Histoire des colonies belges qui s'établirent en Allemagne pendant le XIIe et le XIIIe siècle,* Brussels, 1865 (Mém. Acad. de Belgique).—R. Schroeder, *Die Niederländischen Kolonien im Norddeutschland zur Zeit des Mittelalters,* Berlin, 1880. —E. O. Schulze, *Niederländische Siedelungen in den Marschen an der unteren Weser und Elbe im XII und XIII Jahrhundert,* Hanover, 1889.

and a growing number of individuals, compelled to leave the paternal holding, had to seek fresh means of subsistence. In particular the lesser nobility, whose fiefs were inherited by primogeniture, were burdened with a multitude of younger sons. The Norman adventurers who conquered Southern Italy, followed Duke William to England and furnished the majority of the soldiers of the first crusade, were recruited from among these. The immigration from the country to the nascent towns and the formation of the new class of merchants and artisans, which took place about the same time, would be incomprehensible without a considerable increase in the number of inhabitants. That increase was still more striking at the beginning of the twelfth century and continued without interruption to the end of the thirteenth. Two important phenomena resulted from it: on the one hand, a denser population in the regions of old settlements, on the other, the colonisation by German emigrants, of the Slav countries on the right bank of the Elbe and the Saale. Finally, the growing density and the expansion of the population was accompanied by a profound change in its economic condition and legal status. With more or less rapidity in different countries, there began a process of evolution which, in spite of variations in detail, showed the same general trend throughout the West.

We have already seen that the idea of profit was completely foreign to the patriarchal organisation of the great estate. It functioned only for the subsistence of the lord and his people. Regulated by custom which fixed immutably every man's rights and obligations, it was incapable of adapting itself to the new conditions. Nowhere do we see the great landowners taking the first step to bring it into harmony with its changed surroundings. They were obviously disconcerted by them, and allowed themselves to be carried along, without seeking to profit by the advantages which the enormous landed capital at their disposal might have given them. Clearly it was not they but their tenants who inaugurated the changes, which already in the first half of the twelfth century in the most advanced countries, brought about the decay of the manorial system. But this was true only of the old estates of the lay aristocracy and of the bishops and Benedictine monasteries, established in accordance with the principles which had prevailed in the Carolingian era. On the other hand, the Cistercian abbeys founded in the eleventh century, that is to say, at a time when the first symptoms of a breach in the traditional equilibrium were beginning to manifest themselves, show an entirely new type of economic administration. Since all cultivable lands were already occupied at the time of their appearance, they almost always established themselves in wild and uncultivated country, in the midst of woods, heaths and marshes. Their benefactors made them large grants from the wastes in which their demesnes abounded and the monks were thus able to work with their hands as their rule ordained. Unlike the Benedictine monasteries, which had mostly been heavily endowed with lands already under cultivation, the Cistercians applied themselves from the beginning to the work of clearing the land. In this work they were assisted by lay brothers, or *conversi,* to whom they entrusted the exploitation of the large farms or granges which were the innovations of their agricultural economy. These embraced a considerable area, usually 500 to 700 acres, which, instead of being divided into holdings, was farmed under the supervision of a monk (*grangiarius*), by the *conversi,* or even by men from outside, employed as agricultural labourers.

Serfdom which up to then had been the normal status of the peasants, was almost entirely absent on Cistercian lands, nor do we meet there corvées nor the oppressive and incompetent supervision of the hereditary *villici.* Nothing could have been more different from the demesnes of the old manorial estates than these fine Cistercian farms, with their centralised administration, compact form, and rational exploitation. Thus the "new lands" that the monasteries put under cultivation brought with them a new kind of economic organisation. Here is an intelligent system which discovered how to profit to the full by the increase of population. It appealed to that surplus of workers for whom there was no employment under the old division of land. It was certainly from among them that it recruited its lay brothers, whose numbers continued to grow up to the second half of the thirteenth century. The Abbey of the Dunes had thirty-six of them in 1150 and twelve hundred and forty-eight a hundred years later; and side by side with them, the free labour furnished by the *hôtes* grew at a corresponding rate.[8]

The term *hôtes* (literally "guests"), which appears more and more frequently from the beginning of the twelfth century, is characteristic of the movement which was then going on in rural society. As the name indicates, the *hôte* was a new-comer, a stranger. He was, in short, a kind of colonist, an immigrant in search of new lands to cultivate. These colonists were undoubtedly drawn either from the vagrant population, from which at the same period the first merchants and the artisans of the towns were being recruited, or from among the inhabitants of the great estates, whose serfdom they thus shook off. For the regular status of the *hôte* was one of freedom. To be sure, he was almost always born of unfree parents, but as soon as he had managed to put a distance between himself and the estate where he was born, and to elude the pursuit of his lord, who could tell what was his original status? No one any longer had any claim on his person and he was henceforward his own master. For these *hôtes* there were vacant lands in abundance. Immense "solitudes," forests, woodlands and marshes remained outside the bounds of private ownership, depending on the justiciary authority of the territorial princes alone. A simple permission to

[8] On the organisation of Cistercian estates see, for instance, *Le polyptyque de l'abbaye de Villers* (mid 13th century), edited by E. de Moreau and J. B. Goetstouwers, in the *Analectes pour servir à l'histoire ecclésiastique de la Belgique,* tt. XXXII and XXXIII (1906–7), and E. de Moreau, *L'abbaye de Villers en Brabant,* Brussels, 1909.

settle there was all that was required, and why should it be refused, since the new-comers were infringing no established rights? Everything goes to show that in many cases they started on their own initiative to clear and drain the land, like colonists in new countries. From the beginning of the twelfth century, for instance, free immigrants established themselves in the vast spaces of the "forest of Theux" held by the prince-bishop of Liége, without having been invited by the latter to do so. They were the first to penetrate into these wilds, the settlement of which was so much the work of free pioneers that down to the end of the Ancien Régime serfdom was still unknown there.

It is, of course, obvious that this primitive mode of occupation could not last very long. The holders of all virgin lands outside the manorial *communia* soon began to take advantage of the growing increase of manual labour. The very simple idea of attracting *hôtes* and settling them there in return for a rent could not fail to suggest itself. *Mutatis mutandis,* they employed the same method of settling and populating the land which we see so often in the Far West of America in the nineteenth century. The resemblance of the "new towns" of the eleventh and twelfth centuries to the towns laid out in advance by American contractors all along a railway line, is indeed striking, even down to details. Both sides sought to attract the immigrant by offering him the most advantageous material and personal conditions, and both had recourse to publicity to entice him. The charter of the *ville neuve* which was to be founded was promulgated throughout the country, just as in our days the press publishes the most flamboyant prospectuses about the future resources and amenities of a town which is in process of formation. The name of "new town" is not less significant than that of the *hôtes,* for whom it was destined. It clearly indicates that it was intended for new-comers, strangers and immigrants, i.e., for colonists. In this respect it at once presents the strongest possible contrast to the large manorial estate, a fact which is all the more remarkable since the founder of the new town was almost always the lord of one or more manors. He was familiar with manorial organisation and yet carefully refrained from imitating it, for the obvious reason that he considered it unsuitable to the wishes and needs of the people whom he proposed to attract. Nowhere do we observe the least connection between the old manors and the new towns, the smallest effort to attach the latter to the *curtes* of the former, or to submit them to the jurisdiction of the *villici*. They were as completely independent of one another as two different worlds.

From the agrarian point of view, the chief characteristic of the new towns was free labour. Their charters, which are so numerous from the beginning of the twelfth to the end of the thirteenth century, leave everywhere the same impression. Personal serfdom is completely unknown. What is more, the serfs who came from outside are to be enfranchised after a year and a day's residence, though occasionally the founder excepts from this rule the serfs on his own manors, lest these should become depopulated to the advantage of the new town. It was the same with labour services. After all, these services were used for the cultivation of the lord's demesne, and here there was no demesne land. The entire soil was covered with peasant holdings and each peasant devoted the whole of his labour to his own land. At most, a few collective labour dues were here and there imposed on the population, such, for example, as the obligation found in the charter of Lorris (1155) of transporting the King's wine once a year to Orléans. As to the old manorial rights of mortmain, heriot and formariage, there was naturally no longer any question of them. Tallage and the obligation of military service remained, but they took on the nature of public charges and were moreover limited and regulated. The *banalités* of the wine-press and the mill did not disappear, but they were not rights which debased personal status, nor could their exercise be considered as an exploitation, since the plant involved was indispensable and no one but the lord could have constructed it.

Here it is important to observe that if the peasants of the new town differed from manorial *vilains,* they also had many points of resemblance with burgesses. The charters by which they were governed were directly influenced by urban law, so much so that the inhabitants of the new towns are frequently described as burgesses. Like burgesses, indeed, they received an administrative autonomy corresponding to their needs. The mayor who was placed at their head in no way resembled the manorial *villici;* he was the guardian of the village interests, and often, as in the numerous *villes neuves* whose charters of enfranchisement were modelled on that of Beaumont in Argonne (1182), he was nominated by the peasants. Similarly, in imitation of the towns, each *ville neuve* had its own council to administer law and justice to its inhabitants. Thus the new rural class benefited by the earlier progress of the bourgeoisie. So far from the towns having sprung from the villages, as has sometimes been thought, it was, on the contrary, the free villages which were endowed with municipal law, in so far as it was applicable to them. It is a curious fact that for the greater part of the time it was the large towns, and not the secondary semi-rural ones, whose laws spread all over the countryside. In Brabant, for instance, the dukes founded the charters given in 1160 to Baisy, in 1216 to Dongelberg, in 1222 to Wavre, in 1228 to Courrières, and in 1251 to Merchtem, upon that of Louvain. A few charters of new towns proved so excellent in practice that they spread far and wide. That of Lorris, at the beginning of 1155, was conferred on eighty-three places in Gatinais and Orléanais, that of Beaumont, at the beginning of 1182, on over five hundred villages and *bourgs* of Champagne, Burgundy and Luxembourg, that of Priches (1158) on numbers of new towns in Hainault and Vermandois. In the same way the laws of Breteuil in Normandy were disseminated widely in the course of the twelfth century, in England, Wales and even in Ireland.

Nevertheless the analogy must not be carried too far and we must beware of exaggerating the resemblance between the peasant of the *villes neuves* and the burgess of the towns proper. The personal liberty of the peasant was still limited by the rights which the lord preserved in respect of the village land. The *hôte*, in fact, enjoyed only the hereditary use of the land in return for a rent (*cens*), but the actual ownership continued to reside in the lord and all matters relating to the tenures were subject to seigneurial jurisdiction. It may be said with truth that in the *villes neuves* peasant farming went hand in hand with the great estate. The latter formed the legal substratum of the whole edifice; though it no longer determined the condition of men, it continued to determine that of the land. Doubtless, in the long run, the peasant's possession of his holding became so strong as to appear almost in the light of a proprietary right, encumbered merely by a nominal payment to the lord. Nevertheless peasant ownership never completely threw off the bonds that shackled it until the end of the *Ancien Régime*.

The *villes neuves* were only one manifestation of the great work of land reclamation which from the end of the eleventh century transformed the soil of Europe. Moreover, they are to be found, in the form which we have been describing, nowhere except in the north of France between the Loire and the Meuse. South of the Loire may be compared with the *bastides*, which were similarly due to the initiative of princes or great lords. In Spain, the *poblaciones* of the regions retaken by the Christians from the Moslems present the rather different character of a military colonisation. As to Italy, it seems very probable that the development of cultivation was mainly accomplished by the mere increase of the number of inhabitants in the old agricultural divisions, dating from ancient times, of which the people regained possession at the end of the Saracen devastations and the civil wars of the tenth century. But in spite of differences in detail, the general phenomenon was everywhere the same. Throughout the area occupied by the old Carolingian Empire, the growing density of the population brought about a great increase in the number of inhabited centres, from which free labour pushed its way energetically across the waste-lands to conquer fresh fields.

In the Low Countries it undertook a simultaneous fight against the sea and the rivers. Over-population, here very conspicuous, was unquestionably the cause of the first attempts at drainage. We know from the sources that during the eleventh century the county of Flanders began to find difficulty in feeding its inhabitants. Numbers of Flemings, indeed, are known to have enlisted in 1066 in the army of William the Conqueror, and when the expedition ended they remained in England, where, for a hundred years, bands of their fellow-countrymen keep on coming to join them. A little later the same country furnished the first crusade with one of its largest armies, and it was from· it again that the neighbouring princes recruited those mercenaries who, under the name of *geldungi, cotereaux,* or *Brabançons,* played in the military history of the eleventh and twelfth centuries the same rôle as the Swiss in that of the sixteenth.[9] Finally, the extraordinarily rapid growth of Flemish towns in the same period obviously implies a characteristic flow of the rural population into urban centres. The same necessity to find new means of existence must have called forth the oldest dikes. The counts of Flanders early took steps to encourage and keep them up. Indeed, the marshes (*meerschen,*

[9] H. Pirenne, *Histoire de Belgique,* t. I, 5th ed., p. 156. The Romance countries adjoining Flanders also appear to have been exceedingly thickly populated in the twelfth century and they sent many emigrants to Silesia and even to Hungary. The town of Gran seems to have owed its origin to them. In the twelfth century there was a *vicus latinorum* there, inhabited chiefly by people from Lotharingia and Artois. K. Schünemann, *Die Entstehung des Stadtwesens in Südosteuropa* (Breslau, 1929).

broeken) and the alluvial soil were subject to the princely authority, which was bound to gain by their being brought under cultivation. Under Baldwin V. (1035–67) the progress made was already considerable enough for the Archbishop of Rheims to be able to congratulate the Count on having transformed regions, until then unproductive, into fertile lands, rich with grazing herds. From that time, the whole maritime region was dotted with vaccaries and sheepfolds (*vaccariae, bercariae*), and, at the end of the century, their revenues were sufficiently large to be the subject of elaborate accounts drawn up by professional notaries.

This suffices to show that the counts did not introduce manorial organisations into the "new lands" of maritime Flanders. The areas to be drained or diked were granted, like the ground of the *villes neuves* of the interior, to *hôtes* who came to settle there. Their status again, as in the *villes neuves,* was that of freemen, bound simply to the payment of rents in money or in kind. But the peculiar circumstances created by the struggle with the sea demanded from these men a very much closer degree of co-operation than that of the peasants on the mainland. Although the associations of *wateringues,* i.e., obligatory groups formed in order to regulate the flow of the waters and to keep up the dikes in the same maritime district, do not appear in the earliest texts, there is not a doubt but that they must have existed from the beginning. In the twelfth century we already encounter on every side, in the estuary of the Scheldt and along the coast of the North Sea, *polders,* a word by which was designated the alluvial soil, diked and reclaimed from the sea. In this period the abbeys imitated the example of the Count and began energetically to drive back the waters in the swampy parts of their estates. Among them, the Cistercians took the lead. In the territory of Hulst alone, in the middle of the thirteenth century, the Abbey of the Dunes possessed 5,000 measures of diked land and 2,400 of non-diked (about 5,500 and 2,750 acres respectively).

In the north of Flanders, the counties of Zealand and
Holland gave proof of the same activity. For want of
documents, we know no details, but the results which it
obtained and the reputation which it won leave no room
to doubt its progress. So great in fact was the renown of
the people of the Low Countries as constructors of dikes
that the German princes invited them at the beginning of
the twelfth century to drain the banks of the Lower Elbe,
whence they soon penetrated into Brandenburg and Mecklenburg, where the configuration of the ground still preserves traces of their works. The princes who sent for
them naturally left them in possession of their personal
liberty and granted them land on conditions analogous to
those customary in their own country. The law which they
brought with them was known as *flämisches Recht,* and
revealed to Germany the class of free peasants, of which
they were such energetic representatives. From this time
the grant of *flämisches Recht* was the equivalent of enfranchisement to the rural population. Flemish colonists
penetrated in the same way into Thuringia, Saxony, Lausitz, and even into Bohemia. Thus they may be regarded
as the forerunners of the great colonial expansion pro-
jected by Germany in the territories on the right bank of
the Elbe and the Saale. Here, settlement was simply the
sequel and result of conquest. The dukes of Saxony and
the margraves of Brandenburg, by driving back and mas-
sacring the Slav population of these regions, opened them
to German occupation. Furthermore, it is certain that this
occupation could never have gone forward so widely and
with such vigour, if the soil of the mother-country had
not at this time been insufficient for its inhabitants. From
Saxony and Thuringia peasants set out to install themselves between the Elbe and the Saale. Westphalians soon
followed and together they poured into Mecklenburg,
Brandenburg and Lausitz. By the end of the twelfth century Mecklenburg was completely colonised; and in the
thirteenth Brendenburg also. It was reserved to the Teutonic Order to pave the way by force of arms, from 1230,

for a German advance in East Prussia, Livonia and Lithuania and to carry it as far as the Gulf of Finland. But Bavarians and Rhinelanders were also advancing at the same time into Bohemia, Moravia and Silesia, into the Tyrol and as far as the borders of Hungary, superimposing themselves on, or settling down side by side with, the original Slav inhabitants of these countries.

The movement was directed with as much skill as energy. The princes apportioned the conquered territories to *locatores,* great colonising agents whose business it was to attract people and to distribute land to them. The Cistercian monasteries were liberally endowed with these areas won from the "barbarians" and at once set up their farms and granges there. The condition of the inhabitants was also the same as that of the *hôtes* of the *villes neuves.* After all, these immigrants of colonial Germany were also and pre-eminently new-comers, *hôtes* on this foreign soil where they were taking the place of Slavs. They received it by hereditary right in return for a moderate *cens,* and they were granted personal liberty, which was indeed indispensable in all colonial territories. Thus the new Germany not only differed from the old Germany in the distribution of its land, but also in the status of its inhabitants.

The great transformation of the rural classes in the twelfth and thirteenth centuries was not only the result of the growing density of population. It was due, also, in large measure to the revival of trade and the growth of the towns. The old manorial organisation, framed for an age in which the absence of markets compelled the produce of the soil to be consumed on the spot, had necessarily to give way when permanent markets assured it a regular sale. This was what happened from the moment that the towns began to demand the country produce, which was essential to their existence. It is entirely inaccurate to represent the first urban agglomerations as semi-rural centres, capable of provisioning themselves. From the beginning, the bourgeoisie appeared as a class of merchants and artisans and it retained this character in all its greatest centres. Thus it was, in the language of the eighteenth century physiocrats, a sterile class, since it produced nothing which could directly serve to maintain life. Its day-to-day existence, its daily bread, depended on the peasantry of the neighbourhood. Up to then the peasants had tilled the soil and reaped the harvest only for themselves and for their lords; now they were urged, and urged increasingly as the number and importance of the towns grew, to produce a surplus, for the consumption of the burgess. The corn came out of the granaries and entered in its turn into circulation, either being carried to the neighbouring town by the peasant himself, or being sold on the spot to merchants who traded in it.[10]

This mobility of the fruits of the earth necessarily brought with it the progress of monetary circulation in the country—the progress, not the beginning, for nothing could be more contrary to truth than the belief, which has too often been held, that the first centuries of the Middle Ages, i.e., those subsequent to the eighth century, were an era of exchange, not in money, but in kind. Properly speaking, what is called natural economy (*Naturalwirtschaft*) never existed in its pure form. There is no doubt that the dues payable to the lord from the *familia* of the great estates were usually paid in products of the soil. Nothing could be more understandable or more practical in a system where the sole purpose of such rents was to provision the landowner; but as soon as the harvest became an object of exchange, its price was expressed and paid in money. This was already the case in the intermittent trade to which it was necessary to have recourse in times of famine; there is no sign that the

---

[10] The influence of the towns on the country was particularly powerful in Italy, where the countryside fell under the domination of the large communes. For the most recent account of this phenomenon see A. Doren, *Italienische Wirtschaftsgeschichte*, t. I, p. 193 *et seq.*

much-needed corn was ever bartered instead of being bought for ready money. Moreover, it is enough to open the Carolingian capitularies to be convinced of the regular use of money in the most trifling transactions effected by *deneratas* in the small markets of the time. It is true that the use of money was limited, but that is not because it was unknown, but because the economic structure of the period, being incompatible with genuine commercial activity, reduced it to a minimum. But as soon as this activity became normal and regular again, monetary circulation, which had never disappeared, advanced side by side with trade. Dues in kind did not disappear—they have never disappeared in any period, not even in our own—but they were less often used, because they were less useful in a society where exchange was increasing. What happened was not the substitution of a money economy (*Geldwirtschaft*) for a natural economy, but simply the fact that money gradually took its place as a measure of value and an instrument of exchange.[11]

The very fact that it was in general use increased the volume of currency. The stock of money in circulation was infinitely more considerable in the twelfth and thirteenth centuries than it had been from the ninth to the end of the tenth century, and the result was a rise in prices which, naturally, turned everywhere to the advantage of the producers. Now this rise in prices went hand in hand with a way of life whose demands became more costly. In every direction where commerce spread, it created the desire for the new articles of consumption which it brought with it. As always happens, the aristocracy wished to surround themselves with the luxury, or at least with the comfort befitting their social rank. We see at once, for instance, by comparing the life of a knight in the eleventh century with that of one in the twelfth, how the expenses necessitated by food, dress, household furni-

[11] H. Van Werveke, *Monnaie, lingots ou marchandises? Les instruments d'échange aux XI*e *et XII*e *siècles,* in *Annales d'histoire économique et sociale,* 1932, p. 452 *et seq.*

ture and, above all, arms, rose between these two periods. They would have risen still higher if revenues had shown a similar rise, but in a landowning class, such as the nobility, these remained, in the midst of a rise in the cost of living, what they had been before; fixed by custom, the rents payable by the land were unalterable. The landowners certainly received from their tenants enough to continue in the old way of life, but not to live as they now wished to do. They were the victims of an obsolete economic system, which prevented them from drawing from their landed capital a rent proportionate to its value. Tradition made it impossible even to think of increasing the dues of their tenants or the labour services of their serfs, since these were sanctioned by age-old usage and had become rights which could not be attacked without causing the most dangerous economic and social repercussions.

Equally incapable of resisting their new needs and of finding the wherewithal to satisfy them, numbers of the nobility were reduced first to debt, and then to ruin. In the middle of the thirteenth century, Thomas de Cantimpré relates that in his native parish the number of knights had dropped from sixty, at the end of the preceding century, to one or two,[12] and this is certainly only a local instance of a general phenomenon. The Church itself was affected by it. At about the same time, Eudes Rigaud, archbishop of Rouen, describes the situation of the majority of small monasteries in his diocese as exceedingly embarrassed.[13] The great lay and ecclesiastical landowners were clearly in a better position to withstand the crisis, but only at the price of a more or less complete rupture with the traditional manorial organisation. Though it had been in existence too long to permit of change, costs could at least be reduced and a rather more

[12] Thomas de Cantimpré, *Bonum Universale de apibus*, II, 49, p. 446, in the Douai ed., 1605.
[13] *Journal des visites pastorales d'Eudes Rigaud, archevêque de Rouen* (1248–69), ed. Th. Bonnin (Rouen, 1852).

profitable yield extracted from it. Many of its institutions had become superfluous with the revival of commerce. Of what use now were the domestic workshops (*gynecea*) which on each important manor used to maintain a few score serfs to manufacture textiles or farming tools, not half so well as they were now made by the artisans of the neighbouring town? They were allowed to disappear almost everywhere in the course of the twelfth century. The same reason prompted the sale of the remote estates which monasteries in countries with no vineyards owned in wine-growing regions.[14] Since wine could be obtained in the market, why continue to supply it at great expense on one's own lands? As to the lord's demesne, it was advisable to turn as much of it as possible into holdings, for labour services were unproductive and it was better to lease the land in return for cash rents, than to store the harvests at the risk of spoiling or being lost by fire.

Clearly the aim of the most prudent owners from now onwards was to increase their cash revenues as much as possible. This naturally led them to abolish or to modify serfdom. To enfranchise a man in return for a sum of money was doubly profitable, since he paid for his liberty, while giving up the ownership of his person did not entail giving up the cultivation of his holding. If he wished, he could keep it on conditions more advantageous to the lord; if he preferred to go, nothing was easier than to put another farmer in his place. Numerous as they were during the twelfth century, however, enfranchisements did not, as we know, put an end to the existence of a servile class. But although it was maintained it lost much of its primitive character; peasants were allowed to commute the labour services and other dues with which they were burdened for money, and although the old names of *mortmain, heriot* and *formariage* were occasionally retained

---

[14] In 1264, the Abbé of Saint-Trond sold the monastery of Himmerode his vineyards at Pommeren and Briedel on the Moselle. See the texts relating to this matter in Lamprecht, *Deutsches Wirtschaftsleben*, t. III, p. 24 *et seq.*

down to the end of the *Ancien Régime,* in practice they were very much softened. Even though they continued to be levied, the corvées were light in comparison with the obligations which they had entailed of old. Seigneurial authority nowhere disappeared, but its power grew steadily less and little remained of its former patriarchal character. The result of this evolution was that the position of the great landowners approximated more and more closely to that of a *rentier* of the soil, a landlord in the modern sense. The majority of the emancipated peasants became tenants to whom the soil was granted in return for a *cens,* which was almost always hereditary. And in the course of the thirteenth century leases for a period of years spread in the most advanced regions. Many of the old demesnes were farmed to wealthy agricultural labourers. Eudes Rigaud advises the abbots in his diocese to lease their lands as often as possible.[15] In the south, in Rousillon, for example, land leases for two to six years were customary, and alongside of these the *métayer* lease, or payment of a share of the crop, was also in general use.[16]

It is characteristic that the decay of the seigneurial system advanced in proportion to the development of commerce. In other words, it was much more rapid in the countries with large towns and a great trade like Lombardy, Tuscany, the north of France, Flanders, or the banks of the Rhine, than in central Germany or England. It was only at the end of the thirteenth century that the manorial system began to break down in the latter, while there were already numerous signs of its disintegration in Flanders from the middle of the twelfth century. Here, economic progress would seem to have brought about the disappearance of serfdom more than anywhere else. In

[15] See his *Journal,* cited in n. 13. In 1268 he advised an abbot "quod quam melius posset, maneria ad firmam traderet" (p. 607). He himself let several manors for two, three or four years to burgesses and clerks. *Ibid.,* p. 766 *et seq.*

[16] J. A. Brutails, *Étude sur la condition des populations rurales du Rousillon au Moyen Age,* p. 117 *et seq.*

1335, the *échevins* of Ypres could write, "Oncques n'avons oy de gens de serve condicion, ne de morte main, ne de quel condicion qu'il soient." [17]

The growing influence of commerce had the further result, at least along the great routes of transit and in the hinterland of the ports, of bringing about a specialisation of cultivation in accordance with the nature of the soil and climate. As long as traffic had been absent or insignificant, it had been necessary to make each manor produce the greatest possible variety of cereals, since they were unprocurable in the markets. But at the beginning of the twelfth century the progress of trade brought about a more rational economy. Everywhere where export could be depended on, the soil was farmed for what it was suited to supply best and most cheaply. From the twelfth century onwards the Cistercian abbeys in England specialised in the production of wool; woad, the indigo of the Middle Ages, was cultivated in the south of France, in Picardy, Lower Normandy, Thuringia and Tuscany. Above all, vineyards spread, to the detriment of corn, all over those countries, where they produced good wine, plentiful and easily transported. Salimbene observed very acutely that if the villagers in the valley of the Auxerre "neither sowed nor reaped," it was because their river carried their wine to Paris where it had a "noble" sale. [18] The Bordeaux district presents the most typical example of a region where commerce determined cultivation. Through the estuary of the Gironde, by way of la Rochelle, its wines were exported more and more widely to the shores of the Atlantic, to England and to the basins of the North Sea and the Baltic. At the end of the twelfth century they had already spread from the port of Bruges to Liége, where they competed with the Rhine and Moselle wines. At the other end of Europe, Prussia on its side applied itself to the cultivation of corn, which the Hanse ships carried to North European ports.

[17] Beugnot, *Les Olim.*, t. II, p. 770.
[18] Marc Bloch, *op. cit.*, p. 23.

Finally, it is important to observe that the greater intensity of the economic movement gave to the land a mobility which upset the traditional holdings into which it was divided. The primitive equality of the *mansi* and *Hufen* yielded little by little to holdings of diverse size, each composed of parcels acquired by one tenant and forming a single individual farm. Now that the peasant found a market for his goods in the neighbouring town, the taste for saving came to him with the taste for profit and there was no better use for savings than to acquire land. But the bourgeoisie also was in search of land; to the wealthy merchants of the town it was the best possible investment for the profits realised in trade. In the thirteenth century a great number of them purchased *censives* in the countryside. In Flanders capitalists interested themselves in draining polders; in Italy the Sienese and Florentine bankers bought up manors and in the fourteenth century the partners who looked after their business in France, England and Flanders showed themselves equally desirous of getting land into their hands.

But we must not generalise too much in regard to phenomena which were peculiar to a few countries, where capitalism was able to develop all its consequences. In reality, the changes in agricultural organisation and in the condition of the rural classes were very slow in all those parts of Europe which were not opened up by the great trade routes. Moreover, even where progress had been most rapid, the sway of the past remained powerful. The area of cultivation seems to have been larger than at any former period, but it was still infinitely less than it is to-day. Methods of cultivation appear to have remained stationary: the use of manure was unknown except in a few privileged regions, and everywhere men remained faithful to the traditional system of rotation. However much serfdom may have been modified, the peasant was still subject to seigneurial jurisdiction, tithes, banalities, and all the abuses of power against which governments did not protect him, or protected him inadequately. All things considered, the rural masses, who numerically formed the overwhelming majority of the population, played a purely passive rôle. The *vilain* had no place in the social hierarchy.

Four

COMMERCE TO THE END OF THE THIRTEENTH CENTURY

I. THE MOVEMENT OF TRADE [1]

The commercial vitality of the Middle Ages appears the more remarkable in view of the difficulties which confronted the movement of people and things during this period. Nothing could have been worse than the condition of the roads from the ninth century. All that remained of the admirable network of Roman roads now finally disappeared. Yet not only where the tolls by which they should have been kept up still in existence, but numbers of new ones had been created, all alike being known by the ancient name of *teloneum,* or market-toll. But these were only unprofitable and vexatious survivals of a tax which had been completely diverted from its original public purpose. The *tonlieu* of the Middle Ages, usurped by the territorial princes, became simply a fiscal imposition

---

[1] BIBLIOGRAPHY.—A. Schulte, *op. cit.,* p. ix.—W. Vogel, *op. cit.,* p. 17, n. 4.—W. Götz, *Die Verkehrswege im Dienste des Welthandels,* Stuttgart (1888).—T. H. Scheffel, *Verkehrsgeschichte der Alpen,* Berlin (1908–13), 2 vols.—R. Laur-Belart, *Studien zur Eröffnungsgeschichte des Gotthardpasses,* Zurich, 1934.—J. E. Tyler, *The Alpine Passes in the Middle Ages* (962–1250), Oxford, 1890.—R. Blanchard, *Les Alpes françaises,* Paris, 1925.—Ch. de La Roncière, *Histoire de la marine française,* Paris, 1899–1932, 6 vols.—E. H. Byrne, *op. cit.,* p. 24, n. 9.—Ed. von Lippmann, *Geschichte des Magnetnadels bis zur Einführung des Compasses,* Berlin, 1932. —A. Beardwood, *Alien Merchants in England, 1350–1377. Their Legal and Economic Position,* Cambridge (Mass.), 1931.

which was a cruel burden on transit. Not a single farthing of it was set aside for road-mending or for the rebuilding of bridges. It weighed as heavily on commerce as the seigneurial rights weighed on the soil. The merchant who paid it regarded it simply as an "exaction," an "evil custom," an unjust levy on his goods, in a word, as an abuse; and it was really nothing else. Of all the obstacles placed in the path of traffic none was more annoying or more general.

Obviously one of the first demands made by the rising towns was that their citizens should be freed from it, either partially or throughout the territory under their prince's jurisdiction, just as many abbeys before them had obtained exemption for reasons of piety. From the twelfth century onwards the wealthiest communes even succeeded in obtaining the privilege of freedom of toll in foreign countries frequented by their merchants.[2] But however numerous these remissions may have been, tolls continued to be a hindrance on all the highways of traffic. At the end of the fifteenth century, there were still sixty-four of them on the Rhine, thirty-five on the Elbe, and seventy-seven on the Danube in its course through Lower Austria alone.[3]

Traffic was thus retarded and handicapped by fiscal exploitation as well as by the bad state of the roads. In winter, it must have been almost impossible to move from place to place along roads that were quagmires of water and mud. The care of them was left to those through whose lands they passed or who had an interest in their upkeep. The public authorities of Lombardy do not seem to have made any attempt to improve the passage through

[2] In 1127, the burgesses of Saint-Omer obtained from William of Normandy the promise to obtain their exemption from the King of England. The statement of Galbert of Bruges in the same period shows the importance that these towns attached to the abolition of the market-toll.

[3] Kulischer, *op. cit.*, t. I, p. 301. In 1271, I counted 22 tolls on the Scarpe and the Scheldt, between Douai and Rupelmonde. Warnkoenig and Gheldorf, *Histoire de la Flandre et de ses institutions*, t. II, p. 460 *et seq.*

the Alps, so essential for the communication of Italy with
Northern Europe. Any progress accomplished in this
matter appears to have been due solely to the initiative o
travellers, pilgrims and merchants. The passes of Mont-
Cenis, Brenner, Septimer and Saint-Bernard were the most
frequented in early times, and at the beginning of the
thirteenth century that of Saint-Gothard began to be used.
The first suspension bridge of whose existence we have any
knowledge was thrown across it by a nameless inventor,
at the expense no doubt of the users, and so opened the
most direct route between Milan and the valleys of the
Rhine and the Danube. But it was only in the kingdom
of Naples, where the absolute monarchy of the Hohenstaufen and the Angevins had profited by the example of
the Byzantine Empire and Moslem Sicily, that administrative authority took any measures for repairing the highways.[4] In France, the royal government left the charge
to those who used them, even in the environs of the
capital. In 1332, the people of Ghent had to repair the
road from Senlis at their own expense, so as to hasten the
passage of their merchandise to Paris.[5]

The building of bridges excited more interest than the
upkeep of the roads. Without them the great rivers also
would have been exceedingly inconvenient obstacles.
But all which were of real importance and consequently
entailed considerable expense, were erected in towns, and
no doubt largely at the expense of the burgesses. Such
were the bridges at Maastricht, Liége, Huy, Namur and
Dinant on the Meuse, at Paris and Rouen on the Seine,
at Avignon on the Rhône, and London bridge on the
Thames, etc.

The means of transport had naturally to be adapted to
the bad state of the roads. Light two-wheeled wagons
were generally used for the conveyance of goods, but a

[4] G. Yver, *Le commerce et les marchands dans l'Italie
méridionale*, p. 70.
[5] *Cartulaire de la ville de Gand. Compte de la ville et des
baillis*, ed. J. Vuylsteke, p. 801 (Ghent, 1900).

great deal was carried on horseback. To send heavy
merchandise by road in those times it was absolutely
essential to distribute the load between a number of ve-
hicles or animals. Certainly, heavy four-wheeled wagons
could have had but a very restricted use on unpaved roads.
The improvement in draught horses in the tenth century
could not have had the results which it did had the means
of communication been less imperfect.[6]

This deficiency of land transit made waterways the trade
routes *par excellence,* although the droughts in summer,
the frosts in winter, and the spring and autumn floods often
prevented their navigation. But such as they were, they
were the great instruments of exchange and transport.
No efforts were spared to improve them. Dikes were constructed and quays and landing-places built at convenient
spots. In the Flemish plain, where the land-locked waters
flowed very slowly, it was possible to dig canals fed by the
rivers and so bring them into communication. The oldest
of these *vaaten* date back to the twelfth century, but it was
in the course of the thirteenth that their number increased
to a degree which bears striking witness to the commercial
activity of the region. The water level was maintained
at the necessary height by wooden dams graded at intervals. Boats crossed them by means of inclined planes over
which they glided with the aid of ropes operated by a
windlass. The entire installation was called an *overdrag.*
The necessary expenses for the construction of canals were
sometimes borne by the towns, sometimes by groups of
merchants. Taxes, very different from the seigneurial *tolls,*
were levied on the passing boats and the proceeds were
used to pay the expenses of installation and upkeep.[7]

Maritime trade naturally assumed an even greater

---

[6] On the deficiency of animal traction before the tenth
century, see Lefebvre des Noëttes, *L'attelage et le cheval de
selle à travers les âges* (Paris, 1931).

[7] H. Pirenne, *Les overdraghes et les portes d'eau en Flandre
au XIII° siècle,* in *Essays in Medieval History presented to
Thomas Frederick Tout* (Manchester, 1925).

importance than river trade. Up to the fourteenth century
in the Mediterranean and the fifteenth in the North Seas,
that is to say, up to the time when the use of the mariner's
compass became general, ships were forced to coast along
the shores. Except for very short voyages, they sailed in
company, often convoyed by warships, an indispensable
precaution in an era when piracy was so common that
merchants themselves did not scruple to engage in it,
when occasion offered. The freightage varied from 200 to
600 tons.[8] In the Mediterranean, galleys were chiefly used.
The French *nef* and the *cogge* of the North Sea and the
Baltic were merely sailing vessels, high in the water and
with rounded sides. The perfecting of the rudder at the
beginning of the thirteenth century improved the sailing
qualities of all the vessels.[9] But they never risked a voyage
in the winds of winter. Down to the beginning of the
fourteenth century it was the exception for Italian ships
to cross the Straits of Gibraltar, but in 1314 Venice and
Genoa organised fleets to go to Flanders and England.[10]
As for the Hansards, who, from the twelfth century, took
the place of the Scandinavians in Northern waters, their
ships went no farther south than the Bay of Biscay, where
they put in at the Bay of Bourgneuf for salt and at La
Rochelle for wine.

The establishment of ports permitted of sheds, cranes
and lighters for the unlading of the ships. In the South
those of Venice, in the North those of Bruges, were considered the safest and the best managed in Europe. The

[8] For the Mediterranean boats, see Byrne, *op. cit.*, p. 9
et seq. His researches have shown that their capacity was
much larger than was formerly believed. Many were able to
carry 1,000 to 1,100 passengers.

[9] Lefebvre des Noëttes, *Le gouvernail. Contribution à
l'histoire de l'esclavage*, in *Mémoires de la société des anti-
quaires de France* 1934, p. 24 *et seq.* The author's conclusions
seem to exaggerate the importance of the improvement.

[10] A. Schaube, *Die Anfänge der venezianischen Galeeren-
fahrten nach der Nordsee*, in *Historische Zeitschrift*, t. CI
(1908).

church towers, campaniles and belfries served to mark the navigable channels as land was approached. Sometimes beacon lights were set at the top of these towers to serve as lighthouses. After being unladed the ships were usually dragged on to the banks where repairs were effected.

Hampered as was all traffic by the multiplication of internal tolls, some compensation at least was to be found in the absence of all obstacles on the political frontiers. It was not until the fifteenth century that the first symptoms of protection began to reveal themselves. Before that, there is no evidence of the slightest desire to favour national trade by protecting it from foreign competition. In this respect, the internationalism which characterised medieval civilisation right into the thirteenth century was manifested with particular clarity in the conduct of the states. They made no attempt to control the movement of commerce and we should seek in vain for traces of an economic policy deserving of the name. Naturally the political relations of princes had their repercussions in the economic sphere. In time of war, the enemy merchants were arrested, their goods confiscated and their vessels seized. The prohibition of trade was a common means of coercion. In the thirteenth and fourteenth centuries, the kings of England, in their conflicts with Flanders, stopped the export of wool to that country, in order to provoke an industrial crisis which would compel it to give in. But these were mere recourses to force, expedients of no lasting duration. When peace was established, all was as before; there is nowhere any idea of trying to ruin the enemy by robbing him of his markets or appropriating his industry. In short, the princes of the Middle Ages were still without the slightest tinge of mercantilism, with the exception, perhaps, of Frederick II and his Angevin successors in the kingdom of Naples. Here, indeed, under the influence of Byzantium and the Moslems in Sicily and Africa, we may detect at least the beginnings of State intervention in the economic system. The king reserved to himself the monopoly of the wheat trade and set up a regular customs administration on the frontiers. His interest in the matter was no doubt purely fiscal, but the fact remains that in bringing commerce under his control, he embarked on a new course, which seems to foreshadow the policy adopted by modern monarchies of modern times.[11] But the kings of Naples were too much in advance of their time and working within too narrow a limit to find any imitators and their work does not seem to have survived the catastrophe of Charles of Anjou in 1282.

The idea of exploiting commerce for the benefit of princely finances naturally occurred to all governments. Everywhere the foreigner was subject to special taxes, and, unless he were protected by treaties, his goods ran a great risk of being requisitioned by the territorial prince in case of need. But if the prince oppressed him, he protected him too. On all sides the merchant, like the pilgrim, was under the special protection of the lord through whose land he was travelling. He was under the safeguard of the public peace. More than one prince earned a well-deserved name as a pitiless judge of robbers and highwaymen. Although down to the end of the Middle Ages, and even later, there still existed a fair number of knights and barons who were the terror of merchants, it is true to say that by the beginning of the thirteenth century these redoubtable types of *Raubritter* were to be found only in lonely regions, or in countries given over to anarchy. From then onwards robbery in times of peace was certainly the exception, wherever governments had firmly established the jurisdiction of their courts and the authority of their officials. At the same time, a number of practices which had become incompatible with economic progress were modified. The right of "wreckage," by virtue of which the lord could claim all that the sea cast up on the shore, was abolished or regulated by treaties. Similarly, an increasing number of agreements were drawn up, guaranteeing foreign merchants from arrest for the debts of their lord

[11] For the economic policy of the kingdom of Naples, see G. Yver, *op. cit.*

or their fellow-countrymen. All these principles were laid down with increasing pressure and emphasis in the course of the thirteenth century, but their application was intermittent and uncertain, owing to the lack of any sanction to enforce them. Nevertheless, the feeling of security was growing and the rôle of brute-force diminishing; and a state of mind was being gradually created which was particularly favourable to the progress of international trade and labour.

In the beginning, the diverse perils by which they were threatened had compelled merchants to travel in armed bands in great caravans. Security was only to be had at the price of force, and force was only to be obtained by union. The same thing happened in Italy, and in the Low Countries, the two countries where commerce was developing most rapidly. There was no difference in this respect between the Romance and the Germanic peoples. Whatever the names by which the unions are called, whether it is a question of *frairies, charités, compagnies, gildes* or *hanses*, the reality is the same. Here, as elsewhere, what determined economic organisation was not national genius but social necessity. The primitive institutions of trade were as cosmopolitan as those of feudalism. The sources permit us to form a pretty clear picture of the troops of merchants, who were to be met with in greater and greater numbers in Western Europe from the tenth century onwards. Their members, armed with bows and swords, surrounded the packhorses and the wagons loaded with sacks, bales, cases and casks. At the head marched the standard-bearer (*schildrake*), and a leader, the *Hansgraf* or the *Doyen*, exercised his authority over the company, which was composed of "brothers" bound together by an oath of fidelity. A spirit of close solidarity animated the whole group. The merchandise, apparently, was bought and sold in common and the profits divided *pro rata* according to each man's share.[12] The longer the

---

[12] C. Koehne, *Das Hansgrafenamt*, Berlin, 1893. W. Stein, *Hansa*, in *Hansische Geschichtsblätter*, 1909, p. 53 *et seq.*

journey, the greater the prospect of profit in an age when prices were chiefly dependent on the rarity of the imported goods and where this rarity was increased by distance. It is easy to understand that the desire for gain was strong enough to counterbalance the hardships and risks of a wandering existence. From the beginning of the twelfth century the men of Dinant were going as far as the mines of Goslar to get supplies of copper, the merchants of Cologne, Huy, Flanders and Rouen frequented the port of London, and numbers of Italians were already to be seen at the Ypres fair. Except in winter, the enterprising merchant was continually on the road, and it was with good reason that he bore in England the picturesque name of "dusty-foot" (*pedes pulverosi, piepowders*).[13]

Soon, amidst these roving masses, there appeared a number of groups, for commercial activity inevitably became specialised in proportion as it increased. In the valley of the Seine, the Paris Hanse of water-merchants devoted itself to inland navigation as far as Rouen.[14] In Flanders, in the twelfth century, an association of city gilds, engaged in trade with England, was formed under the name of the London Hanse.[15] In Italy, the attraction of the Champagne fairs led to the formation of the *Univer-*

---

[13] See above, ch. II, n. 13.—The following passage admirably illustrates the character of the travelling merchants of the Middle Ages. In 1128, the people of Bruges formulated their grievances against Count William Cliton, stating: "Nos in terra hac (Flanders) clausit ne negociari possemus, imo quicquid hactenus possedimus, sine lucro, sine negotiatione, sine acquisitione rerum consumpsimus, unde justam habemus rationem expellendi illum a terra." Galbert of Bruges, *Histoire du meurtre de Charles le Bon*, ed. H. Pirenne, p. 152.

[14] E. Picarda, *Les marchands de l'eau. Hanse parisienne et compagnie française*, Paris, 1901. G. Huisman, *La juridiction de la municipalité parisienne de saint Louis à Charles VII* (Paris, 1912); H. Pirenne, *A propos de la hanse parisienne des marchands de l'eau*, in *Mélanges d'histoire offerts à M. Charles Bémont*, Paris, 1913.

[15] H. Pirenne, *La hanse flamande de Londres*, in *Bulletin de la Classe des Lettres de l'Académie royale de Belgique*, 1899, p. 65 *et seq.*

sitas mercatorum Italiae nundinas Campaniae ac regni Franciae frequentantium. The so-called hanse of seventeen towns came to include merchants from a number of cloth towns in the North of France and the Low Countries, who also traded with Champagne.[16]

The merchant was a vagabond in maritime as well as in land commerce. Here also he did everything in his own person, himself taking ship for the places where he could see his goods and purchase his home freights. But as time went on, an advancing capitalism demanded the presence of the heads of businesses at the centre of their affairs, peace and security made it more possible to rely on expeditions getting safe into port, and merchants became better educated and so able to conduct their business by correspondence. Then the need of personally convoying merchandise grew less urgent and commercial life more stationary: transport was detached as a special branch of activity possessing its own personnel.[17] The directors of the big commercial houses were represented in their foreign branches by partners or agents ("factors"). This system was already well advanced in Italy in the second half of the thirteenth century and thenceforth became increasingly prevalent in all countries. Save at sea, where merchant vessels on a long voyage were compelled by piracy to arm themselves for centuries, commerce was henceforth able to dispense with the military equipment with which it had been surrounded in its early days.

[16] H. Laurent, *Nouvelles recherches sur la Hanse des XVII villes,* in *Le Moyen Age,* 1935.

[17] On this change, see F. Rörig, *Hansische Beiträge zur deutschen Wirtschaftsgeschichte,* p. 217 *et seq.* (Breslau, 1928).

II. THE FAIRS [18]

One of the most striking features of the economic organisation of the Middle Ages was the important rôle played
by the fairs, more especially down to the end of the
thirteenth century. They abounded in all countries, and
everywhere had the same fundamental character, so that
they may be considered an international phenomenon,
inherent in the very conditions of European society.
They were at their height in the era of peripatetic commerce; in proportion as the merchants became sedentary,
they dwindled. Those which were created at the end of
the Middle Ages were of an altogether different type and,
all things considered, their importance in economic life
was not comparable with that of their predecessors.

It would be fruitless to seek the origin of the fairs
(*nundinae*) in those small local markets, which by the
beginning of the ninth century were appearing in ever-
increasing numbers over the whole of Europe. Though
the fairs were subsequent to the markets, they were not
connected with them by any link and indeed present the
most complete contrast to them. The aim of the local
markets was to supply the provisions necessary for daily
life to the population settled in the district. This explains
their being held weekly, their very limited circle of attrac-

[18] BIBLIOGRAPHY.—Huvelin, *op. cit.*, p. viii.—F. Bourquelot,
Étude sur les foires de Champagne, Paris, 1865, 2 vols.—C.
Bassermann, *Die Champagnermessen, Ein Beitrag zur Geschichte des Kredits*, Leipzig, 1911.—G. Des Marez, *La lettre
de foire à Ypres au XIII⁰ siècle*, Brussels, 1901 (Mém. Acad.
Belgique).—H. Laurent, *Documents relatifs à la procédure en
foire de Champagne contre des débiteurs défaillants*, in *Bulletin
de la Commission des anciennes lois et ordonnances de Belgique*, t. XIII (1929).—H. Pirenne, *Un conflit entre le magistrat
yprois et les gardes des foires de Champagne*, in *Bulletin de
la Commission royale d'histoire de Belgique*, t. LXXXVI
(1922).—A. Sayous, *Les opérations des banquiers italiens en
Italie et aux foires de Champagne pendant le XIII⁰ siècle*, in
Revue historique, t. CLXX (1932).

tion and the restriction of their activity to small retail operations. The fairs, on the contrary, were periodical meeting-places for professional merchants. They were centres of exchange and especially of wholesale exchange, and set out to attract the greatest possible number of people and of goods, independent of all local consideration. They may perhaps be compared with international exhibitions, for they excluded nothing and nobody; every individual, no matter what his country, every article which could be bought or sold, whatever its nature, was assured of a welcome. Moreover, it was impossible to hold them more than once, or at most twice a year in the same place, so great was the necessary preparation involved. It is true that the radius of most of the fairs was limited to a more or less extensive region. Only the Champagne fairs in the twelfth and thirteenth centuries attracted merchants from the whole of Europe. But the important thing is that in theory each fair was open to all trade, just as each seaport was open to all shipping. Between the fair and the local market the contrast was not simply a difference in size, but a difference in kind.

With the exception of the fair at Saint Denis, near Paris, which dates back to the Merovingian era and which, during the agricultural period of the Middle Ages, merely vegetated and found no imitators, the fairs date from the revival of trade. The oldest amongst them were in existence in the eleventh century; in the twelfth their number was already large and it continued to increase further during the thirteenth. Their sites were naturally determined by the great movements of commerce. They increased in number, in proportion as trade in each country became more active and more important. Only the territorial prince had the right to found them. Very often he granted them to towns, but by no means all great urban centres possessed them; some towns of the first importance, like Milan and Venice, had none; in Flanders, although there were fairs at Bruges, Ypres and Lille, there were none in so active a centre as Ghent, while they are to be found at

Thourout and Messines, which were never more than small market-towns. It was the same in Champagne as regards places like Lagny and Bar-sur-Aube, which were as insignificant as the fairs held in them were famous.

Thus the importance of a fair was independent of the place where it was set up, and this is easily understood, since the fair was nothing more than a periodic meeting-place for a distant clientèle and attendance at it did not depend on the density of the local population. It was only in the second half of the Middle Ages that fairs were founded for the mere purpose of furnishing certain towns with supplementary resources, by attracting a temporary throng of people. But it is clear that in these cases considerations of local trade were paramount and that the institution was turned from its original and essential object.

The law gave the fairs a privileged position. The ground on which they were held was protected by a special peace, carrying with it particularly severe punishments in case of infringement. All who went there were under the *conduit,* that is to say, the protection, of the territorial prince. "Guards of the fairs" (*custodes nundinarum*) maintained order and exercised a special jurisdiction there. Letters of obligation sealed with their seal were recognised as specially binding, and a number of privileges were designed to attract the greatest possible number of participants. At Cambrai, for example, special permission was given to throw dice and play cards during the fair of Saint Simon and Saint Jude. "Feasts and plays were the chief attractions." [19] But the most effective advantages consisted in the "franchise," which exempted merchants going to the fair from the right of reprisal for crimes committed or debts contracted outside it, and from the right of escheat, and which suspended lawsuits and measures of execution as long as the peace of the fair lasted. Most precious of all was the suspension of the canonical prohibition of usury

[19] Huvelin, *op. cit.*, p. 438.

(i.e., loans at interest) and the fixing of a maximum rate of interest.

If we examine the geographical distribution of the fairs, it is at once apparent that the busiest among them were grouped almost half-way along the great trade route, which ran from Italy and Provence to the coast of Flanders. These were the famous "fairs of Champagne and Brie" which followed each other through the whole course of the year. First came the fair of Lagny-on-the-Marne in January, next on the Tuesday before mid-Lent that of Bar, in May the first fair of Provins, called the fair of Saint Quiriace, in June the "warm fair" of Troyes, in September the second fair of Provins or the fair of Saint Ayoul, and finally, in October, to end the cycle, the "cold fair" of Troyes. In the twelfth century, these assemblies continued for about six weeks, leaving only the necessary interval for the removal of wares. The most important, because of the season in which they took place, were the fairs of Provins and the warm fair of Troyes. The success of these fairs was undoubtedly due to their excellent position. It seems clear that as early as the ninth century the rare merchants of the time frequented the plain of Champagne if, as everything appears to indicate, the *sedem negotiatorum Cappas* mentioned in a letter of Loup de Ferrières[20] is to be placed at Chappas, in the department of Aube. As soon as trade revived, the increasing passage through Champagne induced its counts to secure the maximum advantage for their country by offering the merchants the convenience of fairs set up at places near together. In 1114 those of Bar and Troyes had already been in existence for some time and undoubtedly it was the same with those of Lagny and Provins, near which others (which did not, however, enjoy the same success) were to be found at Bar-on-the-Seine, Châlons-on-the-Marne, Château-Thierry, Nogent-on-the-Seine, etc. Corresponding to these Champagne fairs, at the end of

[20] A. Giry, *Études carolingiennes,* in *Études d'histoire du Moyen Age dédiées à Gabriel Monod,* p. 118 (Paris, 1896).

the line which led from them to the North Sea, were the five Flemish fairs of Bruges, Ypres, Lille, Thourout and Messines.

The twelfth century saw an extraordinarily rapid growth in the prosperity of this commercial system. There is no doubt that already in 1127 a very active intercourse was going on between the fairs of Flanders and those of Champagne, for Galbert has described the terrified flight of the Lombard merchants from the fair of Ypres, on the news of the assassination of Count Charles the Good. On their part the Flemings found in Champagne a permanent market for their cloth, which was despatched from there either by themselves, or by their Italian and Provençal buyers, to the port of Genoa, and thence exported to the seaports of the Levant.[21] From Champagne, in return, the Flemings imported woven silk-stuffs, gold and silver goods and especially spices, with which the sailors of the North supplied themselves at Bruges at the same time as Flemish cloth and French wines. In the thirteenth century, commercial relations reached the height of their development. At each of the Champagne fairs the Flemish drapers had their "tents," grouped according to towns, where they exhibited their cloth, and "Clerks of the fairs" rode without interruption between Champagne and Flanders, carrying the merchants' correspondence.[22] But if the Champagne fairs certainly owed much of their importance to the contact which they early established between Italian commerce and Flemish industry, their influence radiated over all parts of the West. "At the fairs of Troyes there was a German house, and markets and inns belonging to merchants from Montpellier, Barcelona, Valencia, Lérida, Rouen, Montauban, Provins, Auvergne, Burgundy, Picardy, Geneva, Clermont, Ypres, Douai and Saint-Omer." At Provins, the Lombards had

[21] See above, p. 37.
[22] G. Espinas gives lively details regarding these clerks in *Une guerre sociale inter-urbaine dans la Flandre wallonne au XIIIe siècle*, pp. 24, 35, 72, 82, 83, etc. (Paris-Lille, 1930).

their special lodgings, and one of the quarters of the town was called *Vicus Allemannorum,* just as there was a *Vicus Angliae* at Lagny.[23]

Nor was it only trade in merchandise which attracted people from afar to the Champagne fairs. So numerous and important were the settlements of accounts which took place there, that they soon became, to use a happy phrase, "the money market of Europe." [24] At every fair, after a preliminary period devoted to sales, there followed one of payments. These payments not only involved the clearing of debts contracted at the fair itself, but often settled credits contracted at preceding fairs. From the twelfth century onwards this practice led to the establishment of an organisation of credit, in which we must apparently seek the origin of bills of exchange. In this the Italians, who were more advanced than the continentals in the matter of commercial usages, doubtless took the initiative. As yet the bills were nothing more than simple written promises to pay a sum of money in a place other than that in which the debt was contracted, i.e., in legal terminology, "paper payable to order at a specified place." The signatory, in fact, undertook to make payment in another place to the obligee or to his *nuntius,* i.e., his representative (active order clause), and sometimes also himself to pay these through a *nuntius* acting for him (passive order clause). The Champagne fairs were so widely frequented that most debts were made payable at one or other of them, no matter where contracted. This was the case not only with commercial debts, but with simple loans contracted by individuals, princes or religious houses. Furthermore, the fact that all the marts of Europe were in contact with the fairs of Champagne brought about the introduction there, in the thirteenth century, of the practice of settling debts by *"compensation,"* i.e., by clearing arrangements. Thus in the Europe of that day the fairs

[23] Huvelin, *op. cit.,* p. 505.
[24] L. Goldschmidt, *Universalgeschichte des Handelsrechts,* p. 226.

played the part of an embryonic clearing house. When it is remembered that people flocked there from all parts of the Continent, it is easy to realise how they must have initiated their clients into the perfected credit processes in use among the Florentines and Sienese, whose influence was preponderant in the trade in money.

The Champagne fairs may be considered to have reached their height in the second half of the thirteenth century. The beginning of the following century saw their decline. The essential cause was undoubtedly the substitution for peripatetic commerce of more sedentary practices, at the same time as the development of direct shipping from the Italian ports to those of Flanders and England. No doubt, too, the long war which set the County of Flanders and the kings of France by the ears from 1302 to 1320 also contributed to their decay, in depriving them of the most active group of their northern customers. A little later the Hundred Years' War dealt them the decisive blow. Henceforth those great business centres, to which for two centuries all the merchants of Europe had bent their steps, were no more. But the practices learned there now opened the way to an economic life, in which the general use of correspondence and the operations of credit enabled the business world to give up its journeys to Champagne.

III.   MONEY [25]

German economists have invented the term *Naturalwirtschaft*, natural economy, to describe the period prior to the invention of money. It is not our business to consider

[25] BIBLIOGRAPHY.—M. Prou, *Les monnaies carolingiennes*, Paris, 1896.—A. Luschin von Ebengreuth, *Allgemeine Münzkunde und Geldgeschichte*, Munich-Berlin, 2nd ed., 1926.— W. A. Shaw, *The History of Currency*, 1252–1894, London, 1895.—A. Blanchet and A. Dieudonné, *Manuel de numismatique française*, Paris, 1912–30, 3 vols.—H. Van Werveke, *Monnaie, lingots ou marchandises?*, in *Annales d'histoire économique et sociale*, t. IV (1932).—*Id., Monnais de compte et*

whether the phrase is really applicable to the nature of exchange during the earliest phases of economic development; but it is important to enquire how far it can be properly used, as it often is used, of the early Middle Ages before the renaissance of the twelfth century. The writers who describe this period as one of natural economy obviously do not intend the term to be understood in any absolute sense. They are well aware that ever since its invention money has been in continuous use among all the civilised people of the West and that the Roman Empire handed it on without interruption to its succession states. Thus when the early Middle Ages are described as a period of natural economy, all that is meant is that the part played by money was then so small as to be almost negligible. Undoubtedly there is a good deal of truth in this contention; but at the same time we must be on our guard against exaggeration.[26]

To begin with, it would be a mistake to think that barter now took the place of money as the normal means of exchange. Barter has always been used in social intercourse and for that matter is still frequent in our own day, as in the past. But never since the invention of money has it usurped the latter's function. When people resorted to it, they did so for motives of convenience or as a mere accident of practice; they used it as a temporary substitute for money, not to replace it. The sources leave us in no doubt on the point. From the ninth to the twelfth century

---

monnaie réelle, in *Revue belge,* 1934.—A. Landry, *Essai économique sur les mutations des monnaies dans l'ancienne France de Philippe le Bel à Charles VII,* Paris, 1910.—E. Bridrey, *La théorie de la monnaie au XIVᵉ siècle. Nicole Oresme,* Paris, 1906.

[26] A. Dopsch, *Naturalwirtschaft in der Weltgeschichte* (Vienna, 1930), has clearly shown the co-existence in different eras of natural economy and money economy, but without sufficiently taking into account economic evolution and the repercussions which it produced not only on the form but on the nature of exchange. *Cf.* the observations of H. Van Werveke in *Annales d'histoire économique et sociale,* 1931, p. 428 *et seq.*

they invariably express prices in money, nor do they appear to contemplate cases in which payment may be made in kind. The most cursory reading of the capitularies shows that small transactions in the local markets, in which exchange in kind would have been particularly easy, were carried on *per deneratas*, nay more, the obligation to accept money is formally laid down. Moreover, it is well known that after the Carolingian period the grant of a market by the sovereign goes hand in hand with the grant of the right to coin money to the lord of the market, and this combination is clear truth that money was in normal use as the measure of value and the means of purchase. What is true of small payments is equally true of large ones. During times of famine it was by means of hard cash that the abbeys procured the necessary provisions from outside and similarly, in times of plenty, it was not for other provisions but for money that they exchanged their surplus wine and corn.

In face of such clearly established facts, it is impossible to attach any credence to those traditions of a later age which, for instance, represent Baldwin III, Count of Flanders (958–62), as regulating sales carried on without money, two hens for a goose, two geese for a sucking pig, three lambs for a sheep, three heifers for an ox.[27] In short, it is undoubted that during the agrarian period of the Middle Ages, wherever there was a commercial exchange there was an exchange in money. In this respect tradition was unbroken and it is incorrect to speak of the substitution of a natural economy for a money economy.

But we have already seen that the commerce of these times was insignificant, and just as there was but little movement of merchandise, so necessarily there was little movement of money, which could operate only within the restricted circle of trade. The most essential economic dues, those which were paid on the great domains, upon which the social equilibrium then rested, escaped it almost

[27] It is surprising that Huvelin, *op. cit.*, p. 538, should have accepted the truth of these stories.

entirely. Here the tenants paid their obligations to their lord in kind. Every serf, and every owner of a *mansa,* owed a fixed number of days of labour and a fixed quantity of natural products or of goods manufactured by himself, corn, eggs, geese, chickens, lambs, pigs, and hempen, linen or woollen cloth. It is true that a few pence had also to be paid, but they formed such a small proportion of the whole that they cannot prevent the conclusion that the economy of the domain was a natural economy. It was a natural economy because it was not an exchange economy; it was deprived of markets and thus operated in a closed sphere, without communications with the world outside, bound to a traditional routine and producing only for its own consumption. In such a system the most practical course for a lord living on his land was obviously to get it cultivated by tenants and to receive from them the produce which he could not procure elsewhere. Where, moreover, could the villeins themselves have obtained enough money to represent the value of their dues, since they sold nothing outside the estate? The very conditions under which it functioned imposed upon the great estate of the Middle Ages the necessity to make its payments and receive its dues in kind. Since it did not engage in commerce it had no need to make use of money, without which commerce, on the contrary, could not maintain itself. So fundamental is this truth, that when the domanial economy dissolved under the influence of trade, the essential mark of its transformation was the substitution of money payments for dues in kind.

Thus it is both false and true to describe the period between the ninth and twelfth centuries as a period of natural economy. It is false, if by that we mean that money ceased to be the normal instrument of exchange, for it continued to be so in all commercial transactions. But it is true, if we mean that its circulation and rôle were limited, since the whole organisation of the great estate at this time dispensed with it. In other words, in every payment made as the result of a sale, money was

employed, while natural economy determined the method
of all payments in fulfilment of dues involving no return.

It is a fact of the greatest importance, and one which
might well appear paradoxical, that the whole monetary
system of Europe under the *Ancien Régime* and of the
huge British Empire to-day was established at a time
when the circulation of money had declined to the lowest
level which it ever reached. It is impossible to doubt that
there was a profound decadence in this respect from the
Merovingian to the Carolingian period. When the Moslem
invasion closed the Tyrrhenian Sea it brought about a
rupture between the Western world and the economy of
antiquity, which in all its essential traits had lasted until
then. All the barbarian kingdoms, which divided the
Western empire among themselves, kept Constantine's gold
solidus as their monetary standard. Although struck in the
name of their kings, it none the less formed a real international coinage, universally accepted from Syria to Spain
and from Africa to the northern frontiers of Gaul.[28] But it
was not destined to survive the great upheaval caused by
the bottling up of the West. From the beginning of the
ninth century it disappeared in the Carolingian monarchy,
which was now an agricultural state engaging in no commercial activity. Only in the districts where some remnants
of trade still survived, in Frisia and on the Spanish frontier,
were a few gold coins struck in the reign of Lewis the
Pious.[29] Then the turmoil of Norman and Saracen invasions put an end to this last vestige of the ancient coinage.
Gold, which the cessation of Mediterranean trade banished
from Western Europe, ceased for many centuries to serve
as an instrument of exchange. From the reign of Pepin the

[28] See the works cited above, Introduction, n. 2.
[29] It is impossible to discuss here the texts quoted by M.
Dopsch, *op. cit.*, p. 87, n. 24, to prove that the circulation of
money and gold coinage did not suffer a considerable setback
in the Carolingian era. I shall return elsewhere to this important question.

Short silver money was substituted for that of gold, and in this as in so many other respects Charlemagne completed his father's work and gave it its final form.

The monetary system, which he established and which was the most permanent of all his reforms, since it has lasted to this day wherever the pound sterling is in circulation, represented a definite break with the monetary system of Rome. In it, as in all the great emperor's policy, may be observed a clear desire to fit in with the actual state of affairs, to adapt legislation to the new conditions which were being imposed upon society, to accept facts and submit to them, in order to bring order out of disorder. Nowhere more plainly than here does Charlemagne appear as a creative and realistic genius. He undoubtedly recognised the function which money must henceforth perform in a society sinking back again into a state of agriculture, and resolved to provide it with a coinage appropriate to its needs. His monetary reform was precisely that which suited an age of rural economy without markets, and its greatness and originality lie in its recognition of this fact.

The Carolingian monetary system may be briefly defined by calling it a silver monometallism. Officially the State, while still tolerating for a year or two the making of occasional gold coins, struck only silver metal. The basis of the coinage was a new pound, much heavier than the Roman pound, because it weighed *c.* 491 grammes, instead of *c.* 327.[30] It was divided into 240 deniers or pence (*denarii*) of pure metal. These silver pence, each weighing about 2 grammes, and the halfpence (*oboli*), were the only real tangible coins, hard cash. But side by side with them there existed money of account, mere numerical expressions, each of which corresponded to a fixed number of pence. These were the sou or shilling (*solidus*), which was equivalent to 12 pence, and the livre or pound (*libra*), containing 20 sous, and thus equal to the 240 pence con-

tained in the pound weight.[31] The low value of the sole
circulating money, the *denarii* and *oboli,* was perfectly
suited to the needs of an age in which the great majority
of transactions consisted in small retail payments. This
currency was obviously not designed for large-scale commerce: its chief mission was to serve the clientèle of those
little local markets which are so often mentioned in the
capitularies and in which sales and purchases are made
per deneratas.

Moreover, the State took the greatest pains to keep up
the standard of weight and alloy of its coins. It reserved
for itself the sole right of coinage and concentrated it in
a small number of mints working under its own supervision. Extremely severe penalties were promulgated against
counterfeiters and those who refused to receive the legal
deniers in payment were punished. Furthermore, the
circulation of money was very limited. The stock of metal
from which it was struck must for the most part have come
from ancient silver coins of small denomination dating
from the Merovingian or even from the Roman period,
from the booty taken from the barbarians, and from the
few argentiferous seams of Gaul, such as those of Melle in
Aquitaine. The money in circulation was moreover constantly recast and redistributed by the royal mints with a
fresh stamp, no doubt with the object of circumventing the
counterfeiters.

Charlemagne's monetary system remained that of all the
states which were born of the break-up of the Carolingian
Empire. They all retained the silver denier as real money
and the sou and the livre as money of account. Whether
the first be called *pfennig* or *penny,* the second *shilling,*
the third *pfund* or *pound,* the reality behind the different

---

[31] Consequently in Latin documents adjectives indicating the
kind of money of account being reckoned must be read in the
genitive plural. Thus: *V libras tur.* should read: *V libras
turonensium* and not: *V libras turonenses,* because this term
means 5 pounds weight of *denarii* struck at Tours. Similarly
V sol. tur. means *V solidos turonensium.*

words is the same. A gold currency was preserved in the West only in lands under Byzantine rule, such as the South of Italy and Sicily before their occupation by the Normans, or in the regions conquered by Islam, such as Spain. The Anglo-Saxons also struck a few gold coins, before the invasion of 1066 brought England too under the general rule.

Nevertheless, the dissolution of the Carolingian Empire and the collapse of the royal administration in the second half of the ninth century were bound to have their influence on monetary organisation. If its essential characteristics were everywhere maintained, there were everywhere profound alterations in practice. Amid the anarchy which overshadowed the royal power, the feudal princes were not slow to usurp the right of coinage, while the kings, on their side, granted it to numbers of churches. Soon throughout the West there were as many different deniers in circulation as there were great fiefs enjoying the right of *haute justice,* and as a result there was enormous confusion. Not only did the types of coins multiply, but in the absence of any effective control, their weight and fineness became more and more debased. Charlemagne's pound was replaced by others in the different territories. From the beginning of the eleventh century a new monetary weight was introduced throughout Germany, the mark of 218 grammes, which was probably Scandinavian in origin and itself gave birth to other marks, the best known of which are those of Cologne and Troyes. To all these causes of confusion the exploitation of the coinage by the princes added yet another, the most serious of all. Periodically the money was "called down," that is to say, withdrawn from circulation. It had to be taken to the mints, which reissued it to the public only in coins which were of less weight and increasingly debased with alloy; the princes pocketed the difference. Thus the intrinsic value of the currency became rapidly less and Charlemagne's fine silver pennies were replaced by coins even more heavily alloyed with copper, so that by the middle of the thirteenth century most of the deniers were no longer silver, but almost black (*nigri denarii*).

This confusion was the result not only of political anarchy but also of the economic conditions of the age. Since commerce had almost disappeared, it was immaterial that the diversity of currencies was an obstacle to the circulation of money. In a society in which almost all transactions took place in local markets, men were perfectly content with money which was current only within the frontiers of this or that territory. The paucity of commercial exchange involved a similar paucity of monetary circulation and a poor quality of the coinage did not greatly trouble the people of an age in which trade was reduced to the extreme minimum.

Naturally, however, the economic activity which sprang up at the end of the eleventh century was bound to restore the mobility of money which had hitherto been stagnant round the centres from which it was issued. It began to travel with the merchants; from all sides coins of every kind were drawn by commerce into the towns and fairs; the increased circulation of money made up for the insufficiency of the supply of metals. Moreover, the discovery of the silver mines of Freiburg, in the middle of the twelfth century, brought new supplies to feed it. Nevertheless, until the end of the Middle Ages it was always insufficient. It was not until the middle of the fifteenth century that the exploitation of the argentiferous deposits of Saxony, Bohemia, the Tyrol, Salzburg and Hungary materially increased the annual production of silver.

This increased circulation of money could be used by the princes for their own profit. Possessing as they did the sole right of coinage, they considered themselves authorised to use it in the interest of their treasuries, heedless of the fact that this was to enrich themselves at the public cost. The more indispensable money became to economic life, the more it was debased by those who enjoyed the monopoly of the mint. It became increasingly customary, especially from the thirteenth century, to multiply new issues of money, the value of which became less each time; money was continually being recalled, recast and redistributed in a worse state than before. Such transactions were particularly frequent in Germany, where, during the thirty-two years of Bernard of Ascania's reign, the coinage was altered, or rather debased, on an average three times a year.[32]

The position was naturally better in lands in which the influence of the urban population imposed some restraint upon the arbitrary dealings of the princes in a matter so incompatible with the interests of commerce and industry. In Flanders in 1127, for instance, the burgesses of Saint-Omer obtained from Count Thierry of Alsace a grant of the right of coinage. It was revoked the next year,[33] but all the same it bears witness to a state of opinion which should not be overlooked and in consequence of which Flemish money, though it did not escape the general degeneration which befell all medieval currencies, was always distinguished for its relative superiority. The deniers of Cologne, which were widely used in the Rhenish lands, likewise showed a remarkable stability in the twelfth and thirteenth centuries.[34] In England the right of coinage belonged to the king alone and English money maintained its quality better than that of any other country and suffered less from the abuses which resulted on the Continent from the numbers of princes who had usurped the coinage.

Against this usurpation the monarchy naturally reacted as soon as it was able. While in Germany and Italy the decline of its power from the thirteenth century deprived it of all will to restore its regalian rights in this as in other respects, and indeed led it to abandon them more and more to a crowd of princes and towns, in France, on the other

[32] Kulischer, *op. cit.*, t. 1, p. 324.

[33] A. Giry, *Histoire de la ville de Saint Omer*, p. 61.

[34] W. Hävernick, *Der Kölner Pfennig im XII und XIII Jahrhundert*, Stuttgart, 1930.

hand, the royal power began to regain ground steadily from the reign of Philip Augustus. Here, more than in any other country, its monetary prerogative had been seized by the feudal baronage. Under the early Capetians some 300 vassals had appropriated the right of coinage, and it was one of the Crown's most constant objects to recover that right when it should be powerful enough to do so. So successful was it, that at the beginning of the fourteenth century no more than about thirty feudatories retained their own mints, and in 1320–1 Philip the Long formed a premature project for the establishment of a single currency for the whole kingdom.[35]

In the recovery of their monetary regalia, the kings were moved solely by considerations of sovereignty. The idea of putting an end to the abuses of the feudatories and of maintaining the standard of the currency was so completely alien to them that they considered the coinage merely as one of their most valuable sources of revenue. Thus when the coinage once more became royal, it was not much more stable than before. From reign to reign the quality of the coins issued became baser. Ordinance after ordinance was issued calling up its nominal value in accordance with the needs of the crown, while its intrinsic value grew steadily less. Money was called up or down according as the king was creditor or debtor. In this Philip the Fair was merely conforming to a current practice. There were perpetual fluctuations and the chronic disorder of the circulation might have led us to suppose that commerce must have been impossible, if our own age had not provided us with an example of equally severe disturbances due to other causes.

The rudimentary technique of coinage only increased the chaos, since it was unable to secure an identical weight and standard for the coins issued from the mint. It was therefore easy for clippers to glean their harvest from the money in circulation, nor did the prospect of being boiled

alive deter counterfeiters from the temptation of exploiting
a state of affairs so favourable to them.

From the end of the twelfth century the disorder of the
currency had reached such a point that a reform became
absolutely necessary. It is significant that the initiative
came from the greatest commercial centre of the age,
Venice. In 1192 the doge, Henry Dandolo, caused an
entirely new kind of coin to be struck there, the groat, or
gros or *matapan*, weighing a little over 2 grammes of silver
and of the value of 12 of the old deniers. This groat was
thus equivalent to the Carolingian sou, with the difference
that the sou, originally a money of account, now became a
real coin. Charlemagne's system was not abandoned and
the innovation maintained his scale of coinage. All it did
was to take advantage of the continual fall of the denier,
to substitute for it a new denier, of twelve times the value
(whence its name of *grossus*), which in fact corresponded
exactly to the old sou, which from a mere figure now
became an integral part of the currency. In other words,
the new system remained faithful to the old, except that
it gave it a metallic value which was twelve times higher.
The old denier was not suppressed; the groat took its
place beside it as the money of commerce, reducing the
denier in practice to the rank of small change.

The Venetian groat answered the needs of the merchants so well that it was immediately imitated in all the
towns of Lombardy and Tuscany. But north of the Alps,
too, attempts were made to remedy the debasement of the
coinage, which was by now intolerable. In Germany,
where it seems to have been worst of all, the *Heller* (so
called from the town of Halle in Swabia where they were
first struck) brought into use a new denier superior in
weight and fineness to the old. In England the *sterling*
coin which appeared at the end of the twelfth century was
also an improved denier. But it was France which, inspired by the Italian example, discovered the real remedy.
In 1266 Louis IX created the *gros tournois* (*grossus
denarius turonensis*). A little later it was joined by the

gros parisis, which was worth about a quarter more than the *gros tournois*. These two coins immediately spread all over Europe, just as Gothic art and the literature of chivalry and courtesy were spreading from France at the same time. The fairs of Champagne certainly played an important part in this dispersion, which gave these coins the rank of an international currency. They were at once struck in Flanders, in Brabant, in the Liége country and in Lorraine. From 1276 the *gros tournois*, which was known in Germany as the *Groschen*, appeared in the valley of the Moselle; before the end of the thirteenth century it reached Cologne and thence it spread all over the German lands beyond the Rhine, as well as in the Northern Netherlands.

The remarkable good fortune of the *gros tournois* was almost equalled by that of the English sterling coinage, improved at the end of the thirteenth century and likewise imitated almost at once in Germany and the Low Countries. Thus with the appearance of these groats a new phase opened in monetary history. There was no breach with the Carolingian system, but simply an attempt to adapt it to the needs of commerce; and soon the return to a gold currency is yet another proof of the necessity for providing commerce with an instrument of exchange sufficient for its growing requirements.

Ever since the eleventh century Mediterranean trade had begun to disseminate Byzantine and Arab gold coins first in Italy and then north of the Alps. But these coins, known as bezants or marabotins, were usually hoarded by those into whose possession they came and seem only to have been used as a means of payment in exceptional cases, demanding an extraordinary outlay.[36] In 1071, for example, Countess Richilda of Hainault pledged her

[36] On the use of gold before the revival of coinage, see M. Bloch, *Le problème de l'or au Moyen Age*, in *Annales d'histoire économique et sociale*, 1933, p. i *et seq*. The author lays stress on the counterfeiting of foreign gold pieces by certain princes. But there is no trace of their having ever been in commercial circulation, and they seem to have been chiefly used for payments and loans to the great, i.e., in exceptional cases.

estate of Chevigny to the abbot of Saint-Hubert for the enormous sum of 500 gold bezants.[37] In ordinary commercial dealings gold does not seem to have been used at this time, although Italian seamen must early have discovered its advantages from their transactions with the Levant and must have desired to see it introduced into their own countries.

In 1231 Frederick II had the admirable gold Augustales struck in Sicily; they are the *chef d'œuvre* of medieval numismatics, but they never spread beyond the frontiers of southern Italy. It was not until 1252 that Florence, by striking the first florins (*fiorino d'oro*), so called because they were stamped with a lily, the emblem of the town, opened the way for the spread of a gold currency in Europe. Genoa soon followed and in 1284 Venice produced a replica of the florin in her ducat or *zechin*. These two fine coins, each weighing 3½ grammes, corresponded to the value of a silver pound *gros*, just as the groat itself had corresponded to the value of a sou. Thus by the introduction of gold the pound, like the sou, was transformed from a money of account into a real coin. The denier, which had been the only money in actual circulation in the Carolingian age, was henceforth only a coin of small denomination. The closing of the Mediterranean in the eighth century had imposed a silver currency on Western Europe for a long period; now its opening enabled a gold currency to resume its old rôle there.

The economic advancement of Italy is sufficient explanation of the lead which it took in putting out a gold currency, as of its lead in putting out the groat. But in both cases Europe could not be slow in following its example, and imitation came even more rapidly in the case of gold than it had come in that of the groat, a fact which is doubtless attributable to the growing progress of commercial relations. It was in all probability in 1266, i.e., in the same year that the *gros tournois* appeared, that Louis

[37] *La chronique de Saint Hubert, dite Cantatorium,* ed. K. Hanquet, p. 68 (Brussels, 1906).

IX issued the first gold deniers to circulate north of the Alps, and they were followed by the uninterrupted production of a rich gold currency under his successors. In the course of the fourteenth century the movement thus inaugurated spread over the whole Continent. In Spain the regular coinage of gold goes back to Alfonso XI of Castile (1312–50); in the Empire, Bohemia took the lead in 1325; in England Edward III issued a gold florin in 1344. A gold currency was struck in various parts of Flanders where commerce was so active; in Flanders under Louis de Nevers before 1337, in Brabant under John II (1312–55), in the Liége country under Englebert de la Marck (1345–64), in Holland under William V (1346–89), in Guelders under Renaud III (1343–71).

The creation of the groat and of a gold currency brought monetary circulation back to a more healthy condition, but the abuses to which it had been subject still continued. Kings and princes went on debasing the currency and giving it an arbitrary valuation. The value of money still followed a descending curve. The general policy sacrificed economic to fiscal interests and the first appeal for a better understanding of these matters, made by Nicholas Oresme in the fourteenth century, was destined to fall upon deaf ears. Many centuries were yet to elapse before governments began to follow the principles of a true monetary administration.

IV. CREDIT AND THE TRAFFIC IN MONEY[38]

The theory according to which commercial development is divided into three successive phases, the first characterised by barter (*Naturalwirtschaft*), the second by

[38] BIBLIOGRAPHY.—L. Goldschmidt, *op. cit.*, p. viii.—M. Postan, *Credit in Medieval Trade*, in *The Economic History Review*, vol. I (1928).—R. Génestal, *Le rôle des monastères comme établissements de crédit*, Paris (1901).—L. Delisle, *Les opérations financières des Templiers*, Paris (1889).—H. Van Werveke, *Le mort-gage et son rôle économique en Flandre et en Lotharingie*, in *Revue belge de philol. et d'histoire*,

money (*Geldwirtschaft*) and the third by credit (*Kredit-wirtschaft*), has had a long vogue. Nevertheless, a study of the facts should soon have made it plain that it has no foundation in reality and is merely one more example of that love of systematisation which has so often influenced the study of economic history. While it is incontestable that credit has played an increasingly considerable rôle, it is equally true that it may be observed at work in all periods. The difference between them in this respect is merely quantitative and not qualitative.[39]

Naturally, during the agrarian period of the Middle Ages there could be no question of commercial credit in the proper sense of the term, which could not possibly have developed in an age of sporadic and occasional commerce and in the absence of a class of professional merchants. But on the other hand it is clear that, even though limited

t. VIII (1929).—G. Bigwood, *Les financiers d'Arras*, *ibid.*, t. III (1924).—R. L. Reynolds, *The Merchants of Arras*, *ibid.*, vol. IX (1930).—H. Jenkinson, *A Moneylender's Bonds of the Twelfth Century*, in *Essays in History, Presented to R. Lane Poole*, ed. H. W. C. Davis, London (1927).—G. Bigwood, *Le régime juridique et économique du commerce de l'argent dans la Belgique du Moyen Age*, Brussels, 1921–2, 2 vols. (Mém. Acad. Belgique).—S. L. Peruzzi, *Storia del commercio e dei banchieri di Firenze* (1200–1345), Florence (1868).—A. Sapori, *La crise delle compagnie mercantili dei Bardi e dei Peruzzi*, Florence, 1926.—*Id.*, *Una compagnia di Calimala ai primi del trecento*, Florence (1932).—*Id.*, *I Libri di commercio di Peruzzi*, Milan (1934).—A. Ceccherelli, *Le scritture commerciale nelle antiche aziende fiorentine*, Florence, 1910.— E. H. Byrne, *Commercial Contracts of the Genoese in the Syrian Trade of the XIIth Century*, in *The Quarterly Journal of Economics*, vol. XXXI (1916).—A. E. Sayous, *Les opérations du capitaliste et commerçant marseillais Etienne de Man-duel, entre 1200 et 1230*, in *Revue des Questions historiques* (1930).—*Id.*, *Les transformations des méthodes commerciales dans l'Italie médiévale*, in *Annales d'histoire économique et sociale*, t. I (1929).—*Id.*, *Dans l'Italie médiévale a l'intérieur des terres; Sienne de 1221 à 1229*, *ibid.*, t. III (1931).—*Id.*, *Les méthodes commerciales de Barcelone au XIIIᵉ siècle*, in *Estudis universitaris catalans*, t. XVI (1932).—*Id.*, *Les mandats de Saint Louis sur son trésor*, in *Revue historique*, t

to the needs of a society based on a rural economy without markets, the action of credit was nevertheless considerable; so much so, indeed, that it is difficult to see how this landed aristocracy, which was the basis of the whole social organisation, could have maintained itself without its aid. It was by means of credit, indeed, that society was able to survive the disaster into which it was periodically plunged by famine.

The Church was the indispensable moneylender of the period. We have already seen that it possessed a liquid capital which made it a financial power of the first order. Chronicles are full of details about the wealth of the monastic shrines, teeming with reliquaries, candlesticks, censers, and sacred vessels made of the precious metals,

CLXVII (1931).—F. Arens, *Wihelm Servat von Cahors als Kaufmann zu London*, in *Vierteljahrschrift für Social-und Wirtschaftsgeschichte*, t. XI (1913).—W. E. Rhodes, *The Italian Bankers in London and their loans to Edward I and Edward II* in *Owens College Essays*, Manchester (1902).—W. Sombart, *Die Juden und das Wirtschaftsleben*, Leipzig (1911).— A. Sayous, *Les Juifs ont-ils été les fondateurs du capitalisme moderne?*, in *Revue économique internationale* (1932).—W. Endemann, *Studien in die romanisch-kanonistische Wirtschafts-und Rechtslehre*, Berlin (1874–83), 2 vols.—F. Schaub, *Der Kampf gegen den Zinswucher, ungerechten Preis und unlauteren Handel*, Freiburg (1905).—H. Pirenne, *L'instruction des marchands au Moyen Age*, in *Annales d'histoire économique et sociale*, t. I (1929).—A. Schiaffini, *Il mercante Genovese del dugento*, in the review *A compagna*, an. 1929.—F. Rörig, *Das älteste erhaltene deutsche Kaufmannsbüchlein*, in *Hansische Beiträge zur deutschen Wirtschaftsgeschichte*, Breslau (1928).—F. Keutgen, *Hansische Handelsgesellschaften vornehmlich des XIV Jahrhunderts*, in *Vierteljahrschrift für Social-und Wirtschaftsgeschichte*, t. IV (1906).—J. Kulischer, *Warenhändler und Geldausleiher im Mittelalter*, in *Zeitschrift für Volkswirtschaft, Sozialpolitik und Verwaltung* (1908).— A. P. Usher, *The Origins of Banking. The Primitive Bank of Deposit*, in *The Economic History Review*, vol. IV (1934).

** "Sale credit of which the existence has been generally denied, in reality formed the financial basis of the medieval trade. As to the other forms of credit their existence was never doubted but their function was wrongly interpreted." Postan, *loc. cit.*, p. 261.

offerings both great and small, which the piety of the faithful lavished on the earthly representatives of those all-powerful saints, whose intervention was most surely to be obtained by generosity to their servants. Every church of any reputation had thus at its disposal treasures, which not only increased the pomp of its services, but were an abundant hoard of capital. In case of need it had only to melt down a few pieces of goldsmith's work and send the metal to a neighbouring mint, to procure an equivalent sum of money, and this was a practice to which the monasteries had recourse, not only on their own behalf, but on that of others. If a bishop had to make an extraordinary payment, whether for the purchase of an estate or in the royal service, he turned for help to the abbeys of his diocese. There are innumerable examples of such loans. When, for instance, Otbert, bishop of Liége, bought the castles of Bouillon and Couvin in 1096, it was the churches of the diocese which met the costs of the transaction.[40]

But it was above all in times of dearth that the monastic treasuries were called into requisition. They played the part of credit establishments for neighbouring lords, whose reserves were exhausted and who had to obtain the essential means of livelihood for cash. They advanced the necessary funds against a land gage by the borrower, guaranteeing payment of the debt. It was called a "live gage" (*vif gage*) when the revenue from the property pledged contributed to the repayment of the principal, and a "dead gage" or mortgage when the revenues went to the creditor without any deduction of the principal debt. In both cases the prohibition of usury was respected, since the money originally lent did not by itself produce any interest.

In operations of this sort, which were innumerable up to the mid-thirteenth century, the loans were all loans for consumption, that is to say, they were contracted as a result of some urgent necessity; the money received would be spent at once, so that each sum borrowed represented a

[40] H. Pirenne, *Histoire de Belgique,* t. I, 5th ed., p. 132.

dead loss. When it prohibited usury for religious reasons, the Church therefore rendered a signal service to the agrarian society of the early Middle Ages. It saved it from the affliction of consumption debts, from which the ancient world suffered so severely. Christian charity could here apply with the utmost rigour the principle of lending without remuneration; the precept *mutuum date nihil inde sperantes* was perfectly attuned to a period in which, money not yet being a means of wealth, any remuneration for its use could appear only as an exaction. But the revival of commerce, by discovering the productivity of liquid capital, gave rise to problems to which men sought a satisfactory solution in vain. Right up to the end of the Middle Ages society continued to be torn with anxiety over the terrible question of usury, in which business practice and ecclesiastical morality found themselves directly opposed. For want of a better solution, it was evaded by means of compromises and expedients.

The rarity of our sources makes it impossible to discover the conditions under which commercial credit first began, but there is no doubt that already in the eleventh century there was in existence a considerable number of merchants disposing of liquid capital. Of such were the merchants of Liége, who in 1082 lent the abbot of Saint-Hubert the sum which he required for the purchase of an estate.[41] Although we know nothing of the contract between the parties, it is impossible to believe that the loan was a gratuitous one. The lenders obviously agreed to it only in return for advantages which they considered sufficiently remunerative, and it is difficult to believe that they abstained from any sort of usury. In any case the practice of usury appears in full vigour in the middle of the twelfth century. We possess enough details of the career of a burgess of Saint-Omer, William Cade (who died about 1166), to suspect that he engaged simultaneously in trade in merchandise and trade in money. We see him engaging in real credit operations, buying the wool of their sheep in

ᵃ *Chronique de Saint-Hubert,* ed. Hanquet, p. 121.

advance from the English abbeys, and in so acting he was without doubt only conforming to the practice of all the great merchants of his age. Moreover, there is no lack of evidence for purchases and sales on credit in the wholesale trade in spices, wine, wool, cloth and other commodities.

The insufficiency of monetary circulation would render the possibility of large-scale commerce incomprehensible, except on the supposition that it made use of credit as a normal operation. Of this use Italy, where the economic advance began much earlier than on the continent, provides unexceptionable proofs. Already in the tenth century the Venetians were investing money in maritime ventures, and as soon as Genoa and Pisa devoted themselves to navigation, numbers of nobles and burgesses began to risk their capital on the sea. The smallness of the sums involved ought not to blind us to the importance of these investments. In order to distribute the risks, men took "parts" in several ships at a time. The *commenda,* already flourishing in the twelfth century, shows very clearly the part played by commercial credit. The lender (*commendator*) advanced to the borrower for a share in the resultant profits (usually three-quarters) a capital sum which the latter was to put to use abroad.[42] Maritime insurance, which Genoese documents show us in operation from the twelfth century, is another application of credit. In order to describe the many and various forms which it assumed from this time onwards, it would be necessary to trespass further than is here possible into the field of commercial law. Its earliest development would appear to have been due to Italian and more especially Genoese shipowners. It was through them that insurance spread from maritime transactions into general financial practice.

Societies devoted to land commerce developed rather less rapidly than those which originated in sea trade, but in the twelfth century they appear in full vigour in all the

[42] According to Byrne, the normal profit of the Genoese companies in the twelfth century amounted to 25 per cent.

mercantile cities of Italy. Letters of credit were then in regular use; we have already seen what an essential part they played in the business conducted at the Champagne fairs. The documents of obligation, out of which the bill of exchange developed, were drawn up either by notaries, as in Italy and the south of France, or by municipal scribes in Flanders.

The development of instruments of credit presupposes a knowledge of reading and writing among the merchants. The activity of commerce was no doubt the reason for the foundation of the first schools for the children of the bourgeoisie. At first these children must have had to rely entirely upon monastic schools, where they learned the rudiments of Latin necessary for commercial correspondence. But it is obvious that neither the spirit nor the organisation of these schools would allow them to devote enough attention to the kind of practical knowledge which was required by pupils, who were destined for a commercial career. Thus from the second half of the twelfth century the towns began to open little schools, which may be considered as the starting-point of lay education in the Middle Ages. The clergy, of course, opposed this intervention of the secular power in a domain which had hitherto been their exclusive property. Though they did not manage to put a stop to an innovation which had become indispensable to social life, they did almost everywhere succeed in submitting the town schools to the supervision of their own theologians, although the municipal authorities retained the right of nominating the schoolmasters.

The majority of merchants engaged in international commerce in the thirteenth century undoubtedly possessed a more or less advanced degree of instruction. It was certainly largely as a result of their initiative that the vulgar tongues took the place of Latin in private instruments. At all events it is worthy of note that this practice began in those countries which were economically the most advanced, that is to say, in Italy and Flanders. The earliest charter drawn up in French comes from the latter. In

Italy the practice of writing was so much a part of commercial life that the keeping of books by merchants seems to have been general, if not obligatory, in the thirteenth century. From the beginning of the fourteenth century it was general all over Europe. The account books of the Bonis brothers at Montauban begin in 1339,[43] and that of Ugo Teralh at Forcalquier[44] covers the years 1330–2. From Germany there have come down to us, among others, the *Handlungsbücher* of Johann Tölner of Rostock,[45] of Vicko von Geldernsen of Hamburg,[46] of Hermann and Johann Wittenborg of Lübeck;[47] the oldest of all, that of the Warendorps, also comes from Lübeck.[48] At the beginning of the thirteenth century Leonardo Pisano (Leonardo Fibonaci) composed a treatise on arithmetic for the use of merchants.

The knowledge of foreign languages, too, was certainly widespread among men of business, among whom French played much the same part that English plays to-day in economic affairs. The fairs of Champagne no doubt did much to bring this about. There have been preserved a number of little conversation books, composed at Bruges in the middle of the fourteenth century in order to teach

[43] E. Forestié, *Le livre de comptes des frères Bonis, marchands montalbanais du XIVe siècle* (Paris-Ausch, 2 vol., 1890–3).

[44] P. Meyer, *Le livre journal de maître Ugo Teralh, notaire et drapier à Forcalquier* (1330–2), in *Notices et extraits des manuscrits de la Bibliothèque Nationale*, etc., t. XXXVI (1898).

[45] K. Koppmann, *Johann Tölners Handlungsbuch von 1345–1350* (Rostock, 1885).

[46] H. Nirrnheim, *Das Handlungsbuch Vickos von Geldernsen* (Hamburg-Leipzig, 1895).

[47] C. Mollwo, *Das Handlungsbuch von Hermann und Johann Wittenborg* (Leipzig, 1901).

[48] F. Rörig, *Hansische Beiträge*, etc., cited p. 118, Bib.— For Bruges there remain only the fragments of an account-book of Collard de Marke (1366–9). R. de Roover, *Considérations sur le livre de comptes de C. de M.*, in the *Bulletin de l'école supérieure de commerce Saint-Ignace à Anvers* (1930).

this language.[49] Side by side with it Latin continued to fulfil the rôle of an international language, especially in relations between the romance and germanic peoples.

The advance of education appears to have been intimately connected with that of credit, and the example of Italy shows that the further credit was developed, the more rapid was this advance. The commercial documents which have been preserved show that long-term payments were very common; the most cursory glance at the account books mentioned above will make this plain. Moreover, these books are concerned only with retail trade. Analogous documents dealing with wholesale operations would certainly be still more striking. It is impossible to believe that the merchants who bought hundreds of bales of wool in England could have paid for them before they had sold the cloth made from it. Moreover, we possess enough evidence to warrant the conclusion that great merchants were in continual relations of debt and credit with one another. In fact, instead of the almost negligible function which it had been customary to attribute to commercial credit in the Middle Ages, we shall have to admit that it played a preponderant part.

Of course it was not equally advanced in all countries. It was much less widespread in Germany beyond the Rhine than in Flanders and above all in Italy, and it is an error of methodology to generalise from that country to the whole of Europe, as has too often been done. In order to understand the scope of a given phenomenon, it must be studied where its manifestations are most vigorous. The economic activity of the great Flemish and Italian cities cannot be reduced to that of second-rate towns like Frankfort-on-Main. It would be equally unjustifiable to exaggerate the importance of commercial credit in the Middle Ages by comparing it with that of our own day, or even of the end of the fifteenth century. Essential as it was,

[49] *Le livre des métiers de Bruges et ses dérivés. Quatre anciens manuels de conversation,* ed. J. Gessler (Bruges, 1931).

it had to operate within the limits of an economic territory bounded on the West by the shores of the Atlantic and on the East by the Mediterranean, Black Sea and Baltic coasts. It was not, then, upheld by the power of great states, nor was it able, for reasons which will appear later, to influence at all seriously the organisation of industrial production.

Commercial credit employed only a part of the liquid capital available. By far the greater part was used for loans to public authorities or to individuals. The banking operations of the Middle Ages were essentially loan operations, and almost the whole history of the trade in money at this period is concerned with these. This trade was itself only a result of the commercial revival of the eleventh and twelfth centuries. Of the first medieval bankers, some were descendants of the exchangers (*cambitores*), who came into existence at an early date as a result of the diversity of currencies and rapidly grew rich in the exercise of a profession which necessarily escaped all control, while others, many more numerous, were great merchants, who found a use for their surplus capital by lending it to others. It may be observed, moreover, that banking was never entirely divorced from trade in merchandise, upon which it was, so to speak, grafted. It was simply one way of utilising reserves of capital.

As a general rule the medieval banker was both moneylender and merchant. The foundation of great commercial fortunes in the course of the twelfth century inevitably drew the attention of kings, princes, aristocracy and even of the church. They were all suffering from an insufficiency of revenue, as a result of the increasing economic activity and the continual growth of expenses, which were the fruit of more refined standards of life. It was much more convenient for them to get an advance of the money they needed from those merchants who were rolling in it, rather than to pledge their lands to abbeys or to send their plate to the mint. And how could the merchants have withstood their demands? It would have been too dangerous to refuse borrowers whose political and social influence was considerable. It is true that their very power might endanger the repayment of the sums risked in their hands, but it was a sufficient guarantee to demand a rate of interest high enough to compensate the losses due to debts unpaid. All things considered, if the risks were great (and were they any greater than those involved in international commerce, subject to all the hazards of war and shipwreck, pirates and robbers?) the profits in prospect were attractive. From the thirteenth century onwards they must have tempted almost all the *nouveaux riches*. It is obvious that only small traces remain of the loans which they made, the title deeds of which were destroyed on repayment. We owe entirely to chance the preservation of the few sources of information which have come down to us, and which, despite their rarity, enable us to appreciate the vast credits which the merchants placed at the disposal of their clients.

Round about 1160 William Cade was furnishing considerable sums to the king of England and to a number of nobles.[50] John Rynvisch and Simon Saphir of Ghent performed the same office for John Lackland.[51] About the same time Arras was famous for its moneylenders,

> Atrebatum . . . urbs . . . plena
> Divitiis, inhians lucris et foenore gaudens.[52]

The richest of them all, the Louchards, left a name which was legendary in the Low Countries and the Crespins enjoyed an almost equal reputation. Artesian poetry still preserves for us the impression that their wealth and their

---

[50] On these operations see H. Jenkinson's article, quoted p. 117, Bib.

[51] Already in 1176 English prelates were borrowing considerable sums from the "mercatores Flandriae." A. Schaube, *Handelsgeschichte der Romanischen Völker*, p. 393.

[52] Guillaume le Breton, *Philipidis. Mon. Germ. Hist. Script.*, t. XXVI, p. 321.

love of gain made upon contemporaries.[53] From the beginning of the thirteenth century all the great nobles of the Scheldt basin were in debt to the bourgeoisie of the towns. Side by side with the men of Artois we hear of the burgesses of Lens, Douai, Tournai, Ghent, Valenciennes and Ypres as lenders, and the list of their debtors includes the Countesses Jeanne and Marguerite of Flanders, Count Gui de Dampierre, his sons, Robert and Jean, bishop of Liége, Count Robert II of Artois, the sire de Termonde and many others. The sums advanced vary from 60 to 14,000 livres, but the same persons continually return to the charge. From 1269 to 1300, the known debts of Gui de Dampierre reached a total of 55,813 livres, in the county of Flanders alone, and we do not know how many more he may have contracted. Repayment was usually stipulated for in a year's time and under the guarantee of sureties, who were sometimes rich bourgeois, sometimes great personages, such as the *avoués* of Arras and of Bethune and the lord of Audenarde, sometimes (and most often) the town of Bruges. Sometimes, too, the guarantee was provided by the real property of the debtor. Towns were as ready to borrow as the nobility. Large and small, they continually had recourse to the merchant's moneybags. From October 1284 to February 1305 on ten separate occasions Bruges obtained advances which amounted in all to over 460,000 livres.[54] The needs of religious establishments were less considerable, but they too continually sought for credit and the journal of his visitations kept by Archbishop Eudes Rigaud (1248–69) shows that almost all the monasteries of Normandy were in debt.

These illustrations will suffice to show the extent of the credit operations, which arose out of the existence of

[53] A. Guesnon, *La satire à Arras a XIII* siècle, in *Le Moyen Age* (1889 and 1900). On the reputation for cupidity and wealth enjoyed by the Artesians at the beginning of the twelfth century, see Guibert de Nogent, *Histoire de sa vie,* ed. G. Bourgin, p. 223.

[54] G. Bigwood, *op. cit.,* t. I, p. 99.

liquid capital derived from commerce. The picture presented by the Low Countries was reproduced all over Europe, with differences due to the greater or less activity of economic life in the different regions. Everywhere money was assured of a more profitable investment in proportion as the demand for it was greater. Each sum advanced by the lender meant a remuneration which was simply usury, or, to use the modern expression, interest. Neither municipal accounts nor individual memoranda recoil before the odious word usury; but in documents intended for the public the reality was dissimulated. The borrower habitually agreed to repay, on the expiration of the term, a sum greater than that which he had in fact received; the difference formed the interest. In loans with damages (*ad manaium*) the debt acknowledged is exactly that originally contracted. On the nominal day of payment the damages are paid and if the principal is not paid at the same time the debt is renewed until the debtor finally discharges himself. It must have been understood that the debtor would not pay up on the agreed date, so that usury was here concealed under the guise of a penalty for delay.[55] In general the rate of interest varied between 10 and 16 per cent. Sometimes it fell as low as 5 per cent, or rose as high as 24 per cent and even more. The degree of risk involved in the transaction naturally affected the stipulated rate.

The trade in money as it was practised by the merchants of Northern Europe, Cade, Louchard, Crespin and their like, was very primitive in form, in spite of its wide extent. It seems to have been confined to individual contracts between capitalists and borrowers. The financiers of Arras and of the other Flemish towns do not appear to have formed companies. "They either acted alone, or else, more often, in groups of two or three, among whom a temporary association no doubt existed, but not a regular company." [56] They had neither representatives abroad, nor

[55] G. Bigwood, *op. cit.*, t. I, p. 441.
[56] *Ibid.*, p. 178.

corresponding establishments. They do not even seem to have been in relations with the bankers and exchangers of the Champagne fairs, for they regularly stipulate that the money advanced is to be repaid at their own domiciles. Furthermore, they undertook neither to receive deposits, nor to make payments abroad, nor to discount bills of exchange. The Italians, on the contrary, were familiar with all these operations from the twelfth century and from the thirteenth had brought them to the highest degree of development compatible with the social conditions of the age. So great was their superiority over the Northern financiers that the latter had to yield place to them, and the financiers became, from the end of the thirteenth century, no more than wealthy rentiers, *otiosi,* who occupied themselves with the administration of their own fortunes, the acquisition of real property and the purchase of rents.

As we have already seen, the merchants of the North and of Italy were frequenting the fairs of Champagne and Flanders from the thirteenth century. The cloth industry, the products of which they exported in ever-growing quantities to the South of Europe, was so important for them that many of them were led to settle in the centres of production and even to enter into affiliations with the bourgeoisie. But no sooner were they there, than they began to compete successfully with the natives, over whom their organisation and superior technique gave them a great advantage in finance. The powerful companies to which they belonged supported them with capital from abroad and from the end of the thirteenth century all had their representatives in the Low Countries. We find there associates or factors of the Salimbene, the Buonsignori and the Gallerani of Siena, the Frescobaldi, the Pucci, the Peruzzi and the Bardi of Florence, the Scoti of Piacenza, and side by side with them Genoese, Pistoians and Cahorsins from Languedoc. All these southerners possessed a commercial education, a routine of exchange and credit business and a knowledge of the great mercantile centres of Europe with which they were in constant relations, which placed them beyond competition. It is not surprising that, after the Battle of Bouvines, Countess Jeanne had recourse to Italian credit for the sum which she needed to ransom her husband, Ferrand de Portugal, from the hands of Philip Augustus. In 1221 she had received 29,194 livres at a cost of 34,626. It was good business for the moneylenders and doubtless the Countess, on her side, could congratulate herself on their *savoir faire*.[57] At all events, from this time onwards the practice of borrowing from the *ultramontani* spread rapidly.

The advance of credit is shown by the variety of the forms which it assumed. The fairs of Champagne were usually fixed as the place of repayment and determined the term of the loan. But the Italian bankers also acted as intermediaries in making payments abroad, and their mastery of exchange operations and "clearing house" practice, i.e., the mutual setting off of debts, gave them, from the end of the thirteenth century, a monopoly of banking north of the Alps. The kings of France and England, territorial princes, bishops, abbots, towns, all provided them with an international clientèle. The Papacy made use of them to manage the enormous sums at its disposal, to collect Peter's Pence and the ever-increasing taxation of every kind with which it burdened the Church.[58] In fact, they managed the finances of the whole of Europe. Kings called them into their councils, entrusted them with their mints, charged them witth the supervision and collection of their taxes. They farmed the excises in many towns, and everywhere princes authorised them to keep loan establishments (*tables de prêts*). Besides banking they engaged in all kinds of commercial operations. They bought wool and sold cloth, spices, goldsmiths' work, brocade,

---

[57] *Ibid.*, p. 180.

[58] G. Schneider, *Die finanziellen Beziehungen der florentinischen Bankiers zur Kirche* (Leipzig, 1899); ed. Jordan, *Le Saint-Siège et les banquiers italiens*, in *Congrès internationale des catholiques*, 5th section, p. 292 (Brussels, 1895).

and silks. They owned ships on the one hand and hostels in Paris, Bruges and London on the other. As their business grew they became increasingly bolder, for the profits realised more than compensated for the risks. They had no hesitation in squeezing the debtors, who were forced by necessity to apply to them and not infrequently exacted interest of 50 per cent, and even over 100 per cent, from abbeys or individuals in distress. But in big business, and in transactions with clients whose power or solvency were their recommendation, the rate was usually round about 10 per cent.

Compared with the efflorescence and ubiquity of Italian credit, that of the Jews appears a very small affair and the part which they played in the Middle Ages has certainly been much exaggerated. In actual fact, the more economically advanced a country was, the fewer Jewish moneylenders were to be found there. In Flanders there were never more than a negligible number, but they became increasingly numerous towards the East of Europe. In Germany their numbers grew with the distance from the Rhine and in Poland, Bohemia and Hungary they were to be found in quantities. In the agrarian period of the Middle Ages, as was shown above, they acted as pedlars of oriental goods.[59] Through Moslem Spain, where their coreligionists had early acquired great economic influence, they introduced into Northern Europe spices, precious stuffs and goldsmiths' work. They even seem to have engaged in a clandestine traffic in Christian slaves up to about the end of the tenth century. A certain number of them had acquired lands, vineyards and mills in the South of France. But the Church, without persecuting them, always sought to prevent all contact between these "miscreants" and the faithful, and the outburst of mysticism, which was contemporaneous with the first crusade, unleashed popular hatred against them and inaugurated that

[59] See above, p. 11.—*Cf.* M. Hofmann, *Der Geldhandel der deutschen Juden während des Mittelalters bis zum Jahre 1350* (Leipzig, 1910).

long series of pogroms, of which they were so often henceforth to be the victims. At the same time the revival of
Mediterranean commerce in the eleventh century made
it possible to dispense with them as intermediaries with
the Levant. It was only at Barcelona that Jewish traders,
who had grown rich during the Moslem period and remained in the town after the *reconquista,* took part in
maritime trade as owners or sleeping partners in the ownership of ships. Everywhere else the Jews of the West
were reduced to mere pawnbroking, lending money at
interest on the security of pledges. They were unaffected
by the prohibition of usury, which applied only to Christians, and they profited by and undoubtedly abused this
freedom. For no one came to their doors save in case of
need and necessity enabled them to exploit their clients
as much as they liked. Their connections with their coreligionists, not only in Europe but in the Islamic lands
of the South, made it easy for them to procure the ready
money which they required for their business, and individuals in distress could always obtain assistance from them;
the more urgent the need, the less likely was the client to
haggle over the price. Moreover, borrowing from the Jews
had the appreciable advantage of secrecy. It was so convenient that even ecclesiastical establishments resorted to
it.

Wherever they settled the Jews were under the protection of the territorial sovereign, which is as much as to
say that they were dependent on his good-will. In 1261
Duke Henry of Brabant, on his death-bed, ordered all
usurers to be expelled from his country and his widow
only resigned herself to tolerating them, after seeking the
advice of St. Thomas Aquinas.[60] Edward I expelled them
from England in 1290. Philip the Fair followed his example in France in 1306, but his successors allowed their

[60] H. Pirenne, *La duchesse Aleyde de Brabant et le.* "*De
regimine Judaeorum*" *de Saint Thomas d'Aquin,* in *Bulletin
de la Classe des Lettres de l'Académie royale de Belgique*
(1928)

gradual return to the kingdom, whence they were once more banished in 1393. Moreover, the people periodically rose against them, instigated by debtors, for whom it was only too easy to excite the masses by appealing to their credulity.[61] The Jews were suspected of every sort of horror and sacrilege. In 1349 they were massacred all over Brabant; in 1370 they were finally expelled, after a rumour that they had profaned the host.[62]

As pawnbrokers the Jews encountered powerful competition from the Christians themselves from the thirteenth century. The earliest in date would seem to have been men from Cahors, who were scattered all over France and the Low Countries and were so active there that from the middle of the century the word "Cahorsin" became equivalent to moneylender.[63] However, Lombards, or more exactly Italians, soon took their place in this class of business. In return for a rent, princes and towns granted them the right to set up "loan tables"; the earliest of these grants in the Low Countries goes back to 1280. The grantees of these establishments enjoyed a monopoly to the exclusion of others, such as "toscans u coversins u juis," [64] and it may be surmised that it was often their representations which contributed to bring about the expulsion of the Jews, whose place they took. Although the earliest grants stipulated that loans should be made "bien et loiaument sans malengien et sans usure," all that is intended is obviously the prohibition of excessive interest. Later texts leave no doubt on this point; they merely for-

[61] For a curious example at Paris, in 1380, see the *Chronique du religieux de saint Denys,* ed. Bellaguet, t. I, p. 54.

[62] They could not have been very numerous, for the confiscation of their possessions produced only 7,065 Brabantine florins. Henne and Wauters, *Histoire de Bruxelles,* t. I, p. 133, n.

[63] In 1367, at Bruges, the word "cauwersinen" was applied to the Lombards. Gilliodts van Severen, *Inventaire des Archives de Bruges,* t. II, p. 140.—The Cahorsins, too, dealt both in money and in merchandise. See F. Arens, *Wilhelm Servat von Cahors als Kaufmann zu London,* in *Vierteljahrschrift für Social-und Wirtschaftsgeschichte,* t. XI (1913), p. 477 *et seq.*

[64] Bigwood, *Le commerce de l'argent* t. I p. 340.

bid "evil covenants" or oblige the lenders to conform to "the usages and customs according to which the Lombards are accustomed to lend." [65] Thus they officially recognise the exaction of what is regarded as a reasonable rate of interest. The ordinary rate was two deniers per livre per week, that is to say 43⅓ per cent per annum, which was almost double the rate of commercial interest. The Lombard "tables" were, moreover, far from confining themselves exclusively to the practice of loans at interest; they also received and made payments on behalf of their clients and engaged in commercial operations.

The exchangers also took part in the trade in money and the handling of credit. Money-changing was a lucrative business and the right to exercise it was granted by princes only in return for rents and to a limited number of persons, who thus enjoyed a semi-official position. The trade in precious metals was reserved for them and obviously produced abundant profits, in addition to the commission on the exchanges. It soon become customary to entrust them with sums for safe-keeping and these services were doubtless not gratuitous. They also received deposits and funds under arrest, and it can easily be understood that they frequently acted as agents of payment and that some of them even became moneylenders.

On the other hand, ecclesiastical establishments, which had played the part of real credit establishments in the first centuries of the Middle Ages, only rarely lent money from the beginning of the thirteenth century. Unlike laymen, they could not evade the prohibition of usury, though they occasionally permitted themselves to break it.[66] Moreover, they had not enough ready money to compete with the merchants, and above all with the Italian financiers, even if they had wanted to do so. Indeed, it was usually they who had recourse to the good offices of these financiers and they were almost always in debt to

[65] *Ibid.*, p. 451.
[66] In 1228, the Abbé of Saint-Bertin lent money *ad usuram.* Bigwood, *op. cit.*, t. II, p. 263.

them. Only the Order of the Templars, by reason of its
relations with the Christian East, succeeded in becoming a
real financial power in the course of the thirteenth century. Its commanderies were all in correspondence with
each other, whether they were established in Syria or in
the Western states. Their prestige and military power led
the nobility to use them as places of safe deposit, or for the
transmission of money to and from the Levant. In France
the Templars were entrusted by the kings with all kinds
of Treasury business, until Philip the Fair decided to bring
about the dissolution of an order, whose wealth he cov-
eted and whose tutelage he desired to shake off.

Real credit (i.e., credit connected with landed estate)
developed in a way which gave it, in the towns at least,
an essential importance. Merchants who had grown rich
on commerce did not employ all their profits in business
or in loans. The safest investment was to buy land, which
with the rapid growth of the urban population became
building sites, to be rented to the new inhabitants. Already, at the beginning of the twelfth century, the *Gesta
episcoporum cameracensium* show us the first great merchant of the Low Countries whose name has been preserved by history, Werimbold, acquiring more and more
rents as his fortune grows,

> Census accrescunt censibus
> Et munera muneribus.[97]

To the early land rents drawn by the owners of the soil
there were soon added new rents, drawn from the houses
which the occupants had put up there. The creation of these
house rents was one of the most general and frequent
forms of medieval credit. If a householder wanted to
borrow for a long term, he sold a rent on the house, that
is to say, engaged to pay the moneylender a rent, which
was sometimes permanent but more often redeemable,
and which represented the interest on the capital bor-

---

[97] *Gesta episcoporum Cameracensium Continuata,* ed. G.
Waitz, *M.M.G.G., SS.,* t. XIV, p. 215.

rowed on the security of the house property. This interest, which was much more moderate than commercial interest and had the advantage of not falling under the prohibition of usury, usually varied round about 10 to 8 per cent up to the fifteenth century.[68]

Very different from these rents on real property were the life rents, which came into general use as a result of loans contracted by the towns. From the beginning of the thirteenth century the towns resorted increasingly to the practice of selling rents for one or two lives, in order to raise extraordinary sums, such rents forming the interest on the borrowed capital. They were payable to the lender to the time of his death or the death of his heirs (rents for two lives). They were thus investments which were from an early date much sought after by the bourgeoisie, and since everyone was permitted to purchase rents of this kind, each town came to possess rentiers, sometimes distributed very widely. To preclude fraud special prizes were promised to whoever would notify the death of beneficiaries of these rents, who incidentally bear an obvious resemblance to the modern holders of public debt. Sometimes, also, special agents were appointed by the town government to keep count of holders of life rents.[69] Certain towns assigned the administration of a part of their revenues to their creditors, who repaid themselves out of the profits. In Italy this custom was already much in vogue in the middle of the twelfth century. In 1164 Genoa

[68] W. Arnold, *Zur Geschichte des Eigentums in den deutschen Städten* (Basle, 1861). G. Des Marez, *Étude sur la propriété foncière dans les villes du Moyen Age et spécialement en Flandre* (Ghent, 1898); J. Gobbers, *Die Erbleihe und ihr Verhältniss zum Rentenkauf im mittelalterlichen Köln*, in *Zeitschrift der Savigny Stiftung für Rechtsgeschichte, Germ. Abth.* (1883).

[69] The abbeys also created life rents in favour of their creditors. See, for example, in 1267, the list of *pensiones que post vitas hominum ad ecclesiam revertentur*, in *Le livre de l'abbé Guillaume de Ryckel*, ed. H. Pirenne, p. 68.—On life rents in towns, see G. Espinas, *Les finances de la commune de Douai*, p. 321 *et seq.* (Paris, 1902).

handed over some of its revenues for a period of eleven years to a society (*monte*) of eleven persons. By the thirteenth century the city had already consolidated its debt and recognised the right of its creditors to sell their holdings to third parties. The famous Bank of St. George (*casa di S. Georgio*), which was to become so powerful in the fifteenth century, originated in this way.

The foregoing sketch of the history of credit and the trade in money, slight and incomplete as it is, will nevertheless have given some idea of their importance and of the many forms which they had assumed before the end of the thirteenth century. Without them the economic life of the Middle Ages would be incomprehensible. But, save in the great Italian cities, where the governing institutions of financial markets and the banks of the future were already beginning to take shape, their vigour was greater than their technical perfection. It has been truly pointed out that no such thing as a money market, in the proper sense of the term, existed at this period. Every credit operation was, in effect, the subject of a contract determined by the particular circumstances, a private agreement between a lender and a borrower. In fact, commercial loans were not yet clearly differentiated from consumption loans.[70]

One is naturally led to ask how far these weaknesses are to be attributed to the prohibition of interest. The fact that this prohibition passed from ecclesiastical into civil legislation certainly made it still more of a hindrance. In actual practice, however, it was impossible to enforce its literal observance and it was applied in full rigour only in cases of "manifest usury," i.e., of consumption loans upon pledges, in which an excessive rate of interest was stipulated. The need for credit was too great and too general for men to think of discouraging lenders. From the thirteenth century onwards the canonists were seeking to modify the absolute prohibition laid down in the text

[70] Bigwood, *op. cit.*, t. I, p. 456.

Mutuum date nihil inde sperantes by various expedients.[71]
It was discovered that in any advance of money involving
either an eventual loss (*damnum emergens*), or a cessation of gain (*lucrum cessans*), or a risk of the capital
(*periculum sortis*), an indemnity, or, in other words,
interest (*interesse*), was justifiable. Thus interest was simply legitimate usury, and it is easy to understand how
delicate was the distinction between this tolerated usury
and the prohibited usury, and what scope it left for inter-
pretation by the judges. In commerce the "letting out"
of money was authorised by current practice. It was the
rule at the fairs of Champagne and in general in the operations of commercial societies. In the fourteenth century
the theologian, Alvarus Palagius, states that the prohibition
of usury is not applicable to the latter.[72]

The fact remains, however, that the censure of the
Church was always hanging like a permanent menace
over all who concerned themselves with credit. Very often
debtors were absolved by the Church from the obligation
to pay interest on their debts. Consequently the utmost
ingenuity was expended upon dissimulating the dangerous
interest. Sometimes the lender deducted it in advance of
the sum borrowed, sometimes it was concealed under the
guise of a penalty for delay in repayment, sometimes the
debtor acknowledged the receipt of a much greater sum
than he had really received. Altogether the legislation
against usury does not seem to have prevented it in practice very much more than the Volstead Act in America
prevented the consumption of alcohol. It was a hindrance
but not a barrier. The Church itself was continually
obliged to borrow from the financiers whose actions it

[71] W. Endemann, *Studien in die romanisch-kanonistische
Wirtschafts-und Rechtslehre,* 2 vols. (Berlin, 1874–83). E.
Schreiber, *Die volkswirtschaftlichen Anschauungen der Scholis-
tik seit Thomas von Aquin,* Jena, 1913.—A. Fanfoni, *Le origini
del spirito capitalistico in Italia,* Milan, 1932. A. Sapori, *Il
giusto prezzo nella dottrina di S. Tomoso é nella pratica del
suo tempo,* in *Archivio storico Italiano,* 1922.

[72] E. Lipson, *Economic History of England.*

reproved. It was to them that the Papacy entrusted the collection and management of the revenues, which came to it from all parts of Christendom; and it is very plain that the Popes could not have been ignorant of the sort of business in which their bankers were engaged.

$\mathfrak{Five}$

INTERNATIONAL TRADE TO THE END OF THE THIRTEENTH CENTURY

I. COMMODITIES AND DIRECTIONS OF INTERNATIONAL TRADE[1]

Strange though it may seem, medieval commerce developed from the beginning under the influence not of local but of export trade. It was this alone which gave birth to

[1] BIBLIOGRAPHY.—See the works of W. Heyd and A. Schaube cited below in the general Bibliography, p. 221, and those of R. Häpke and R. L. Reynolds above, p. 26, Bib.—H. Simonsfeld, *Der Fondaco dei Tedeschi in Venedig und die deutsch-venetianischen Handelsbeziehungen* (Stuttgart, 1887), 2 vols. —W. Stein, *Beiträge zur Geschichte der deutschen Hanse* (Giessen, 1900).—E. Daenell, *Geschichte der deutschen Hanse in der zweiten Hälfte des XIV Jahrhunderts* (Leipzig, 1897). —Id., *Die Blütezeit der deutschen Hanse* (Berlin, 1905–6), 2 vols.—G. A. Kiesselbach, *Die wirtschaftlichen Grundlagen der deutschen Hanse und die Handelsstellung Hamburgs bis in die zweite Hälfte des XIV Jahrhunderts* (Berlin, 1907).—P. A. Meilink, *De nederlandsche hanzesteden tot het laatste kwartaal der XIV⁰ eeuw* (La Haye, 1912).—F. Rörig, *Hansische Beiträge zur deutschen Wirtschaftsgeschichte* (Breslau, 1928).— Id., *La Hanse*, in *Annales d'histoire économique et sociale*, t. II (1930).—Id., *Mittelalterliche Weltwirtschaft*, Jena, 1933.— A. Arndt, *Zur Geschichte und Theorie des Bergregals und der Bergbaufreiheit* (Halle, 2nd ed., 1916).—L. Blancard, *Documents inédits sur le commerce de Marseille au Moyen Age* (Marseille, 1884–5, 2 vols.).—A. Germain, *Histoire du Commerce de Montpellier* (Montpellier, 1861), 2 vols.—C. Port, *Essai sur l'histoire du commerce maritime de Narbonne* (Paris, 1852).—De Fréville, *Mémoire sur le commerce maritime de*

that class of professional merchants which was the chief instrument of the economic revival of the eleventh and twelfth centuries. In both parts of Europe where it started, Northern Italy and the Low Countries, the story is the same. The impetus was given by long-distance trade.[2] This is clear directly we examine the nature of the goods carried, for all were of foreign origin, and indeed early medieval commerce bears a certain resemblance to colonial trade.

Spices were the first objects of this trade and never ceased to occupy the chief place in it down to the very end. They created the wealth not only of Venice, but of all the great ports of the Western Mediterranean. Directly navigation was re-established between the Tyrrhenian Sea, Africa and the ports of the Levant in the course of the eleventh century, they were the cargo *par excellence* of merchant ships. Syria, to which quantities were brought by caravans coming from Arabia, India and China, was the principal objective of European ships, until the day when the discovery of new maritime routes enabled the Portuguese to supply themselves direct. Everything combined to give spices pre-eminence, both the ease with which they were shipped and the high prices they commanded. Thus medieval trade began as a trade in luxury goods, that is to say, a trade bringing in big profits at a relatively small cost, and this character it preserved, as we shall see, almost to the end of its history. Heavy consign-

Rouen (Rouen, 1857), 2 vols.—L. Mirot, *La colonie lucquoise à Paris, du XIII° au XV° siècle*, in *Bibliothèque de l'École des Chartes* (1927–8).—Z. W. Sneller, *De ontwikkeling van den handel tusschen Noodnederland en Frankryk tot het midden der XV° eeuw*, in *Bydragen voor Vaderl-Geschiedenis* (1929). —A. Schaube, *Die Wollausfuhr Englands vom Jahre 1273*, in *Vierteljahrschrift für Social-und Wirtschaftsgeschichte*, t. VI (1908).—E. E. Power, *The English Wool Trade in the Reign of Edward IV*, in *The Cambridge Historical Journal*, t. II (1926).—E. E. Power and M. Postan (ed.), *Studies in English Trade in the Fifteenth Century* (1933).

[2] See above, p. 44 *et seq.*

ments of raw materials or of articles of common consumption, with the enormous freight charges and the huge accumulations of capital which they imply, were unknown in those days, and here is to be found the most striking contrast between medieval and modern trade. The equipment of a medieval port consisted of modest wooden quays, provided with one or two cranes, alongside which ships of 200 to 600 tons could lie. This was all that was needed for the handling, loading and shipment of some hundreds of tons of pepper, cinnamon, cloves, nutmeg, sugar-cane, etc., which formed the precious cargo of the merchant ships.

The Western peoples who, from the end of the Merovingian era, had left off using spices, welcomed them with growing eagerness. They soon recovered their place in the diet of the upper classes of society, and the more commerce exported them north of the Alps, the more the demand for them increased. However fast and often the cargoes arrived, there was no risk of lack of buyers; no medieval shipowner had to fear an accumulation of stocks, or a ruinous fall of prices, for every merchant ship returning to its port of register brought with it the certainty of high profits. But there were many dangers to be faced, continual shipwrecks, piracy, practised in broad daylight as actively as a regular industry, and constant warfare among the Italian cities, each of which was bent on destroying the trade of its rivals, so as to profit by their ruin. Throughout the Middle Ages they fought each other in the Mediterranean as fiercely as Spain, France and England were to struggle in the Atlantic and the Pacific from the sixteenth to the eighteenth centuries. Hardly had Genoa and Pisa started to trade in the Levant than it became the one aim of Venice to expel them from a domain of which till then she had been undisputed mistress. The foundation of the Latin Empire of Constantinople, towards which she had employed all her energy and skill, gave her a temporary superiority over her rivals. She lost it after the Byzantine restoration (1261), which was in part the work of Genoa. From that time, the two great trading cities shared the mastery of the Aegean Sea, continually watching and impeding each other. As to Pisa, she ceased to be formidable after the naval defeat inflicted on her by the Genoese at Meloria in 1284. However, the length and obstinacy of these struggles did not for a moment hamper the prosperity of the combatants, which is a striking proof both of their energy and of the enormous profits which they obtained from this bitterly disputed trade.

Spices gave the impulse to Mediterranean trade, but they did not absorb the whole of it. As relations between West and East, Christian or Moslem, became closer and more frequent, an increasingly large variety of natural or manufactured commodities changed hands. From the beginning of the thirteenth century, imports into Europe consisted of rice, oranges, apricots, figs, raisins, perfumes, medicaments, and dyestuffs, such as Brazil wood (which came from India), cochineal or alum. To these were added cotton, which the Venetians called by its Greek name of *bombacinus* and the Genoese by its Arabic name of *cotone,* which they handed down to all languages. Raw silk was imported from the end of the twelfth century and, like cotton, in growing quantities, as silk and cotton manufactures grew up, first in Italy and shortly afterwards on the Continent. There was also a demand for Eastern manufactured stuffs, which were later imitated in the West, damask from Damascus, baldachins from Baghdad, muslins from Mosul and gauzes from Gaza. The vocabulary of modern European languages is still full of words of Arabic origin, which were introduced by Oriental commerce and bear witness to its activity and variety. In English, for instance, we have words such as divan, bazaar, artichoke, spinach, tarragon, orange, alcove, arsenal, jar, magazine, syrup, taffetas, tare, tariff, and in French *douane, darse, gabelle, goudron, jupe, quintal, recif,* and many others, which have come from Arabic through the medium of Italian.

In return for all these imports, by which a more comfortable and refined standard of living gradually spread throughout Western Europe, the Italians supplied the seaports of the Levant with timber and arms, and Venice, at least for a certain time, with slaves. But woollen goods soon became the chief export, at first fustians woven in Italy, then, from the second half of the twelfth century, cloths from Flanders and Northern France. No doubt the visits paid to the Champagne fairs by Italian merchants brought to their notice the superior quality of these cloths and suggested the possibility of a profitable trade. The port of Genoa was in a good position to export them to the East, and they certainly played a large part in the rapid progress of its trade. Notarial acts in the Genoese archives inform us that before the beginning of the thirteenth century the town was exporting cloth from Arras, Lille, Ghent, Ypres, Douai, Amiens, Beauvais, Cambrai, Tournai, Provins, Montreuil,[3] etc. This list, it will be observed, includes the names of a number of French towns. But in the course of the thirteenth century, their industry yielded place to that of Flanders and Brabant, which henceforth became the cloth region *par excellence* of Europe.[4] Their prominence was due to the perfection of their cloths, which were unrivalled for flexibility, softness and beauty of colour. They were in every sense of the term luxury products and their commercial vogue was the result of the high prices which they fetched. They played among textiles the part which spices played among foodstuffs, and from the thirteenth century the Italian merchants, owing to their command of capital and their

[3] See above, p. 37.
[4] The height of their cloth trade must be placed at the beginning of the fourteenth century. At this time Flemish and Brabantine cloth played a far more important part in large-scale commerce than that of either France or England. In England, it was complained that the Flemings and the Brabanters bought woad, cards and fuller's earth within the kingdom to the detriment of the native artisans. Lipson, *op. cit.*, t. I, p. 399.

superior technique, had a monopoly in the export of Flemish cloth to the South. After the decline of the Champagne fairs, the big Italian commercial companies installed "factors" at Bruges, charged with the wholesale purchase of Flemish and Brabantine cloths. Leaden labels certifying their price and quality were affixed to them at the time of despatch. Florence ordered large quantities of these cloths, before they had received their final dressing, and they were finished within its walls by the famous *arte di Calimala*.[5]

Thus Flemish and Brabantine industry played from afar an essential part in Mediterranean trade, which was itself in constant relations with Bruges. This fact gave Bruges a position such as no other town in medieval Europe could boast. The name, often given to this city, of "the Venice of the North," is a misnomer, for Venice never enjoyed the international importance which made the great Flemish port unique. The power of Venice lay essentially in her shipping, and owed nothing to the foreigner; the Germans alone had a permanent establishment there, the *Fondaco dei Tedeschi*, the activity of which was confined to the purchase of commodities imported by Venetian vessels. Bruges, on the contrary, foreshadowing in a striking way the part which Antwerp was to play in the sixteenth century, lived first and foremost by her foreign clientèle. The large majority of the ships which frequented her port belonged to shipowners from outside; her inhabitants themselves took but a small part in commercial activity and were content instead to serve as middlemen between the merchants who thronged from all parts to the town. From the thirteenth century onwards the Venetians, Florentines, Catalans, Spaniards Bayonnais, Bretons and Hansards all possessed depôts or counting-houses there. It was they who fostered the activity of this great entrepôt, which succeeded the Cham-

[5] A. Sapori, *Una compagnia di Calimala ai primi del trecento;* A. Doren, *Die Florentiner Wollentuchindustrie vom XIV bis zum XVI Jahrhundert* (Stuttgart, 1901).

pagne fairs as the point of contact between the commerce of the North and that of the South, with this difference, that instead of being periodical, as it was at the fairs, the contact was now permanent.

It was not until the first half of the fourteenth century that Genoa and Venice established direct maritime relations with the port of Bruges. Up to then they had communicated with Italy and the south of France only by land. Northern ships, on the other hand, had always come to Bruges and the Scandinavian sailors had already abandoned Tiel in its favour. When in the course of the twelfth century the mastery of the North Sea and the Baltic passed to the German cities, the resultant recrudescence of commercial activity gave a fresh impetus to the fortunes of Bruges.[6] It is very probable that the creation of its outer port of Damme before 1180, and then that of Sluys, at the mouth of the Zwyn, before 1293, is not to be explained solely by the progressive silting up of Bruges harbour, but by the fact that the light, bridgeless Scandinavian barks now gave place to the heavy Hanseatic *coggen,* which required deeper anchorage, and coming in ever-increasing numbers, soon demanded more space. From their advent may also be dated the definite decline of the mercantile marine of Flanders, which had, indeed, never been very considerable. Its disappearance completed the process, by which the commerce of Bruges became a purely passive one.

The efflorescence of the cloth industry in the basin of the Scheldt was the chief reason why the Hansards as well as the Italians established themselves at Bruges. But for the Hansards the advantage of finding themselves in continuous contact with the Italians was itself a powerful attraction, which drew them to the town. The counts of Flanders—not unconscious of their own interests—were swift to show them favour. In 1252, the Countess Mar-

---

[6] A. Bugge, *Der Untergang der norwegischen Schiffahrt im Mittelalter,* in *Vierteljahrschrift für Social-und Wirtschaftsgeschichte,* t. XII (1914), p. 92 *et seq.*

garet, at the request of Lübeck, acting in the name of several towns of the Empire, regulated the collection of tolls at Damme. From the second half of the thirteenth century, the *kontor* founded by the Hansards, or Easterlings, at Bruges, became and remained until the end of the Middle Ages the most important of all those that they possessed outside Germany.

The Teutonic Hanse occupied, in Northern Europe, a position comparable with that occupied by the big Italian ports in the basin of the Mediterranean. Like them, it served as intermediary between Western Europe and the East. But the Italian East and the Hanseatic East were very different things. In the one, the Byzantine and Moslem worlds furnished commerce with all the produce of a lavish nature and of an industry perfected in the course of thousands of years of civilisation. But the East which the Hansards set out to exploit consisted of lands, of which the nearest were still in process of colonisation and the remotest in a state of primitive barbarism, while they had also to face the rigour of a northern climate, a soil still for the most part covered with forests and a sea rendered inaccessible by ice during winter. All along the shores of the Baltic towns sprang up as German colonisation advanced beyond the Elbe. Under the powerful instigation of Lübeck, built in 1158 on the banks of the Trave, they took possession of the islands and the river mouths. About 1160, Wisby was built on the island of Gothland, which had been taken from the Scandinavians. Rostock was founded about 1218, Stralsund and Dantzig about 1230, Wismar about 1269. Riga appeared at the beginning of the thirteenth century, Dorpat between 1224 and 1250, and finally, some twenty years later, the remote Reval. Thus, the commercial middle-classes installed themselves on the coast of the Slav, Lithuanian and Lettish lands even before their conquest was complete. The Teutonic knights had not yet occupied the whole of Prussia or founded Königsberg, but they had already laid the foundations of Elbing. They established a footing at the same time on the coast of Sweden, settled at Stockholm and appropriated the herring fisheries of the peninsula of Skaania.

Among these advance ports in still half-conquered territories, lying on the shores of a sea from which the Scandinavians had only recently been driven, some sort of agreement was necessary for common protection. Led by Lübeck, which round about 1230 concluded a treaty of friendship and free trade with Hamburg, the young towns of the Baltic united in a league, which was immediately joined by the ports of the North Sea and became known as the Hanse, the name commonly applied to associations of merchants. This confederation of German maritime towns, which forms such a striking contrast to the continual wars of the Italian towns of the Mediterranean, gave them a predominance on all the Northern waters, which they were to keep to the end of the Middle Ages. Thanks to their agreement, they succeeded in holding their own against the attacks launched against them by the kings of Denmark and in promoting their common interests abroad.

The bases of Hanseatic trade in Western Europe were the London Steelyard, established in the middle of the twelfth century, and above all the *kontor* at Bruges. In the East, they possessed another at Novgorod, by which they drained the trade of Russia. By the Weser, the Elbe and the Oder their trade penetrated into continental Germany and by the Vistula they dominated Poland and pushed their operations to the confines of the Balkans. On the other hand, the great commercial road, by which in the past the Baltic had communicated with Constantinople and Baghdad *via* Russia, had been closed since the establishment of the Patzinaks on the shores of the Black Sea and the Caspian in the twelfth century, thus giving the Mediterranean the monopoly of relations with the Byzantine and Moslem East.

In striking contrast with those of the Italian ports, the exports of the Hansards inevitably consisted of natural products, which were all that the purely agricultural territories of their hinterland had to offer to trade. These were, above all, wheat from Prussia, furs and honey from Russia, timber, tar, dried fish and salted herrings from the fisheries of Skaania. But to these they added as a return freight the wool that their ships brought back from England and the salt of Bourgneuf ("Bay salt") which they laded in the Bay of Biscay, whence they also took back cargoes of French wines. All this traffic gravitated round Bruges, which was the central staple of Hanseatic commerce, midway between the Baltic and the Bay of Biscay where it stopped. It was there that the spices from Italy and the cloths of Flanders and Brabant were offered to German merchants and carried by them as far as Novgorod and the south of Poland. In all the maritime towns they were piled up in the shops of the *gewandschneider,* for the clothing of the rich bourgeoisie. The volume of Hanseatic trade certainly equalled if it did not surpass that of the Mediterranean, but it certainly involved a smaller capital. The value of the merchandise in which it dealt was not such as to permit of the big profits resulting from the sale of spices; a heavy expenditure was necessary to bring in a small return. Thus it is not surprising that we do not meet in the Hanse towns those powerful financial houses which gave medieval Italy the financial hegemony of Europe. There was a wide gulf between firms like the Bardi or Peruzzi and honest merchants such as Wittenborg at Lübeck, Geldernsen at Hamburg or Tölner at Rostock, and the contrast was equally great between the perfected commercial technique of the former and the unsophisticated methods of the latter.

No other region in Germany attained the same degree of economic vitality as the Hanse. In the thirteenth century the maritime towns took precedence of the Rhenish towns, which had introduced urban civilisation into the Empire. Cologne, still under the Hohenstaufen the great market of Germany, was eclipsed by Lübeck from about 1250, but since the Rhine was one of the chief trade routes between Italy and the Low Countries, the city continued to be of great commercial importance, as did Utrecht downstream, and Mainz, Spires, Worms, Strasburg and Basle upstream. There was also a considerable export of wine from the vineyards of the Rhine and the Moselle and a lively industry in all the chief centres, though it never became more than regional in scope.

As to Southern Germany, although it had contact through Venice with Mediterranean trade, it was still very far from the prosperity which it attained at the end of the Middle Ages. The *Fondaco dei Tedeschi,* which German merchants established in the city of lagoons, cannot be compared in any respect to the powerful Hanseatic *kontor* at Bruges. The working of the mines of the Tyrol and Bohemia had only just begun, and the trade in Salzkammergut and Luneburg salt could not compete with Bourgneuf salt carried everywhere by sea. The magnificent outlet which the Danube opened into the Black Sea remained unused, serving only for transit between Bavaria and Austria by way of Augsburg, Regensburg and Vienna; the undeveloped state of Hungary and the incessant troubles of the Balkans forbade all traffic on its lower stream. Furthermore, the excessive political subdivisions of Germany, the weakness of the emperors, and the struggles of rival dynasties, were singularly unfavourable to the development of economic activity. This is not the place in which to dilate on the advantages that Italy derived from an advanced civilisation and a geographical situation which everywhere enabled the mainland to communicate easily with the sea.

England, which alone in Europe possessed a national government able to exert its authority from one end of the country to the other, without encountering the obstacle of feudal princes, enjoyed an economic administration superior to that of all the continental states. But neither her industry nor her commerce profited by these favourable conditions. Up to the middle of the fourteenth century, she was an essentially agricultural country. Except London, whose port had been largely frequented by continental merchants since the eleventh century, all the towns before the reign of Edward III were content to limit production to the needs of their own citizens and of the surrounding country. With the exception of Stratford during some fifty years of the thirteenth century, they manufactured only as much of the excellent wool produced in the kingdom as was necessary for their own consumption, and that of their local clientèle. The reason for this apparent anomaly is to be found in the extraordinary development of Flemish cloth from the early Middle Ages. Surpassed by their neighbours in the Low Countries, the English were content to supply them with the raw material. They were to the Flemish cloth industry what the Argentine Republic and Australia are to the cloth industry of Europe and America to-day. Instead of competing with them, they devoted themselves to producing more and more wool, for which there was always a sale. The Cistercian monasteries of England became pre-eminent as sheep farmers. The wool trade made the fortunes of the fair of St. Ives on the Ouse, St. Giles at Winchester, Stourbridge, St. Botolph at Boston, Westminster, Northampton and Bristol, while at the same time furnishing the crown with a good part of its revenues and leading to an ever-increasing activity in the ports.[7]

But, surprising as it may seem, English shipping did not advance with her wool exports. To begin with, they were carried chiefly by continental ships and by the thirteenth century had become almost the monopoly of the Teutonic Hanse. The kings of England made no attempt to promote the carrying trade of their subjects before the end of the Middle Ages.[8] On the contrary, they showed

[7] A. Schaube, *Die Wollausfuhr Englands vom Jahre 1273,* in *Vierteljahrschrift für Social-und Wirtschaftsgeschichte,* t. VI (1908).

[8] In 1381, an Act had reserved the trade of the kingdom for English ships. But it was found impossible to enforce it and it was necessary to have recourse as before to the ships of the

themselves full of eagerness to attract foreign merchants to their shores, by the grant of all kinds of privileges. Their policy was obviously determined chiefly by fiscal motives, for their treasury was fed by taxes levied on foreign trade and loans raised by the crown from capitalists established in London. By the thirteenth century the Italians were installed there in large numbers, where they carried on side by side financial operations and a trade in wool, which they resold in Flanders, or despatched direct to the cloth centres beyond the Alps and especially to Florence.

The economic character of France was much more complex than that of England. France was in no sense an economic unity before the end of the Middle Ages. It consisted of a certain number of juxtaposed regions, having no closer relations with each other than with the foreigner. In the south, Montpellier, Aiguesmortes and Narbonne in Languedoc, and, above all, Marseilles in Provence, took part in Mediterranean commerce and in the course of the thirteenth century carried on an active export of Flanders cloths and import of spices. But towards the end of the century the failure of St. Louis' crusade and the competition of Genoa greatly reduced their prosperity, which did not revive until the seventeenth century. Henceforth the trade of Marseilles was confined to the South of France. Its decline almost synchronised with that of the fairs of Champagne, which were, as we saw, from the beginning of the twelfth century, the great entrepôt of Europe. Paris profited largely by this decline, and together with Bruges became the principal seat of Italian firms trading north of the Alps. There they introduced the silk industry and devoted themselves chiefly to banking. But the rôle which Paris

Hanse. Nevertheless, the Act of 1381 must be considered as the beginning of a new policy, foreshadowing the economic intervention of the State. See F. R. Salter in *The Economic History Review* (1931), p. 93.

played in the economic history of the Middle Ages bore
no relation to the prestige of French civilisation and to
the political supremacy of France at the beginning of the
reign of Philip-Augustus. An international city by reason
of her university, she was international neither in her
trade nor in her industry. She attracted no foreigners but
Italians and drapers from the Low Countries, and though
her population increased rapidly, it was chiefly owing to
the presence of the court and to the progress of political
centralisation. The 282 trades which were represented
there at the end of the thirteenth century[9] were carried
on by artisans in small workshops, who provided what
the great city needed, without trying to extend their
market beyond it. From an industrial point of view,
France, unlike Italy and the Low Countries, was not an
exporting country. Her architects and sculptors spread
their art throughout Europe, but the part she took in international trade was due solely to the abundance of her
natural riches.

Among these, wine unquestionably occupied the first
place. It is surprising and regrettable that neither viti-
culture nor the wine trade should have been studied in a
manner worthy of their importance.[10] The part which it
played in the diet of the non-vine-growing countries seems
to have been much greater in the Middle Ages than in
our own time. In England, Germany and the Low Countries especially, it was the usual beverage of the wealthy
classes. At Ghent, a thirteenth-century *keure* contrasted

[9] This total of 282 different trades is taken from the list
furnished by G. Fagniez, *Études sur l'industrie et la classe industrielle à Paris au XIII* et au XIV* siècle*, p. 7 *et seq.* (Paris,
1877), omitting synonyms as well as maids and valets.

[10] H. Pirenne, *Un grand commerce d'exportation au Moyen
Age: les vins de France*, in *Annales d'histoire économique et
sociale*, 1933, p. 225 *et seq.*—Z. W. Sneller, *Wijnvaart en Wijn-
handel tusschen Frankrijk en de Noordelike Nederlanden in de
tweede helft der XV eeuw*, in *Bydragen voor Vaderl, geschiedenis* (1924).

the common man with the bourgeois, *qui in hospitio suo vinum bibere solet*,[11] since Italian wines did not lend themselves to export and the production of those of the Rhine and the Moselle was limited. French wines enjoyed from the thirteenth century an undoubted preponderance in the international trade of the Northern countries. The wines of the Seine valley and Burgundy seem to have been exported only by Rouen ships, but the Bordeaux wines, owing to their abundance, their superior quality and the fact that their proximity to the sea made transport easy, became increasingly popular when the economic renaissance of the twelfth century set in. From the roadstead of Oléron and the port of La Rochelle (from which they got the name of "wines of La Rochelle," by which they were known in commerce), Gascon, Breton and English ships, and above all, from the middle of the fourteenth century, those of the Hanse, carried them to the North Sea and the utmost ends of the Baltic. They penetrated into the interior of Europe by river. At Liége, at the beginning of the fourteenth century, they arrived in such quantities that they were sold more cheaply than the German wines, in spite of the distance.[12] England, of which Gascony was a dependency up to the middle of the fifteenth century, furnished them with an ever-open market. The wine trade laid the foundation of considerable fortunes and to this day the British peerage still includes families which owe their rise to it.[13] The carrying trade in Bordeaux wines was so important that the usages prevailing in the wine fleets gave rise to the maritime law of Northern Europe. The Rolls of Oléron drawn up towards the end of the twelfth century, consisted of "judgments" relating to wine ships and were early translated into Flemish at Damme,

[11] Warnkoenig-Gheldolf, *Histoire de la Flandre*, etc., t. III, p. 284.

[12] Hocsem, *Gesta episcoporum*, ed. G. Kurth, p. 252.

[13] For example, that of the Dukes of Bedford, see G. Scott Thomson, *Two Centuries of Family History* (London, 1930).

whence they spread to England and as far as the Baltic, where they were known as the Sea Laws of Wisby.[14]

By a fortunate geographical coincidence, the salt-mines of Bourgneuf were quite close to La Rochelle, so that the merchant-ships could take in a supply of wine and salt at the same time. In the course of the fourteenth century, Hanseatic ships imported increasingly large quantities of bay salt as the herring fishery on the coast of Skaania progressed. Even in Germany it was soon successfully competing with that of Luneburg and Salzburg.[15]

Side by side with wine and salt, France exported cereals from Artois and Normandy. Woad, which has been called "the indigo of the Middle Ages," was cultivated in Picardy, where the trade in it was concentrated at Amiens, and in Languedoc, where it contributed largely to the prosperity of Toulouse; it found a ready market in the Flemish and Italian cloth industries.

Thus medieval France as a whole had much the same character as the France of to-day. Her industry sufficed for her needs and, except for a few luxury products, such as enamels of Limoges, she took but a small share in European trade. The cloth trade of the Northern towns, it is true, was active enough as long as the Champagne fairs flourished, but after their decline its place in international commerce was taken by that of Flanders and Brabant. Tournai in the extreme north of the kingdom and Valenciennes (which, however, belonged to the Empire) certainly remained textile centres of the first order, but looked towards Bruges and belonged to the economic *milieu* of the Low Countries. The wealth of France consisted, above all, in the abundance, variety and excellence of the productions of her soil. Her wine especially, which appeared on all well-to-do tables by the side of

[14] Th. Kiesselbach, *Der Ursprung der rôles d'Oléron und des Seerechts von Damme*, in *Hansische Geschichtsblätter*, 1906, p. 1 *et seq.*

[15] A. Agats, *Der hansische Baienhandel* (Heidelberg, 1908). *Cf.* H. Hauser, *Le sel dans l'histoire*, in *Revue économique internationale* (1927).

spices, made her, with Italy, the purveyor of luxury foods for Europe. But it should be observed that in contrast to Italy she did not herself export the goods supplied by her to commerce. With the exception of the ships of Marseilles and the Provençal ports, which took an active share in the trade of the Mediterranean, she had, properly speaking, no merchant fleet. She abandoned the navigation of the coasts of the Gulf of Gascony, the Channel and the North Sea almost entirely to foreigners, Basques, Bretons, Spaniards and Hansards. But if there were neither great commercial nor great industrial fortunes to be found in France, she enjoyed in compensation, up to the catastrophe of the Hundred Years' War, a well-being and an economic stability which were to be found nowhere else, and which undoubtedly had their share in the brilliant efflorescence of French civilisation in the thirteenth century.[16]

As the Spanish kingdoms drove out their Arab conquerors they began to play an increasingly large part in economic history. Barcelona in Aragon was known from the thirteenth century for its enterprising spirit and its bold sailors. Thanks to the Jews, who remained there after the *reconquista,* it possessed sufficient capital for its shipping trade and rapidly learned the commercial technique of Italy. At first, like the early Venetians, Barcelona engaged in the slave trade, for which the war against Islam provided an ample supply of Moorish prisoners. The intervention of the kings of Aragon in Sicily naturally gave a fresh impulse to its relations with this country,[17] while the adventurous expeditions of the Catalans to Greece, and a little later to the Aegean islands, similarly stimulated trade with the East, where the natives of Barcelona carried on war and commerce at the same

[16] According to F. Lot, *L'état des paroisses et des feux de 1328,* in *Bibliothèque de l'École des Chartes,* t. XC (1929), p. 405, the population of France (within its present frontiers) reached in 1328 the relatively high figure of 23–24 million souls.

[17] See Sayous' article, listed in bibliography, ch. IV, n. 38.

time. From the beginning of the fourteenth century their vessels ventured beyond the Straits of Gibraltar. At Bruges they met the ships of Galicia and Portugal, which carried on a coasting trade along the shores of the Atlantic, exporting chiefly metals and those Spanish wools which were to take the place of English wools in the cloth manufacture of the Low Countries at the end of the Middle Ages.

If we consider the articles which fed the international trade of the Middle Ages, it will be observed that industrial products are fewer by far than agricultural and food commodities, spices, wines, corn, salt, fish and wools. Only cloth, first that of the Low Countries and later that of Florence, gave rise to a large export trade. The export of woven silks and luxury stuffs manufactured in Italy was limited in scope and almost all branches of industry (pottery, furniture, shoes, clothing, utensils and tools of all sorts) remained within the confines of the towns and were the monopoly of their artisans, feeding nothing wider than a local market.

But a few obvious exceptions may be pointed out. In Germany, at Hildesheim and Nuremberg, in the valley of the Meuse, at Huy and above all at Dinant, metal-working was developed to the extent of contributing to international trade. The copper goods of Dinant, known as *Dinanderies,* enjoyed a European reputation. Nevertheless, one of the greatest contrasts between the economy of the modern world and that of the Middle Ages is to be found in the rudimentary development of medieval metallurgy. The miners of the Tyrol, Bohemia and Carinthia were little more than peasants, combining to excavate a "mountain" by the most primitive process. Not until the fifteenth century did the capitalists of the neighbouring towns establish control over them and develop mining, which even then remained very insignificant. Still less developed was the coal industry, although coal had been used in the neighbourhood of Liége from the end of the twelfth century, and in the following century the Liége miners had attained a remarkable skill in the art of boring subterranean adits, digging shafts and draining water from the pits. But for centuries yet the *terra nigra* was used only for household purposes in the regions where it was plentiful.[18] It was not until the eighteenth century that its application to the smelting of iron was to open a new era in economic history.

In the course of the thirteenth century, the whole of Europe from the Mediterranean to the Baltic and from the Atlantic to Russia was open to international commerce. From its two chief centres, the Low Countries in the North and Italy in the South, it reached the sea coasts, whence it advanced progressively into the interior of the Continent. In view of all the difficulties which it had to conquer, deplorable conditions of circulation, inadequate means of transport, general insecurity and an insufficiently organised monetary system, it is impossible not to admire the magnitude of the results obtained. They are all the more remarkable because the governments contributed nothing to them, beyond protecting merchants for fiscal reasons. The progress accomplished in the domain of international commerce is thus to be explained solely by the energy, the spirit of initiative and the ingenuity of the merchants themselves. The Italians, who, in this respect, were the leaders of Europe, undoubtedly learned much from the Byzantines and the Moslems, whose more advanced civilisation exercised an influence over them analogous to that of Egypt and Persia over ancient Greece. But, like the Greeks, whom they also resembled in the violence of their internal struggles, they were quick to assimilate and develop what they borrowed. They founded commercial societies, created credit, and restored the currency, and the spread of their economic methods in Northern Europe is as striking as that of humanism in the fifteenth and sixteenth centuries.

[18] In the absence of a work on the origin of coal-mining in the Middle Ages, J. A. Nef, *The Rise of the British Coal Industry*, 2 vols. (London, 1932), may be consulted.

In conclusion, one would like to be able to estimate with some exactitude the volume of this international commerce, of which an attempt has been made to outline the principal characteristics.[19] The scantiness of our information is unfortunately such as to oblige us to give up all hope of arriving at any such estimate. To compare it with modern commerce would, of course, be absurd. There is no possible comparison between the world-commerce of to-day, with all the resources of modern science at its command, and that of the Middle Ages, limited to Western Europe and employing only rudimentary methods. The clientèle of the former must be reckoned in hundreds and that of the latter in dozens of millions, and the tonnage of a single twentieth-century ship is equal to that of the whole Venetian or Genoese fleet of the thirteenth century. Nor is there anything to be gained by an attempt to estimate the importance of medieval trade in relation to that of trade subsequent to the fifteenth century. Though the difference is less marked, it is still too considerable, if only because of the discovery of the Indies and America. It has been conjectured that medieval commerce was to that of the sixteenth or seventeenth centuries as five to one, but in the absence of figures this is a meaningless formula. What we need are statistics of this commerce, and these cannot be even approximately drawn up. All we can say is that the volume of medieval commerce corresponded to an economic activity whose magnitude is sufficiently vouched for by ports such as Venice, Genoa and Bruges, by the Italian colonies in the Levant, by the shipping of the Hanseatic towns, and by the development of the Champagne fairs.

[19] On this see Kulischer, *op. cit.*, t. I, p. 263 *et seq.*

II. THE CAPITALISTIC CHARACTER OF INTERNATIONAL TRADE[20]

Economists who have asseverated the insignificance of medieval commerce by looking at it through the wrong end of the telescope, that is, in the light of the twentieth century, have pleaded in support of their argument the absence of a class of capitalist merchants in Europe previous to the Renaissance. They may be disposed to make an exception in favour of a few Italian firms, but it is the exception that proves the rule. It has even been asserted that the typical merchant of the Middle Ages was a small tradesman, solely preoccupied in getting a living and with no idea of profit, or desire to enrich himself. It is of course undeniable that numbers of retail dealers of this kind were to be found among the *petite bourgeoisie* of the towns, but it would be fantastic to reduce the exporters and bankers, whose operations we have been describing, to their level. Only those who are completely blinded to reality by a preconceived theory can deny the importance and influence of commercial capitalism from the beginning of the economic renaissance.

Certainly capitalism and large-scale commerce, which was at once its cause and its effect, did not appear at the same date in all countries and were not developed every-

[20] BIBLIOGRAPHY.—G. von Below, *Grosshändler und Kleinhändler im deutschen Mittelalter,* in *Probleme der Wirtschaftsgeschichte* (Tübingen, 2nd ed., 1926).—F. Keutgen, *Der Grosshandel im Mittelalter,* in *Hansische Geschichtsblätter* (1901).—H. Sieveking, *Die kapitalistische Entwickelung in den italienischen Städten des Mittelalters,* in *Vierteljahrschrift für Social-und Wirtschaftsgeschichte,* t. VII (1909).—J. Strieder, *Studien zur Geschichte kapitalistischer Organisationsformen* (Munich, 2nd ed., 1925).—G. Luzzatto, *Piccoli e grandi mercanti nelle città italiane del Rinascimento,* in *Volume commemorativo in onore del prof. Giuseppe Prato* (Turin, 1930).— W. Sombart, *Kapitalismus,* see p. ix.—H. Pirenne, *Les étapes de l'histoire sociale du capitalisme,* in *Bulletin de la Classe des Lettres de l'Académie royale de Belgique,* 1914.

where with the same vigour. In this respect Germany beyond the Rhine was unquestionably behind Western Europe and above all, Italy. It is no doubt through leaving this out of consideration that so many German scholars have rashly generalised from conclusions which are partially true of their own past. The intrinsic interest of their works won acceptance for these generalisations, until it was observed that in order to correct their exaggeration it is only necessary to apply the same methods to countries where progress was more rapid than that of Germany and where medieval economy attained its most complete development.

Scant as they are, medieval sources place the existence of capitalism in the twelfth century beyond a doubt.[21] From that time long-distance trade unquestionably produced considerable fortunes. The case of Godric has already been quoted. The spirit which animated him was in every sense of the term the capitalistic spirit of all times. He reasoned, he calculated and his sole aim was the accumulation of profits.[22] These are, after all, the

---

[21] See above, p. 46 *et seq.*

[22] The following passages from the *Libellus,* quoted ch. II, n. 7, prove it up to the hilt: "Sic puerilibus annis simpliciter domi transactis, coepit adolescentior prudentiores vitae vias excolere et documenta saecularis providentiae sollicite et exercitate perdiscere. Unde non agriculturae delegit exercitia colere, sed potius quae sagacioris animi sunt rudimenta studuit, arripiendo exercere. Hinc est quod mercatoris aemulatus studium coepit mercimonii frequentare negotium et primitus in minoribus rebus quidem et rebus pretii inferioris coepit lucrandi officia discere. Postmodum vero paulatim ad majoris pretii emolumenta adolescentiae suae ingenia promovere (p. 25) . . . Unde et mercandi gratia frequenter in Daciam ibat et aliquoties in Flandriam navigii remige pervolabat, et dum oportunitas juvabat, littora marina circuiens, multoties ad Scotorum fines deveniebat. In quibus singulis terrarum finibus aliqua rara et ideo pretiosiora reperiens, ad alius secum regiones transtulit, in quibus ea maxime ignota fuisse persensit, quae apud indigenas *desiderabiliora super aurum exstiterant;* et ideo pro his quaeque alia, aliis terrarum incolis concupiscibilia, libentius et studiosissime commutando comparabat. De quibus

essential characteristics of capitalism, of which a certain
school of historians makes so great a mystery, but which,
nevertheless, is to be met with at all periods, fundamentally
the same though in differing degrees of development,
because it corresponds with man's acquisitive instinct.
Godric cannot have been in any way exceptional. Chance,
which has preserved the story of this Scot, might equally
well have furnished us with that of a Venetian or a
Genoese and shown us the same facilities deployed in an
environment singularly more favourable to their expansion.
The real interest of Godric lies in his psychology, which
was that of all merchant adventurers of his time (as his
biographer specifically states). He is the type of those
nouveaux riches who were created by commerce, first on
the sea-coasts and in increasing numbers as it penetrated
farther into the Continent. A large number of them could
be instanced both in Italy and in Flanders before the end
of the twelfth century,[23] and there can be no more striking proof of the importance of commercial capitalism at
this date, when it is remembered that only the *rari nantes*
of its representatives are known to us.

As has already been shown, these capitalists, for the
most part, sprang from the dregs of society, *déracinés*,
who as soon as trade revived took to it with no assets but
their energy and intelligence, their love of adventure and
no doubt also their lack of scruples. With the aid of luck,
many made their fortunes as so many colonists and free-
booters of the seventeenth and eighteenth centuries were
later to make theirs. Nothing could have been more
unlike the small retail dealers of the local markets than
these adventurers. The sole aim of the gilds and hanses
of the early Middle Ages, in which they were grouped, was
to fulfil the needs of long-distance trade. From the begin-

---

singulis negotiando plurimum profecerat et maximas opum
divitias in sudore vultus sui sibi perquisierat, quia hic multo
venundabat quod alibi ex parvi pretii sumptibus congregaverat
(pp. 29–30)."

[23] See above, pp. 48, 49, 120.

ning the profits of this trade were certainly very considerable. The sale of a few hundred pounds of spices or a few dozen pieces of fine cloth was all the more remunerative, in that there was as yet no competition and no market price, while at this early period the demand was certainly always greater than the supply. In these conditions, neither the cost of transport nor the numerous tolls, however high they may have been, could prevent the realisation of considerable profits. In order to get rich, all that was necessary was to form an association with determined companions, to make one's way with them to lands where goods for export could be procured cheaply, and then to take these goods to places of sale. Famines, which were endemic sometimes in one region and sometimes in another, also furnished a certain opportunity of gaining a good deal with very little.[24] People who are dying of hunger do not haggle over the price of a sack of corn and the merchants had no scruples in turning their misfortune to account.[25] From the beginning of the twelfth century the sources leave no doubt as to their practice of cornering grain in times of scarcity.

To take advantage of the numerous opportunities which the commerce of that period afforded, nothing was needed but the will to do so, backed by energy and intelligence. There is no warrant for believing that the precursors of the great merchants of the Middle Ages began their career with a personal fortune. We must stop thinking of them as landed proprietors risking their revenues in trade, or selling their land in order to raise the initial capital. Most of them must have built up their first capital by hiring themselves out as sailors, or dockers, or as assistants in merchant caravans. Others must have had recourse to credit, borrowing a little money from some monastery or lord in their neighbourhood. Others, again, may have begun as

[24] F. Curschmann, *Hungersnöte im Mittelalter*, p. 132 *et seq.* (Leipzig, 1900).
[25] See the sentence about goods *desiderabiliora super aurum*, in the passage quoted above, n. 22.

mercenaries and then used for trade what they had gained from pillage and rapine. The story of the large fortunes of our own day furnishes us with so many examples of the part played by chance in their foundation, that we may safely suppose it to have been the same in an age when social life lent itself even better to the intervention of luck. Consider, for example, the wealth which successful piratical expeditions must have procured for the ancestors of the Pisan and Genoese merchants. Finally, due prominence must be given to the large part played by association in providing this early mercantile capital. In the gilds and hanses purchases were made in common and in the ports ships were chartered by several co-partners. In any case, though we may be ignorant of the precise way in which the first professional merchants set out on their careers, we at least know with certainty that their rise to wealth was very rapid.

Many of them, in the eleventh century, had already realised enough profits to be able to lend big sums to the princes, to build churches at their own expense in their towns and to buy freedom from toll from the lords. In numbers of communes it was their funds which established and fostered the growth of a middle class. Their corporation formed a sort of official municipal administration. At Saint Omer, the gild made itself responsible, with the consent of the castellan (1072–83), for part of the necessary expenses of paving the streets and constructing the enceinte.[26] Elsewhere, as at Lille, Audenarde, Tournai, Bruges, they took part in the organisation of municipal finance.[27] Moreover, the profits realised by the merchants were by no means all invested in trade in merchandise. Side by side with the latter, many of them carried on a trade in money. It is unnecessary to repeat what has been said elsewhere about the financial operations, in

[26] G. Espinas and H. Pirenne, *Les coutumes de la gilde marchande de Saint-Omer,* in *Le Moyen Age,* 1901.

[27] H. Pirenne, *Les périodes de l'histoire sociale du capitalisme,* p. 282 *et seq.*

which the richest among them engaged from the twelfth century onwards, both in Italy and in the Low Countries, and which show them advancing considerable sums to kings and feudal princes. In addition to this, all merchants continued to invest their superabundant reserves in land, the safest of all investments. In the course of the twelfth and thirteenth centuries they acquired most of the ground in the towns.[28] The steady rise of the population, by converting their ground into building sites, sent up their rents to such an extent, that from the second half of the thirteenth century many of them gave up trade and became *rentiers* (*otiosi, huiseux, lediggangers*). Thus, far from movable capital originating in land, it was, on the contrary, the means by which the first landed fortunes of the middle class were founded.[29]

As always happens, the *nouveaux riches* soon formed themselves into closed groups. The statutes of the Flemish Hanse of London (before 1187) forbade entrance into the company to all retail dealers, as well as to "those who have blue nails," [30] that is to say, to workers in the cloth industry. Admittance to large-scale commerce now depended on the groups which monopolised it. In the towns it was concentrated in the hands of a wealthy and arrogant patriciate, which sought to exclude the "common people" and confine them to manual crafts or to retail trade. In all these regions which had taken the lead in the economic renaissance there was a striking contrast between small and great commerce. The capitalistic character of the latter is incontestable.[31] What, if not capitalists, were the im-

[28] See above, p. 84, and H. Pirenne, *Les villes du Moyen Age*, p. 168 *et seq.*

[29] G. Des Marez, *La propriété foncière dans les villes du Moyen Age*, p. 11 *et seq.*, 44 *et seq.* See in G. Espinas, *La vie urbaine de Douai*, t. III, p. 578, and IV, 4, the list of houses acquired in the town by the two drapers, Jehans de France and Jakemes li Blons.

[30] H. Pirenne, *La hanse flamande de Londres*, p. 81.

[31] In Italian documents of the thirteenth century the word *capital* is regularly employed to denote money invested in business.

porters of wool who supplied the Flemish and Brabantine towns with their raw materials, the cloth merchants who sold hundreds of pieces at a time, the Venetian, Genoese or Pisan shipowners who traded in the Levantine ports, the Lombard or Florentine firms whose branches spread throughout Europe and carried on business and banking at the same time? [32] It is true that the distinction between wholesale and retail commerce was not absolute. Many merchants carried on both. In Germany, especially, the *Gewandschneider,* who imported cloths from Flanders, resold them by the ell in their shops,[33] and at Florence many agents of the *Arte di calimala* did the same.[34] Doubtless also commercial specialisation was not yet very marked, the merchant imported, according to circumstances, the commodities which were offered him, provided that he could be sure of a sufficiently remunerative profit. But all this merely shows that commercial capitalism adapted itself to the conditions imposed on it by the market and by the social conditions of the age.

[32] For the dazzling fortune of the Zaccaria of Genoa in the thirteenth century, see Bratianu, *op. cit.,* p. 138 *et seq.,* and Roberto Lopez, *Genova marinara nel duecento Benadetto Zaccaria, ammiraglio e mercante,* Messina-Milan, 1933.

[33] See the account books mentioned above, p. 123.

[34] A. Sapori, *Una compagnia di Calimala.*

𝕾𝔦𝔵

URBAN ECONOMY AND THE
REGULATION OF INDUSTRY

I. THE TOWNS AS ECONOMIC CENTRES.
THE PROVISIONING OF THE TOWNS[1]

Up to and during the course of the fifteenth century the
towns were the sole centres of commerce and industry, to
such an extent that none of it was allowed to escape into
the open country. Between them and the country there
was a sharp division of labour, the latter practising agriculture only, the former trade and the manual arts. Thus
towns were important in proportion to the radius of their
economic influence. There were very few exceptions to
this rule, perhaps none except Rome, Paris and London,
which, as the residences respectively of the head of the

[1] BIBLIOGRAPHY.—G. Espinas, *La vie urbaine à Douai*, Paris
(1913), 4 vols.—W. S. Unger, *De levensmiddelen Voorziening
der Holländsche steden in de middleeuwen* (Amsterdam,
1906).—J. G. Van Dillen, *Het economisch karakter der mid-
deleeuwsche stad* (Amsterdam, 1914).—P. Sander, *Die reichs-
städtische Haushaltung Nürnbergs*, 1431–40 (Leipzig, 1902,
2 vols.).—K. Bücher, *Die Bevölkerung von Frankfurt am Main
im XIV und XV Jahrhundert* (Tübingen, 1886).—J. Jastrow,
Die Volkszahl Deutscher Städte zu Ende des Mittelalters
(Berlin, 1886).—H. Pirenne, *Les dénombrements de la population d'Ypres au XVe siècle*, in *Vierteljahrschrift für Social-
und Wirtschaftsgeschichte*, t. I (1903).—J. Cuvelier, *Les dénombrements de foyers en Brabant, XIV-XVIe siècles* (Brussels,
1912).—G. Pardi, *Disegno della storia demografica di Firenze*,
in *Archivio storico italiano* (1915).—Add the bibliography of
Kulischer, *op. cit.*, t. I, pp. 164–5, and see also above, p. 39.

Church and of the sovereigns of two great kingdoms, exterted an influence far surpassing that which they would otherwise have enjoyed. In the Middle Ages the State was not yet sufficiently centralised, and governments and administration were not yet sufficiently fixed to allow the formation of urban agglomerations such as our modern capitals, or the cities of the ancient world. At the most a few episcopal towns owed to their position as diocesan centres an advantage which increased but did not cause their activity. Nowhere was an ecclesiastical institution sufficient in itself to bring about a great development of municipal life. Places where the townsfolk had only to supply the needs of a cathedral or a monastery never rose to be more than country towns of the second order. It is enough to recall the examples of Fulda and Corbie in Germany, of Stavelot and Térouanne in the Low Countries, of Ely in England, of Luxeuil, Vézelai and many small *cités* in the South of France.

It is a familiar fact that the clergy were a foreign element in the medieval town. Their privileges excluded them from sharing in those of the city. Amidst the commercial and industrial population their economic rôle was simply that of consumers. As to the nobility, it was only in the Mediterranean regions, in Italy, the South of France and Spain, that some of its members lived in the towns. This fact is undoubtedly due to the preservation in these countries of the tradition and, to a certain degree, of the municipal character which the Roman Empire had so deeply stamped on them. Their nobility never entirely abandoned the site of the ancient cities, even at the period of their greatest decadence, and continued to live there when town life revived. High above the roofs of the private houses, they built those towers which still add so greatly to the picturesqueness of many of the old Tuscan towns. Often, indeed, they interested themselves in mercantile business and invested a part of their revenues in it; in Venice and Genoa they took a considerable part in maritime commerce, and it is unnecessary to recall the prominent part which they played in the political and social struggles of the Italian towns. In Northern Europe, on the other hand, almost all the nobles left the towns to settle in their castles in the country. It is only in exceptional circumstances that a knightly family is to be found here and there, isolated and, as it were, astray in the midst of bourgeois society. It was not until the end of the Middle Ages that the aristocracy, by that time less quarrelsome and more eager for comfort, began to build themselves luxurious town houses.

Thus the medieval town was essentially the home of the burgesses; it existed only for them and because of them. It was in their own interest, and in their own interest alone, that they created its institutions and organised its economy. That economy was, of course, more or less highly developed, according as the population, on behalf of which it functioned, was more or less numerous, or more or less actively engaged in commerce and industry. The mistake has too often been made of describing it as if it were everywhere the same, and reducing it to a single type, as though the organisation of a semi-rural *bourg,* or even of a town of the second order like Frankfort-on-the-Main, could possibly suffice for a powerful metropolis such as Venice, Florence, or Bruges. The *Stadwirtschaft,* which a certain German school has elaborated with so much acumen and knowledge, undoubtedly corresponds to certain aspects of reality, but it neglects so many others that it is impossible to admit it without very considerable correction. Once more, its authors have based their ideas too exclusively upon Germany and have arbitrarily extended to the whole of Europe results which are valid only for some of the lands east of the Rhine. To form an adequate idea of urban economy it ought, on the contrary, to be examined in the surroundings where it reached its highest development.

The most urgent need of this economy was obviously to secure food for the population. It is unfortunately impossible to estimate the size of the latter with any degree of accuracy. We possess no statistical data until the fifteenth century, and even those which have come down to us for that period are inadequate and far from clear. Nevertheless, the careful and thorough research which has been based upon them justifies us in concluding that medieval towns were only thinly populated. Strange as it may seem, it has been proved that Nuremberg in 1450 numbered only 20,165 inhabitants; Frankfort in 1440, only 8,719; Basel about 1450, round about 8,000; Friburg in Switzerland, in 1444, only 5,200; Strasburg, about 1475, only 26,198; Louvain and Brussels in the middle of the fifteenth century only about 25,000 and 40,000 respectively.

These are far removed from the fantastic figures that have been accepted for so long, in defiance of all probability. For, unless we claim that Europe from the twelfth to the fifteenth century was able to feed as many people as Europe in the twentieth, it will readily be granted that it is impossible to draw a parallel between the urban population then and in our own day. The data, too, often propagated on the strength of information venerable with age, but entirely devoid of numerical precision, cannot withstand criticism. At an interval of eleven years (1247–58) two documents attribute to Ypres a population of 200,000 and 40,000 inhabitants respectively; but it is doubtful whether the population could ever have attained even half the second figure. Absolutely reliable censuses inform us that the town numbered 10,736 souls in 1412. It had sunk so low at this period that we are justified in supposing that at the height of its industrial prosperity, at the end of the thirteenth century, it may have numbered about 20,000. Ghent, where about 4,000 weavers were working in 1346, may have had approximately 50,000 inhabitants, if we assume, as is likely, that the weavers, with their families, formed a quarter of its population.[2] Bruges was certainly not less important. In Italy, Venice, unquestionably the largest town in the West, could not

[2] G. Espinas and H. Pirenne, *Recueil de documents relatifs à l'histoire de l'industrie drapière en Flandre*, t. II. p. 637.

have fallen below 100,000 inhabitants, and was probably not much larger than cities such as Florence, Milan and Genoa.[3] All things considered, it is very probable that at the beginning of the fourteenth century the population of the biggest urban agglomerations only rarely attained a maximum of 50,000 to 100,000 inhabitants, that a town of 20,000, already passed as a large one, and that, in the great majority of cases, the number of inhabitants fluctuated between 5,000 and 10,000.

If we take the beginning of the fourteenth century as our point of departure in these estimates, it is because it seems to mark almost everywhere a halt in urban demography. Up to then, the population had shown a continuous rise. The first centres of urban life undoubtedly grew with great rapidity, as is clearly shown by the uninterrupted enlargement of the municipal boundaries. Those of Ghent, for example, were successively extended about 1163, and in 1213, 1254, 1269 and 1299, so as to include the suburbs which had grown up round it. Future progress was certainly counted on, for the ramparts built on the last occasion enclosed a surface extensive enough to suffice for a long time for the establishment of new quarters; but these new quarters were not established. The demographic situation was stabilised. We shall have to wait until the sixteenth century before it resumes its forward march.

For their food the towns had to have recourse both to the surrounding country and to large-scale commerce. They themselves were unable to contribute more than an infinitesimal amount towards their own provisioning. Only the small localities, which were endowed with municipal franchises in the second half of the Middle Ages, and

[3] According to Davidsohn, *Forschungen zur Geschichte von Florenz*, t. II, 2nd part, p. 171, Florence numbered about 45,000 inhabitants in 1280 and about 90,000 in 1339. According to F. Lot, *L'état des paroisses et des feux, loc. cit.*, p. 300, at the beginning of the fourteenth century, no town in France, except Paris, reached a population of 100,000. As regards Paris, we must allow about 200,000 souls, if the figure of 61,-000 hearths attributed to this town is correct.

which for the most part always preserved a semi-rural character, were able to subsist without outside help. But nothing would be more erroneous than to compare them to the great mercantile agglomerations which were the cradle of the middle class. From the beginning, these were forced to import all their food. This sufficiently obvious truth is not to be denied by pointing to the byres and pigsties which were to be found in the towns at the period of their highest development, for such were to be found in every town up to the eighteenth century and have not entirely disappeared to-day. Their aim was merely to supplement their owners' food and in no way to provision the public.

The purveyors of the bourgeoisie were first and foremost the peasants of the surrounding districts. As soon as the formation of the first urban commune offered an outlet for their produce, which up to then had had none except the small local markets of the cities and *bourgs,* the economic stagnation of the country was a thing of the past. A connection was established between the peasantry and the nascent towns, which gratified at once the needs of the latter and the interests of the former. The countryside provisioned the town which was its centre, and as the growth of the town gave rise to a still greater demand, the country took measures to satisfy it and to meet a steadily increasing consumption by an increase in its own surplus production.

From the beginning the town government found themselves obliged to regulate the import of foodstuffs. They had not only to obtain them, but also to guard against the dangers of monopoly and an arbitrary rise in prices. They made use of two measures, in order to secure for the townsfolk abundant provisions as cheaply as possible, viz., publicity of transactions and the suppression of middlemen, through whose hands the commodities passed from the producer to the consumer. Their aim was to bring the country vendor and the city buyer face to face, under general control. Edicts and ordinances, of which, unfortunately, only a few have come down to us, had been promulgated from the twelfth century onwards and from the thirteenth the sources are full of meticulous regulations which give a vivid picture of the procedure employed to attain this end. The forestalling and regrating of food-stuffs (i.e., purchasing them from the peasant before he reached the town) was forbidden; all commodities had to be taken direct to the market and exposed for a fixed time, during which they could be sold only to the burgesses. Butchers were forbidden to keep meat in their cellars and bakers to procure more grain than was necessary for their own oven; no burgess was to buy more than he needed for himself and his family. The most minute precautions were taken to prevent artificial increases in the price of food. Often a maximum was fixed; the weight of bread was proportioned to the value of grain; the maintenance of order in the markets was entrusted to communal officials whose numbers were continually increasing. The burgess was protected against fraud, as well as against the abuses of speculation and monopoly. All commodities were carefully inspected and those which were not irreproachable in quality or, in the happy expression used in the documents, "loyal," were confiscated or destroyed, in addition to penalties which often extended to banishment.

All these stipulations (which could be multiplied indefinitely) were obviously governed by the spirit of control and by the principle of direct exchange to the profit of the consumer.[4] This principle was expressed so frequently and was manifested under so many forms that some writers have fixed upon it (not without a certain exaggeration) as the essential characteristic of urban economy. In any case it was certainly widely applied in order to realise the

[4] Naturally, retail dealers existed in more or less large numbers, both for food and for the articles of consumption brought by commerce. Direct exchange was a principle the application of which admitted of numerous exceptions. See, for example, the researches of B. Mendel, *Breslau zu Beginn des XV Jahrhunderts,* in *Zeitschrift des Vereins für die Geschichte Schlesiens* (1929).

"common good" of the citizens, which was the ideal at which it aimed and for the sake of which the most arbitrary measures were used. The liberty of the individual was ruthlessly curtailed, and the sale of foodstuffs subjected to a regulation almost as despotic and inquisitorial as that which was applied, as we shall see later, to small-scale industry.

It must not be thought that only the surrounding countryside was requisitioned to provision the towns. Commerce also played its part. A considerable amount of the food consumed by the large towns (and a town of 2,000 inhabitants must be considered large) arrived by this means. This was certainly in Gui de Dampierre's mind when he observed, in 1297, that "Flanders cannot support herself without provisions from outside." [5] For the rest, there were a great many goods which had necessarily to be imported from outside, such as spices, or saltwater fish in the inland countries, or wine in the North. Here it was impossible to do without the intervention of the merchants, who bought wholesale either at the fairs or at the places of production. In times of scarcity or famine it was thanks to the goods imported by them that the towns, deprived of the resources of their own neighbourhood, succeeded in feeding their population. This import trade could not be subjected to the regulation just outlined, which thus cannot be considered as embracing the whole urban economy. It was made for the municipal market, which it could dominate because it functioned within the orbit of the town walls, but large-scale commerce escaped it. It was entirely successful in preventing a baker from secretly accumulating in his granary a few sacks of corn to resell at the first rise, in ferreting out the "regraters," or in frustrating the manœuvres of middlemen in secret connivance with a few peasants, but it was powerless before the wholesale merchant, who unloaded on the town quays the cargo of several ships laden with rye, cheese, or casks of wine. What influence could it exert

[5] H. Pirenne, *Histoire de Belgique*, t. I, 5th ed., p. 263.

in this case on prices and how set to work to subject wholesale sales to a system made for retail trade? Here it was obviously face to face with an economic phenomenon to which it was not adapted. As soon as capital came into action it foiled municipal regulation, because it was beyond its reach. All that the town government could do was to see that the burgesses had some share in the profits of the importers and were paid for the services they rendered them. Indeed, as a foreigner, the merchant from outside had necessarily to have recourse to the local population. It was through their agency that he bought or sold with people whom he did not know.

In the beginning, no doubt, he took as guide and assistant the host with whom he lodged. The institution of brokers is certainly connected with this custom. What was the result of circumstances became a legal obligation, and the merchant found himself compelled to make all his contracts with the burgesses through the intermediary of an official broker. Venice seems to have set the example in this, as in other matters; from the twelfth century onwards real brokers are to be found there, under the name of *sensales*, borrowed from Byzantium. In the thirteenth century these agents appeared everywhere, as *makelaeren* in Flanders, *Unterkäufer* in Germany and *brokers* in England.[6] Occasionally they even preserved their primitive name of hosts (*Gasten*). In every town they enjoyed such lucrative rights that many of them accumulated considerable fortunes and occupied the upper ranks of the bourgeoisie.

Yet another precaution was taken against the invasion of foreign capitalists by excluding them from retail trade. The latter remained the unassailable monopoly of the burgesses, which they reserved for themselves and defended against all competition. Thus municipal legislation imposed on large-scale commerce those very middlemen whom it refused to sanction in retail trade. The interest

[6] L. Goldschmidt, *Universalgeschichte des Handelsrechts*, p. 230 *et seq.*

of the burgesses explains this apparent contradiction. Though it resulted in a rise in the price of imported goods, at least it encouraged local trade. It is hardly necessary to add that the intervention of brokers and the prohibition to sell by retail applied only to "foreigners." The great merchants of the town itself were exempted.

II. URBAN INDUSTRY [7]

The characteristics that we have just observed in the domain of urban food supplies appear again, but in a much more varied and ingenious form, in the organisation

[7] BIBLIOGRAPHY.—L. M. Hartmann, *Zur Geschichte der Zünfte im frühen Mittelalter*, in *Zeitschrift für Social-und Wirtschaftsgeschichte*, t. III (1896).—R. Eberstadt, *Der Ursprung des Zunftwesens* (Leipzig, 2nd ed., 1915).—G. von Below, *Handwerk und Hofrecht*, in *Vierteljahrschrift für Social- und Wirtschaftsgeschichte*, t. XII (1914).—F. Keutgen, *Aemter und Zünfte* (Jena, 1903).—G. Seeliger, *Handwerk und Hofrecht*, in *Historische Vierteljahrschrift*, t. XVI (1913).—For the German bibliography, cf. Kulischer, *op. cit.*, t. I, p. 165.— G. Des Marez, *La première étape de la formation corporative. L'entr'aide*, in *Bull. de la Classe des Lettres de l'Acad. royale de Belgique* (1921).—E. Martin Saint-Léon, *Histoire des corporations de métiers* (Paris, 3rd ed., 1922).—G. Fagniez, *Études sur l'industrie et la classe industrielle à Paris, au XIIIᵉ et au XIVᵉ siècles* (Paris, 1877).—P. Boissonnade, *Étude sur l'organisation du travail en Poitou* (Paris, 1899).—G. Des Marez, *L'organisation du travail à Bruxelles, au XVᵉ siècle* (Brussels, 1904) (Mém. Acad. de Belgique).—E. Lipson, *op. cit.*, p. viii.—A. Doren, *Das Florentiner Zunftwesen vom XIV bis zum XVI Jahrhundert* (Stuttgart-Berlin, 1908).—*Id.*, *Die Florentiner Wollentuchindustrie* (Stuttgart, 1901).—E. Rodocanachi, *Les corporations ouvrières à Rome* (Paris, 1894), 2 vols.—H. Pirenne, *Les anc. démocr. des Pays Bas*, p. 33, n. 1. —G. Espinas and H. Pirenne, *Recueil de documents relatifs à l'histoire de l'industrie drapière en Flandre* (Brussels, 1906- 24), 4 vols.—G. Espinas, *Les origines du capitalisme*, t. I. *Sire Jean Boinebroke* (Lille, 1930).—*Id.*, *L'industrie drapière dans la Flandre française au Moyen Age* (Paris, 1926).—E. Coornaert, *Un centre industriel d'autrefois. La draperie-sayetterie d'Hondschoote, XIVᵉ-XVIIIᵉ siècles* (Paris, 1930).—*Id.*, *L'industrie de la laine à Bergues-Saint-Winoc* (Paris, 1930).—

of industry. Here also the régime differed according as to whether it was a matter of wholesale or retail trade. The artisans who supplied the local market were treated quite differently from those who worked for export. Let us begin with the former.

Large or small, each town had a number and variety of craftsmen proportionate to its size, for no town population could do without manufactured articles. Though luxury crafts existed only in the large agglomerations, artisans indispensable to daily life, such as bakers, butchers, tailors, blacksmiths, joiners, potters, pewterers, etc., are found everywhere. Just as the great estate, in the agricultural period of the Middle Ages, was forced to produce all kinds of cereals, so every town provided common necessities for its inhabitants and for those of the surrounding country-side. It disposed of its products in the territory from which it derived its food. The peasants who supplied it with provisions took industrial products in exchange, and the customers of the small town workshops were thus drawn both from the local burgesses and from the rural popula-tion of the neighbourhood.

Industrial legislation was necessarily more complex than legislation in regard to food. The latter had only to con-sider the burgess as a consumer, the former had to en-visage him at the same time as a producer. Thus it was necessary to institute a system which protected both the artisan who manufactured and sold and the customer who bought. In every country this was secured by an organisa-tion which, in spite of innumerable differences of detail, was everywhere based on the same principle: that of craft gilds. Under a diversity of names, *officium* or *ministerium* in Latin, *métier* or *jurande* in French, *arte* in Italian,

N. W. Posthumus, *De geschiedenis van de Leidsche lakenin-dustrie*, t. I (The Hague, 1908).—Broglio d'Ajano, *Die Vene-tianer Seidenindustrie und ihre Organisation bis zum Ausgang des Mittelalters* (Stuttgart, 1893).—E. Wege, *Die Zünfte als Träger wirtschaftlicher Kollektivmassnahmen* (Stuttgart, 1932). —F. Rörig, *Mittelalterliche Weltwirtschaft* (Jena, 1933).

ambacht or *neering* in the Netherlands, *Amt, Innung, Zunft* or *Handwerk,* in German, *craft-gild* or *mistery* in English, the institution is everywhere in essence identical, because it answered everywhere to the same fundamental needs. It was in it that city economy found its most general and characteristic expression.

The origin of the crafts has been and continues to be much disputed. It was sought first of all, in conformity with the tendency of scholars at the beginning of the nineteenth century, in the *collegia* and *artes,* into which the town artisans were grouped under the Roman Empire. It was supposed that they had survived the Germanic invasions and that the economic renaissance of the twelfth century revived them again. But no proof has ever been produced of this survival north of the Alps, and what we know of the complete extinction of municipal life from the ninth century is all against it. It is only in those parts of Italy which remained under Byzantine administration in the early Middle Ages that certain traces of the ancient *collegia* were to some extent preserved. But the phenomenon is too local and of too little importance to be the origin of an institution so general as that of the craft gilds.

The attempt to find them a manorial origin has been no more successful. It is quite true that we find at the centre of the great estates, during and after the Carolingian era, artisans of various sorts recruited from among the lord's serfs and working in his service under the supervision of overseers.[8] Unfortunately, no one has been able to prove that at the period of the formation of towns these domestic artisans were authorised to work for the public, and were joined by freemen, and that, little by little, these originally servile groups became autonomous associations.

The majority of modern scholars rightly consider that free association provides a more likely solution of the problem. From the end of the eleventh century we do

[8] See above, p. 61.

indeed see the urban artisans forming fraternities (*fraternitates, caritates*) on the basis of their professions. For this their models would be the merchant gilds and the religious societies formed around the churches and monasteries. The first artisan groups were in fact distinguished by their pious and charitable propensities; but they must at the same time have fulfilled the need of economic protection. The pressing necessity to stand by one another, so as to resist the competition of new-comers, must have made itself felt from the very beginning of industrial life.

But, important as it was, association alone was not sufficient to bring about the formation of crafts. A large part was also played by the public authority or authorities. The regulative character which had dominated the whole economic legislation of the Roman Empire did not disappear with the fall of the latter. It is still clearly recognisable, even in the agricultural period of the Middle Ages, in the control exercised by the kings or the feudal powers over weights and measures, coinage, tolls and markets. When the artisans began to move into the nascent towns, the castellans or the mayors who were established there naturally required them to submit to their authority. We know enough to perceive that from the first half of the eleventh century they maintained certain rights of control over the sale of commodities and the exercise of various professions. In the episcopal cities the bishops were, in addition, concerned with establishing the principles of Catholic morality, which imposed on sellers a *justum pretium* which they might not exceed without incurring the penalty of sin.

It was inevitable that this early industrial regulation should be increasingly absorbed and then perfected by communal authority, at the time of the formation of the urban constitutions. In Flanders, from the second half of the twelfth century, the *échevins* published edicts concerning not only foodstuffs, but also all other merchandise (*in pane et vino et caeteris mercibus*) and consequently industrial products. Now, it was obviously impossible to enact laws relating to products without including the producers, since the only means of ensuring the good quality of the former was to supervise the latter. The most efficacious way of doing this was to form them into groups according to professions and subject them to the control of the municipal authority. Thus the spontaneous tendency which drove the artisans into corporations was reinforced by the interests of administrative control. It may be asserted that by the middle of the twelfth century the division of urban artisans into professional bodies, recognised or instituted by local authority, was already an accomplished fact in a great number of towns. If they are to be met with at this period in places as insignificant as Pontoise (1162), Hagenau (1164), Hochfelden and Swindratzheim (before 1164),[9] they must previously have appeared in more important agglomerations. Moreover, we possess a certain number of documents which show that crafts were in existence at a very early period: in 1099 the weavers at Mainz, in 1106 the fishmongers at Worms, in 1128 the shoemakers at Wurtzburg, in 1149 the coverlet weavers at Cologne, formed official groups. At Rouen, at the beginning of the twelfth century, the tanners formed a gild to which all those who desired to practise their profession were compelled to belong. In England, craft gilds are mentioned in the reign of Henry I (1100-35) at Oxford, Huntington, Winchester, London, Lincoln, and soon spread to all the towns.

From this we may conclude that from the eleventh century onwards the public authorities regulated town industry by dividing artisans into as many groups as there were distinct crafts to supervise. Each of them had the right to reserve to its members the practice of the craft to which it devoted itself. They were thus essentially privileged bodies, as far removed as possible from indus-

[9] F. Keutgen, *Urkunden zur städtischen Verfassungsgeschichte*, p. 136, § 23 (Berlin, 1899).

trial liberty. They were founded on exclusivism and protection. Their monopoly was known in England by the name of *gild*, in Germany by those of *Zunftzwang* or *Innung*.

There is no doubt that this compulsory regimentation of artisans was primarily designed in the interest of the artisans themselves. To protect the consumer against fraud and adulteration it was sufficient to regulate industrial practices and to supervise sales. The professional monopoly enjoyed by the gilds was rather a danger to the buyers, who were completely at their mercy. But for the producers it offered the inestimable advantage of freedom from competition, and it was no doubt a concession made at their demand by the legal authorities. The voluntary associations formed by artisans from the end of the eleventh century possessed, indeed, no legal right which allowed them to forbid the practice of industry by others. Their only weapon against those who were not affiliated to them was the boycott, that is to say, brute-force, a precarious and inadequate weapon. Thus they must quite early have sought the right to compel every artisan to enter their ranks or to shut up shop. The authorities found no difficulty in granting their request, which was in the interests of the public peace, and would facilitate the control of industry. Often the crafts were subject to dues in return for the precious concession; in England they paid the Crown an annual fee for the monopoly which they enjoyed, and this is certainly also the explanation of the taxes imposed on various crafts in the towns of France, Germany and the Low Countries.

Thus the origin of gilds is traceable to the action of two factors: legal authority and voluntary association. The first intervened on behalf of the public, i.e., of the consumers; the second is the result of the initiative of the artisans themselves, i.e., of the producers. Thus in the beginning they were quite opposite movements. They united from the moment that the authorities officially recognised the workers' associations as compulsory trade unions.[10] In its essentials the medieval craft may be defined as an industrial corporation enjoying the monopoly of practising a particular profession, in accordance with regulations sanctioned by public authority. It would be a complete mistake to envisage the right of self-government as inherent in the nature of gilds. In a large number of towns they never shook off the tutelage of the municipal authority and remained mere organisms functioning under its control.[11] In this sense, the German word *Amt*, which means function, describes their character very well. In a centre as active as Nuremberg, for example, they never ceased to be strictly subject to the *Rath* (Municipal Council), which even refused them the right to meet without its authorisation and went so far as to oblige them to submit their correspondence with the artisans of foreign towns to it.

On the other hand, the corporative tendency appears to have been very strong in the majority of towns in Western Europe. In the Low Countries and the North of France, on the banks of the Rhine, in Italy, that is to say, in those regions where city life had had its earliest and its most complete development, artisan associations claimed an autonomy which often involved them in disputes, not only with authority but also with one another. From the first half of the thirteenth century, they demanded the right of

[10] Etienne Boileau thus explains the motives which moved him to collect the craft regulations of Paris: "Pour ce que nous avons veu à Paris en nostre tans mout de plais, de contens par la delloial envie qui est mère de plais et defferenée convoitise qui gaste soy même et par la non sens as jones et as poi sachrans, entre les estranges gens et ceus de la vile, qui aucun mestier usent et hantent, pour la raison de ce qu'il avoient vendu as estranges aucunes choses qui n'estoient par si bones ne si loi aus que elles deussent . . ." Etienne Boileau, *Le livre des métiers*, ed. S. Depping (Paris, 1837), p. 1.

[11] See, for example, J. Billioud, *De la confrérie à la corporation: les classes industrielles en Provence aux XIV*, XV* et XVI* siècles* (Marseilles, 1929). Industry was none the less supervised by the city "consuls."

self-government, of meeting to discuss their concerns, of possessing a bell and a seal, and even of sharing the government of the town with the rich merchants in whose hands it was centralised. Their attempts became so formidable that at Rouen, in 1189, artisan fraternities were already prohibited, and the same thing happened at Dinant in 1255, in the majority of the Flemish towns and at Tournai in 1280, and at Brussels in 1290. But opposition did not discourage them. In the course of the fourteenth century, they were successful in obtaining, although not everywhere, the right to nominate their own *doyens* and *jurés*, to be recognised as a political body and to share authority with the *haute bourgeoisie*.

Though the crafts differed considerably from place to place in the amount of internal autonomy and political influence which they enjoyed, their economic organisation was alike throughout the whole of Europe. Everywhere its fundamental traits were the same. It was here that the spirit of protectionism inherent in medieval urban economy showed itself most vigorously. Its essential aim was to protect the artisan, not only from external competition, but also from the competition of his fellow-members. It reserved the town market exclusively for him, closing it to foreign products, and at the same time it saw that no member of the profession grew rich to the detriment of the others. It was on this account that more and more minute regulations governed a technique which was strictly the same for all, fixed hours of work, settled prices and wages, forbade any kind of advertisement, determined the number of tools and of workers in the workshops, appointed overseers charged with the most meticulous and inquisitorial inspection—in a word, contrived to guarantee to each of its members both protection and at the same time as complete an equality as possible. The result was to safeguard the independence of each by the vigorous subordination of all. The counterpart of the privilege and monopoly enjoyed by the gild was the destruction of all initiative. No one was permitted to harm others by methods which enabled him to produce more quickly and more cheaply than they. Technical progress took on the appearance of disloyalty. The ideal was stable conditions in a stable industry.

The discipline imposed on the artisan naturally aimed at ensuring the irreproachable quality of manufactured products. In this sense it was exercised to the advantage of the consumer. The rigid regulation of the towns made scamped workmanship as impossible, or, at least, as difficult and as dangerous, in industry as was adulteration in food. The severity of the punishments inflicted for fraud or even for mere carelessness is astonishing. The artisan was not only subject to the constant control of municipal overseers, who had the right to enter his workshop by day or night, but also to that of the public, under whose eyes he was ordered to work at his window.

The members of each corporation were divided into categories subordinate to one another, masters, apprentices (*Lehrlingen*) and journeymen (*Knechte, compagnons*). The masters were the dominant class, upon whom the other two depended. They were the proprietors of small workshops, owning their raw materials and tools. Thus the manufactured article belonged to them, together with all the profits from its sale. The apprentices were initiated into the trade under their direction, for no one was admitted to the craft unless thoroughly proficient. Finally, the journeymen were paid workmen who had completed their apprenticeship, but had not yet risen to the rank of master. The number of masters, indeed, was restricted, being governed by the demand of the local market, and the acquisition of mastership was subject to certain conditions (an entry fine, legitimate birth and possession of the freedom of the town), which rendered it rather difficult. The clientèle of each workshop was limited to the inhabitants of the town and its environs. Each workroom was also a shop where the buyer was face to face with the producer. Here, as in the retail food trade, the middleman was reduced to his proper place.

Thus, the master craftsman was in every sense of the term a small, independent *entrepreneur*. His sole capital consisted in his house and the tools indispensable to his craft. His personnel, strictly limited by the regulations, was composed of one or two apprentices and journeymen, whose number very rarely rose above these figures. If by chance some master acquired by marriage or inheritance a fortune superior to that of his fellows, it was impossible for him to augment the sum-total of his business to their harm, since the industrial system left no room for competition. But inequality of fortunes must have been very rare among these *petits bourgeois*. For almost all of them, the economic organisation meant the same kind of existence and the same moderate resources. It gave them a secure position and prevented them from rising above it. It may, in fact, be described as a "non-capitalistic" system.

But urban industry was not everywhere the same. In many towns, and precisely in those which were the most developed, there was, side by side with the craftsmen-*entrepreneurs* living by the local market, an entirely different group, which worked for export. Instead of producing only for the limited clientèle of the town and its environs, these were the purveyors of the wholesale merchants carrying on international commerce. From these merchants they received their raw material, for them they worked, and to them they delivered it in the form of a manufactured article. In relation to their employers they were thus mere wage-earners. Such was the position of the silk workers at Lucca,[12] of the copper-beaters at Dinant, and of the weavers, fullers and dyers at Ghent, Ypres, Douai, Brussels, Louvain, Florence—in short, in all the centres

[12] On the capitalist character of the Lucchese industry, F. M. Edler is preparing a work of which a résumé has appeared, "for private circulation," in *Abstracts of Theses of the University of Chicago: Humanistic Series*, t. VIII (1929–30). For that of the industry of Dinant, see H. Pirenne, *Les marchands-batteurs de Dinant au XIV* et au XV* siècles*, in *Vierteljahrschrift für Social-und Wirtschaftsgeschichte*, t. II (1904), p. 442 *et seq.*

of the cloth industry, which was *par excellence* the "great" industry of the Middle Ages. It is true that all the workers were divided into corporations, like the other artisans. But if the form of association was the same in both, the position of their members was quite different. In the crafts dealing with the local industry, bakers, blacksmiths, cobblers, etc., tools, workshops and raw material all belonged to the worker, and so did the finished article, which he sold direct to his customers. In the great industry, on the contrary, capital and labour were dissociated. The workman, far away from the market, knew only the *entrepreneur* who paid him, and it was through the agency of the latter that the fruits of his labour, after passing through a number of hands, were finally sold in the Levantine ports or at the fairs of Novgorod. Direct exchange, which historians have too often taken as the essential characteristic of urban economy, is here entirely absent.

By their numbers, also, the export workers contrast strongly with .the small town crafts. The ever-growing market served by international commerce required an ever-growing number of workers. In the middle of the fourteenth century, Ghent contained over 4,000 weavers and many more than 1,200 fullers; enormous figures, when it is remembered that the total population was certainly not more than 50,000. The equilibrium established in medieval towns of the ordinary type between the different trades is here completely destroyed in favour of one of them and we are faced with a situation analogous to that of the manufacturing centres of our own times. A single fact will suffice to prove this. At Ypres in 1431, that is to say, at a period when the cloth manufacture was rapidly declining, it still comprised 51.6 per cent of all the trades, while at the same date in Frankfort-on-the-Main, a town of local industry, the cloth-workers formed only 16 per cent.

The working masses in the large industrial towns were at the mercy of crises and stoppages. When, as a result of war or a ban on importation, raw material ceased to arrive, the looms stopped working and bands of unemployed filled the streets, or wandered about the country begging their bread. Apart from these periods of unavoidable misery, the condition of the masters, proprietors, or tenants of workshops was satisfactory, but it was far otherwise with the journeymen employed by them. For the most part these lived in alleys in some room rented by the week and owned nothing but the clothes they wore. They went from town to town hiring themselves out to employers. On Monday morning they were to be met with in the squares and in front of the churches, anxiously waiting for a master to engage them for the week. The working day began at dawn and ended at nightfall. Wages were paid on the Saturday evening, and although the municipal regulations ordered that they should be in cash, the abuses of the truck system were numerous. Thus the workers in the great industry formed a class apart among the other artisans and bore a pretty close resemblance to the modern proletariat. They were recognisable by their "blue nails," their dress and their rough manners. Masters were not afraid to treat them harshly, for they knew that the place of those who had been banished would soon be filled. It is therefore not surprising to find that, from the middle of the thirteenth century, they were organising strikes. The earliest of which we know occurred at Douai in 1245, under the name of *takehan*.[13] In 1274 the weavers and fullers of Ghent went so far as to leave the town in a body to retire to Brabant, where the *échevins*, warned in time, refused to receive them.[14] In the Low Countries from 1245 city leagues began to be formed, for the extradition of runaway workmen, suspects or conspirators. Every attempt to rise entailed banishment or the death penalty.

In one essential particular, the workers in the export industries differed from the wage-earners of our own days.

[13] G. Espinas and H. Pirenne, *Recueil de documents relatifs à l'histoire de l'industrie drapière en Flandre*, t. II, p. 22.
[14] *Ibid.*, p. 379 *et seq.*

Instead of being concentrated in large factories they were distributed in a number of small workrooms. The master weaver or fuller, the owner or more often the hirer of the tools that he used, was a domestic worker, working for a great mercantile capitalist. The control exercised by the municipal authority over industry was very little protection to the workmen, so long as power was in the hands of the *haute bourgeoisie*, for it was from among these capitalists that the city authorities were recruited. It is only necessary to glance through the deeds relating to the inheritance of the wealthy Douai draper, sire Jehan Boinebroke[15] (who died in 1285–6), to observe the extent to which the artisans of the great industry were still exploited at the beginning of the fourteenth century. Ground down by employers who gave out work to them, the masters were compelled in their turn to grind down the apprentices and journeymen. The preponderance of capital, from which urban economy had been able to free the small crafts, pressed with all its weight on those producing for wholesale trade, where it reigned supreme.

[15] G. Espinas, *Les origines du Capitalisme. Sire Jehan Boinebroke, patricien et drapier douaisien*, Lille, 1933.

𝔖𝔢𝔳𝔢𝔫

THE ECONOMIC CHANGES OF THE FOURTEENTH AND FIFTEENTH CENTURIES

I. CATASTROPHES AND SOCIAL DISTURBANCES[1]

The beginning of the fourteenth century may be considered as the end of the period of medieval economic expansion. Up to then progress was continuous in every sphere. The progressive enfranchisement of the rural classes went hand

[1] BIBLIOGRAPHY.—H. S. Lucas, *The Great European Famine of 1315, 1316 and 1317,* in *Speculum* (*Medieval Academy of America, 1930*).—F. A. Gasquet, *The Black Death of 1348 and 1349* (London, 1908).—H. Pirenne, *Le soulèvement de la Flandre maritime de 1323–1328* (Brussels, 1900).—A. Réville, *Le soulèvement des travailleurs d'Angleterre en 1381* (Paris, 1898).—Ch. Oman, *The Great Revolt of 1381* (Oxford, 1906). —E. Powell, *The Rising in East Anglia in 1381* (Cambridge, 1896).—G. M. Trevelyan, *England in the Age of Wycliffe* (London, 3rd ed., 1900).—S. Luce, *Histoire de la Jacquerie* (Paris, 1859).—G. Franz, *Die agrarischen Unruhen des ausgehenden Mittelalters* (Marburg, 1930).—H. Denifle, *La désolation des églises, monastères et hôpitaux en France pendant la guerre de Cent Ans* (Paris, 1898–9), 2 vols.—G. Schanz, *Zur Geschichte der deutschen Gesellenverbände* (Leipzig, 1877).—E. Martin Saint-Léon, *Le compagnonnage* (Paris, 1901).—H. Pirenne, *Histoire de Belgique,* t. II (Brussels, 3rd ed., 1922).—S. Salvemini, *Magnati e popolani in Firenze dal 1280 al 1295* (Florence, 1899).—C. Falletti-Fossati, *Il tumulto dei Ciompi* (Florence, 1882).—L. Mirot, *Les insurrections urbaines au début du règne de Charles VI, 1380–1383* (Paris, 1906).

in hand with the clearing, drainage and peopling of uncultivated or waste lands, and with the Germanic colonisation of the territories beyond the Elbe. The development of industry and commerce completely transformed the appearance and indeed the very existence of society. While the Mediterranean and the Black Sea on the one side and the North Sea and the Baltic on the other became the scenes of a great trade, and the ports and trading posts sprang up all along their coasts and in their islands, continental Europe was covered with towns from which the activity of the new middle-class radiated in all directions. Under the influence of this new life, the circulation of money was perfected, all sorts of new forms of credit came into use, and the development of credit encouraged that of capital. Finally, the growth of the population was an infallible indication of the health and vigour of society.[2]

[2] Nothing is more essential to a sound understanding of medieval economic history than a knowledge of the density of the population of Europe at this period. Unfortunately, the data at our disposal permit only of estimates which are too conjectural to be of any use. The recent work of M. F. Lot, *L'état des paroisses et des feux de 1328*, in *Bibliothèque de l'École de Chartes*, t. XC (1929), according to which the population of France (within its present frontiers) was at this date as high as 23 or 24 million souls, involves too many hypotheses, both as to the number of hearths and as to the coefficient by which they should be multiplied, to carry conviction. It is only at the beginning of the fifteenth century that we begin to have at our disposal documents from which a few more or less accurate statistics can be obtained. Again there are no reliable censuses except for a few towns (see ch. VI, n. 1). The very small population shown for these, compared with that of our own times, makes it probable that the country districts were thinly populated. For the entire Duchy of Brabant, J. Cuvelier has reached the conclusion, which has considerable probability in view of the precise information which has been preserved for us in the lists of hearths in this territory, that the total number of inhabitants in 1437 was about 450,000. To-day, in the same region, it is nearly two and a half millions, that is to say, it has quintupled (J. Cuvelier, *Les dénombrements des foyers en Brabant*, p. cccxxvii). But one hesitates to generalise from this and to conclude that the total

Now during the early years of the fourteenth century there is observable in all these directions not perhaps a decline but a cessation of all advance. Europe lived, so to speak, on what it had acquired; the economic front was stabilised. It is true that it was precisely then that countries which had hitherto been unaffected by the general movement, like Poland and especially Bohemia, began to take a more active part in it. But their tardy awakening did not entail consequences of sufficient importance to effect the whole of the Western world to any appreciable extent. If we consider the latter alone, it is clear that it was entering upon a period of conservation rather than of creation, when social discontent seems to suggest both the desire and the inability to ameliorate a situation which no longer completely harmonised with men's needs. A proof of this interruption in economic growth is to be found at once in the fact that the scope of external commerce ceased to expand. Until the age of the great geographical discoveries in the middle of the fifteenth century, it never advanced beyond the extreme points reached by Italian navigation in the South and that of the Hanse in the North, that is to say, the ports of the Aegean and Black Seas on the one hand, and on the other the Russian fair of Novgorod. Trade was still, of course, extremely active. In certain respects it may even be said to have increased. It was, in fact, from 1314 that the maritime relations of Genoa and Venice with Bruges and London, through the Straits of Gibraltar, began and that the victory of the Hanse over Waldemar of Denmark in 1380 seemed to have definitely secured its control of the Baltic. But all the same the fact remains that they lived on the past without trying to push *plus oultre*. The same is true of the Continent. German colonisation towards the East stopped, as if exhausted, at the frontier of Lithuania and Latvia. It made no further progress either in Bohemia, Poland or

population of Europe at the end of the Middle Ages was five times less than that of Europe to-day. I am inclined to think that it was even less.

Hungary. In Flanders and Brabant, the cloth industry still preserved, without increasing, its traditional prosperity until towards the middle of the century, when it rapidly declined. In Italy, the majority of the large banks which had for so long dominated the trade in money foundered in a series of sensational bankruptcies: in 1327, the Scali failed; in 1341, the Bonnaccorci, the Usani, the Corsini and many others; in 1343, the Bardi, the Peruzzi and the Acciajuoli. The decline of the Champagne fairs began with the early years of the century.[3] It was then, too, that the population ceased to grow, and its check is the most significant symptom of the stabilisation of society and of an evolution which had reached its maximum.[4]

It is only fair to point out that if the fourteenth century did not continue to progress, the catastrophes which overwhelmed it were largely responsible. The terrible famine which laid waste the whole of Europe from 1315 to 1317 seems to have caused greater ravages than any which had preceded it. The figures which happen to have been preserved for Ypres allow us to estimate its extent. From the beginning of May to the middle of October 1316, we know that the town government ordered the burial of 2,794 corpses, an enormous number, considering the fact that the inhabitants probably did not exceed 20,000. Thirty years later, a new and still more appalling disaster, the Black Death, burst on a world which had hardly recovered from the first shock. Of all epidemics mentioned in history

[3] A. Sapori, *La crise delle compagnie mercantili dei Bardi e dei Peruzzi* (Florence, 1926); E. Jordan, *La faillite des Buonsignori,* in *Mélanges P. Fabre* (Paris, 1902).

[4] In the absence of a sufficient number of accurate works on medieval demography, only a general impression can be given here. It is obvious that it cannot be more than approximately exact. In general, the Black Death may be considered as marking not only an arrest, but even a decline in the growth of the population. Nevertheless, even before this catastrophe, the population had already become stabilised everywhere in Western Europe. The first half of the fourteenth century, on the other hand, witnessed a very great growth of the population in the Slav countries of Eastern Europe, especially in Bohemia.

it was indisputably the most horrible. It is estimated that from 1347 to 1350 it probably carried off a third of the population of Europe and it was followed by a long period of high prices, the effects of which will be discussed later.[5]

To these natural calamities, political calamities no less cruel were added. Italy was torn by civil struggles during the whole century. Germany was a prey to permanent political anarchy. Finally, the Hundred Years' War ruined France and exhausted England. All this weighed heavily upon economic life. The number of consumers decreased and the market lost part of its power of absorption.

These misfortunes unquestionably aggravated the social troubles which make the fourteenth century so violent a contrast to the thirteenth, but their chief cause must be sought in the economic organisation itself, which had reached a point when its operation provoked discontent in urban and rural populations alike.

The enfranchisement of the peasants, however generally it had taken place in the course of the previous age, had still left behind more or less deep traces of serfdom. In many countries *corvées* continued to weigh heavily on the peasants and the disappearance of the manorial régime made them a still greater infliction. For the lord had ceased to consider himself the protector of the men on his estate. His position in relation to his tenants was no longer that of a hereditary chieftain whose authority was accepted by reason of its patriarchal character; it had become that of a landlord and recipient of dues.[6] Since all the former wastelands of the great estates were now occupied, no more *villes neuves* were founded and there was no longer any motive for giving the serfs a freedom which,

[5] Hence the appearance in 1350 of the Statute of Labourers in England and in France of the royal ordinance of 1351, both of which regulated wages with a view to lowering prices.— R. Vivier, *La grande ordonnance de février 1351: les mesures anticorporatives et la liberté du travail,* in *Revue historique,* t. CXXXVIII (1921), p. 201 *et seq.*

[6] On all this, see M. Bloch, *Les caractères originaux de l'histoire rurale française,* p. 112 *et seq.*

instead of being profitable to their lord, would have deprived him of the rents and services which he continued to extract from them. Doubtless, the need of money often drove the lords to sell charters of enfranchisement for a good price, or even to free a whole village in return for the cession of a part of the common lands. But the fact remains that now that the period of clearance was over the peasant no longer had any hope of improving his condition by emigrating to virgin lands. Everywhere where serfdom remained, it became all the more odious because, being now exceptional, it took on a derogatory appearance. The free cultivators on their side were impatient of the jurisdiction of the manorial courts, by virtue of which they held their tenures and through which they remained subject to economic exploitation by the lords, whose men they had once been. Ever since the monks, in the course of the thirteenth century, had lost their early fervour and, with it, their prestige, tithes were paid most unwillingly. The large farms established on the demesne lands were a crushing weight upon the villagers. They claimed the greater part of the common lands as pasturage for their flocks, and rounded off their boundaries at the expense of the villagers. It was easy for them to encroach because they were often in the hands of the lord's bailiff or reeve, and thus they were able to oblige a number of the inhabitants to work for them as agricultural labourers. To all these causes of discomfort were added the evils produced by frequent wars. The Hundred Years' War especially, during which mercenaries continued to live on the country after their disbandment, turned many regions of France into deserts "where there was no longer to be heard a cock crowing or a hen clucking." [7]

This desolation was, it is true, a phenomenon peculiar to France, and it would no doubt be incorrect to argue that in the rest of Europe the situation of the peasants became worse in the course of the fourteenth century. The social discontent of which they gave so many proofs

[7] M. Bloch, *op. cit.*, p. 118.

is not to be explained everywhere in the same way. It may equally well have arisen from excessive misery and from a wish to put an end to a state of things all the more shocking because men believed themselves equal to overthrowing it. If the Jacquerie in the Ile de France in 1357 was the uprising of populations driven to extremes by distress and hatred of the nobles who were held responsible for it, it seems to have been quite otherwise with the rising in Western Flanders in 1323 to 1328 and the insurrection of 1381 in England.

The long duration of the former is quite sufficient to prove that it could not have been the work of a miserable and feeble populace. It was, in fact, a genuine attempt at a social revolution, directed against the nobility in order to wrest legal and financial authority from them. The strictness with which the nobles collected the taxes levied to pay the heavy fines imposed on Flanders for the benefit of the King of France, after the war begun by the battle of Courtrai, caused the outbreak of riots, which soon changed into an open revolt against the established order. It was no longer merely a question of putting an end to abuses. The independent spirit of the sturdy peasants of this territory, descendants of the *hôtes* who had brought these swampy lands into cultivation in the twelfth and thirteenth centuries, was roused in the struggle to such a degree as to make them look upon the rich and even upon the Church itself as their natural enemies. It was enough to live on the revenues of the land to be suspect.[8] The villagers refused to pay the tithe and demanded that the monasteries should distribute their grain to the people. The priests did not escape the class hatred which animated the masses; one of the leaders of the movement would have liked, so he declared, to see the last of them hanging on the gallows. By a refine-

---

[8] "Dicebant enim alicui diviti: Tu plus diligis dominos quam *communitates de quibus vivis;* et nulla alia causa in eo reperta, talem exponebant morti." *Chronicon comitum Flandrensium,* in *Corpus Chron. Flandr.,* t. I, p. 202.

ment of cruelty, the nobles and the rich were compelled
to put their own relatives to death under the eyes of the
crowd. Never again either during the Jacquerie, or during
the English rising in 1381, do we see acts of violence such
as then horrified Western Flanders. "The plague of insurrection was such," says a contemporary, "that men became
disgusted with life." In order to put down these rebels
who, "like brutes devoid of sense and reason," threatened
to overthrow the social order, it was necessary for the
King of France himself to take the field. The peasants, full
of self-confidence, advanced boldly to meet him and offered him battle on the slopes of Mount Cassel (August
23, 1228). It was as short as it was bloody. The knights
mercilessly put to the sword the rabble who had dared to
resist them and who had put themselves outside the common law. The king refused to listen to the barons, who
urged him to burn maritime Flanders to the ground and
to slaughter man, woman and child; he contented himself
with confiscating the property of the insurgents who had
fought against him. The social revolt, triumphant for a
moment, was crushed. Its radical tendencies, indeed, cannot be regarded as more than the transient exasperation
of a discontent driven to extremes by circumstances. The
stubbornness and length of the rebellion are also partially
explicable by the fact that it was excited and supported
by the craftsmen of Ypres and Bruges, who made common cause with it and temporarily impressed on the rural
class the revolutionary spirit of the towns.

The English insurrection of 1381 was also, like that of
Western Flanders, the common work of the townspeople
and those of the countryside, and like it, too, may be considered as a violent and fugitive expression of the sense
of contrast between the worker and the man who lives on
his labour. No more than in Flanders was the English
rising due to the misery of the rural classes. It had nothing in common with the Jacquerie. The condition of the
English peasantry had steadily improved during the course
of the thirteenth century, with the growing substitution

of money rents for the labour services. But in all the manors there were more or less pronounced survivals of serfdom, which the villeins found all the more intolerable because the rise in prices and wages following on the Black Death had still further improved their position. There is nothing to prove that their rising was caused by an attempt on the part of the landlords to increase dues and labour services. It would appear rather as an attempt to shake off, for the benefit of the people, what still remained of the manorial system. Possibly the mysticism of the Lollards also helped to excite in their minds hatred of the "gentlemen" who did not exist "when Adam delved and Eve span." Just as in Flanders fifty years before, vague communistic aspirations filled the minds of the insurgents and gave the revolt the appearance of a movement directed against the social order. But the terror which it spread was short-lived. The disproportion was too great between the forces of conservatism and the peasantry who, in their thirst for revenge and hopes of a Utopia, nursed the eternal illusion of a world founded on justice and equality. At the end of a few months order was reestablished. It had been enough for the king to show himself and for the knighthood to arm to end a situation which was more noisy than dangerous.

The rural insurrections of the fourteenth century really owed their appearance of gravity to the brutishness of the peasantry. By themselves they could not succeed. Though the agricultural classes formed by far the largest part of society, they were incapable of combining in a common action and more incapable still of any thought of making a new world. All things considered, these risings were but local and short-lived spurts, outbursts of anger with no future. Although the economic contrast between the peasantry who tilled the soil and the nobility who owned it, was as real as that between the workman and the urban capitalist, it was less felt, by virtue of the very conditions of rural existence, which bound a man by so many ties to the land which he cultivated and which left him, in spite of everything, a much higher degree of personal independence than was enjoyed by the wage-earner in the great industry. Thus it is not surprising that in bitterness, duration and results alike the city agitations of the fourteenth century are in striking contrast with those of the country people.

Throughout the whole of Western Europe the *haute bourgeoisie* had from the beginning monopolised town government. It could not have been otherwise, if we remember that city life, resting essentially on commerce and industry, made it inevitable that those who promoted the latter should at the same time direct the former. Thus during the twelfth and thirteenth centuries, an aristocracy, recruited from among the most notable merchants, had everywhere exercised municipal government. Their government had been a class government in the full sense of the term, and for long it possessed all the virtues of its class, energy, perspicacity, devotion to the public interest, which was indeed identical with and the chief guarantee of their own private interests. The work which it accomplished bears high testimony to its merits. Under it urban civilisation took on the features which were to distinguish it to the end. It created the whole machinery of municipal administration, organised its various services, founded civic finance and credit, built and organised markets, found the necessary money to build strong ramparts and to open schools, in a word, to meet all the needs of the bourgeoisie. But little by little there were revealed the faults of a system which entrusted the economic regulation of the great industry to the very people who lived upon its profits, and were naturally impelled to reduce the share of the workers to a minimum.

We have already seen that in the greatest manufacturing cities of the medieval world, in the Flemish towns, the cloth-workers had begun to manifest a hostility to the patrician *échevins*, which is clearly shown by the outbreak of strikes.[9] To their own discontent was added that of a

[9] See above, p. 187.

growing number of the well-to-do bourgeoisie. For, in the meantime, the patrician régime had in many towns become a plutocratic oligarchy, jealously withholding power from all who were not members of a few families, and exercising it more and more obviously in their own interests. Thus an opposition which was both social and political grew up against the town government. It was the social opposition, obviously the most violent, which gave the signal for a conflict which, with many bloody vicissitudes, was to continue right into the fifteenth century.

The revolt of the crafts against the patrician régime is often styled a democratic revolution. The term is not wholly exact, if by democracy is meant what the word denotes to-day. The malcontents had no intention of founding popular governments. Their horizons was bounded by the walls of their city and limited to the framework of their corporation. Though each craft claimed a share of power it was very little concerned with its neighbours and its action was narrowly circumscribed by particularism. It sometimes happened, of course, that corporations of the same town combined against the common enemy, the oligarchy of *échevins,* but they frequently also turned on each other after the victory. It must not be forgotten that these self-styled democrats were all members of industrial groups possessing the enormous privilege of monopoly. Democracy, as they understood it, was nothing but a democracy of the privileged.

Not all towns were disturbed by the demands of the crafts. Neither Venice, nor the Hanseatic towns, nor the English cities show any traces of agitation. No doubt the reason was that the government of the *haute bourgeoisie* did not degenerate there into a closed and selfish oligarchy. New men, enriched by commerce, were constantly renewing and rejuvenating the ruling class. It is this which explains how the patricians there succeeded in preserving an authority which they were able to impose on everyone by means of their double control of business and of urban government. For centuries, the Venetian aristocracy set an admirable example of the highest virtues of patriotism, energy and skill, and the prosperity which they gained for the republic shone upon all alike, so that the people never dreamed of throwing off their yoke. It seems likely that similar causes preserved the rule of the patriciate in the Hanseatic towns. In England, the control exercised by royal authority over the towns was strong enough to check, if necessary, the efforts of the common people. The same is true of the French towns, which, from the end of the thirteenth century, were increasingly subordinated to the authority of the agents of the Crown, *baillis,* or seneschals. Elsewhere, as for example in Brabant, the territorial prince constituted himself the protector of the great bourgeois.

It was above all in the large industrial towns of the Low Countries, on the banks of the Rhine and in Italy, that municipal revolutions broke out. Here we can attempt only a sketch of their chief features, passing over the innumerable variations due to differences of circumstances, interests and surroundings. Their first cause must be sought in the abuses of the governing oligarchy. Wherever princely power was too weak either to forbid or to control it, nothing remained but to overthrow it, or at least to compel it to share the power which it sought to monopolise. As to this everyone, rich and poor alike, was agreed, merchants who were kept out of commercial affairs no less than craftsmen and wage-earners in the great industry. The movement, which started in the second half of the thirteenth century, reached its conclusion in the course of the fourteenth. In consequence of riots, which almost always developed into armed struggles, the "great" were obliged to cede to the "small" a more or less large share in the municipal administration. Since the majority of the population was grouped into crafts, the reform necessarily consisted in associating these with the government. Sometimes they received the right to dispose of a few seats on the body of *échevins* or the town council, sometimes a new body of magistrates elected by them was formed by the side of the old one; sometimes all measures concerning the finances or political organisation of the city had to be submitted for approval by their delegates in general assembly. Sometimes they even succeeded in seizing the whole of this power from which the patriciate had excluded them so long. At Liége, for example, in 1384, the "great," incapable of continuing a resistance which had lasted for more than a century, ended by capitulating. From then onwards, the craft completely dominated the town. Only those whose names were inscribed on their rolls enjoyed political rights. The council, the jurors of which were nominated each year by them and supervised by their "governors," was no more than a machine whose action they regulated at will. The two *maîtres* (burgomasters), recruited from this council, carried out their orders, for all important questions had to be submitted for consideration to the thirty-two crafts and settled in each of them by a majority vote. Similar constitutions, making the associations of artisans the arbiters of the municipal government, are to be met with at Utrecht and Cologne.

But what was possible in towns, where no one industry had any decided advantage over the others, was impossible where the balance manifestly inclined in favour of one of them. In the large manufacturing cities of Flanders, the numerical superiority of the weavers and fullers, whose crafts counted many thousands of members, prevented them from being satisfied with the rôle assigned to the small corporations which comprised no more than a few score. They were all the more anxious for ascendancy because their condition as wage-earners differed greatly from that of the craftsmen serving the local market. For them, the fall of the patriciate was not only a political question, it was first and foremost a social one. In it they looked forward to the end of their economic subordination, hoping that when the power to regulate conditions of work and rates of wages passed into their hands, the precarious condition to which they were reduced by their profession would be over. Many indulged in confused dreams of equality, in a world where "every man should have as much as another." [10] It was they who, in all the large towns, at the end of the thirteenth century, had given the signal for revolt and maintained the momentous struggle which brought them a temporary ascendancy after the victory of Courtrai. But their domination had soon roused the rest of the bourgeoisie against them. The divergence, or, rather, the incompatibility of their interests with those of the merchants and the artisans, was too great for the latter to submit to being subordinate to the cloth-workers.

Against these wage-earners and proletarians, the capitalists of the great commerce, brokers or exporters, combined with the small independent *entrepreneurs* of local industry. In order to satisfy everybody they tried to establish municipal governments in which a share was reserved for each of the large groups into which the population was divided: the *poorterie* (*haute bourgeoisie*), the mass of small crafts and the cloth-workers. But the equilibrium which it was hoped to attain in this way could not be, and never was; anything but an unstable one. In the eyes of the weavers and fullers, it was nothing but a fraud, since it in effect condemned them to being always in a minority in relation to the other members of the town. To gain their demands, they could only count on force, and they did not fail to use it. Throughout the fourteenth century, we see them constantly rising, seizing power and refusing to give it up except when, starved out by a blockade or decimated by a massacre, they were compelled to yield to the coalition of their adversaries.

Nothing is more tragic than the situation of the Flemish towns, in which social hatred raged with the frenzy of madness. In 1320–32 the "good people" of Ypres implored the king not to allow the inner bastion of the town, in which they lived and which protected them from the

[10] L. Verriest, *Le registre de la Loi de Tournai de 1302*, in *Bulletin de la Commission royale d'histoire*, t. LXXX (1911), p. 445.

"common people," to be demolished.[11] The history of this town, like that of Ghent and Bruges, abounds in bloody struggles, setting the cloth-workers at grips with "those who had something to lose." The struggle took on more and more the appearance of a class war between rich and poor. But it was this in appearance only. There was no common understanding among the mass of workers in revolt. The fullers, whose wages the weavers claimed to fix, or, rather, to reduce, treated the latter as enemies and, in order to escape from their exploitation, supported the cause of the "good people." As to the small-scale crafts, all detested the "odious weavers"[12] who interfered with their work and injured their business, and whose communistic aspirations dismayed them as much as they dismayed the ruler and the nobility. But perpetually in a state of revolt as they were, the exasperation of these people only increased, when they perceived that, in spite of all their efforts and even when they were in authority, their situation did not improve. Incapable of understanding that the nature of the great commerce and of capitalistic industry inevitably condemned them to the insecurity of a wage-earning class and to all the misery of crises and stoppages, they believed themselves to be the victims of the "rich" for whom they laboured. It was not until the ruin of the cloth industry forced them to emigrate to seek a living elsewhere that the struggle which they had waged indomitably up to that moment came to an end.

Fundamentally, the situation in the large manufacturing centres of Flanders was identical with that in all the

[11] "L'effort du commun de la ville d'Ypre demeure dehors les portes, qui maint outrageus et horrible fait et conspiration ont fait sur les boins de la ville . . . si que les portes fussent ostées, li boine gent de la ville seroient en peril de estre mourdri par nuit et de desrobeir leur avoir." *Bulletin de la Commission royale d'histoire*, 5ᵉ série, t. VII (1897), p. 28.

[12] *Chronique rimée des troubles de Flandre en 1379–1380*, ed. H. Pirenne, p. 38 (Ghent, 1902).

towns where export industry preponderated over local industry. At Dinant, the copper-workers exercised an influence as supreme as that of the weavers and fullers at Ghent or Ypres. Florence, which was at once a city of bankers and of drapers, also saw the mass of the workers seize power by main force from the capitalist class. The rebellion of the Ciompi (1379–82), roused and led by the cloth-workers, formed a pendant to the revolutionary agitations in Northern Europe at the same date. It would be no exaggeration to say that on the banks of the Scheldt, as on those of the Arno, the revolutionaries sought to impose the dictatorship of the proletariat upon their adversaries.

Moreover, towards the end of the century a proletariat began to make its appearance in the small crafts, in spite of the fact that their whole organisation was designed to safeguard the economic independence of their members. Between the master-craftsmen and the apprentices or journeymen whom they employed goodwill had lasted as long as it was easy for the latter to rise to the position of masters. But from the moment that the population ceased to grow and the crafts were faced with the necessity of stabilising production, the acquisition of mastership had become more and more difficult. The tendency to make it a close family reserve is shown by all sorts of measures, e.g., long terms of apprenticeship, the raising of the fees which had to be paid for obtaining the title of master and the exaction of a "masterpiece" as a guarantee of proficiency in those who aspired to it. In short, each corporation of artisans was gradually transformed into a selfish clique of employers, determined to bequeath to their sons or sons-in-law the fixed clientèle of their small workshops.

Hence, it is not surprising that we observe from the middle of the fourteenth century, among the apprentices and especially among the journeymen, who saw all hope of ever improving their condition vanishing, a discontent which showed itself first in strikes, in demands for higher wages, and finally in claims to share side by side with the masters in the government of the craft. At Liége, says Jacques de Hemricourt (1333–1403), "quant . . . les mestiers sont ensemble por faire leur offichiens, les garchons servans et les apprendiches ont ortant de vois, en la siiet faisant, comme il hont les maistres et les chiefs d'hosteit." [13] Clearly, the journeyman, hitherto the master's assistant, associated with his life and often destined to marry into his family and to succeed him, was gradually transformed into a mere wage-earner. The craft knew in its turn the opposition of labour and capital. For the family character which had reigned for so long there was substituted the conflict between employer and employed. Among the journeymen, identity of interests and demands soon gave birth to associations for mutual assistance and defence which extended to several towns. Such were the *compagnonnages,* or *gesellenverbände,* loose associations of journeymen, which appeared a little earlier in France and a little later in Germany, with the object of finding work for their members and protecting them against exploitation by the masters. To these offensive organisations, the masters replied on their side by interurban measures of defence. In 1383, the blacksmiths of Mainz, Worms, Speier, Frankfort, Aschaffenberg, Bingen, Oppenheim and Kreuznach, concluded an alliance against the *knechte* of the respective crafts, who were beginning to agitate.[14]

Thus, among the towns there was revealed an economic and social antagonism, so widespread as to prove that it sprang from profound and permanent causes. But strong as it was, it did not succeed in overthrowing the established order, which was too powerful to be imperilled by the craftsmen and labourers. Only here and there did the urban malcontents seek to draw the country districts into their movement. Too many differences of spirit, needs and

[13] J. de Hemricourt, *Le patron de la temporalité des évêques de Liége,* p. 56, in t. III of the *Oeuvres de J. de Hemricourt,* edited by C. de Borman, A. Bayot and E. Poncelet (Brussels, 1931).

[14] Kulischer, *op. cit.,* t. I, p. 214.

interests separated them from the peasants for any under-standing to be possible between people who really be-longed to two distinct worlds. Thus the attempted revolu-tions of the towns were doomed to certain failure. The provinces and the nobility came to the rescue of all those who were threatened by them, great merchants, *rentiers* of the *haute bourgeoisie* and master-craftsmen. During the fifteenth century the wave that had risen in the preceding one fell back upon itself, to break against the inevitable coalition of all the interests which it had united against it.

II. PROTECTIONISM, CAPITALISM AND MERCANTILISM[15]

The period in which the craft gilds dominated or influ-enced the economic régime of the towns is also that in which urban protectionism reached its height. However divergent their professional interests might be, all indus-trial groups were united in their determination to enforce to the utmost the monopoly which each enjoyed and to crush all scope for individual initiative and all possibility of competition. Henceforth the consumer was completely sacrificed to the producer. The great aim of workers in export industries was to raise wages, that of those engaged

[15] BIBLIOGRAPHY.—See above, Ch. VI, n. 7; Ch. VII, n. 1.— W. Schmidt-Rimpler, *Geschichte des Kommissionsgeschäfts in Deutschland*, t. I (Halle, 1915).—A. Schulte, *Geschichte der grossen Ravensburger Handelsgesellschaft*, 1380–1530 (Stutt-gart, 1923, 3 vols.).—W. Stieda, *Briefwechsel eines deutschen Kaufmanns im XV Jahrhundert* (Leipzig, 1921).—H. Am-mann, *Die Diesbach-Watt Gesellschaft* (Saint-Gall, 1928).— A. Grunzweig, *Correspondance de la filiale de Bruges des Medici, I* (Brussels, 1931).—H. Prutz, *Jacques Coeur* (Berlin, 1911).—L. Guiraud, *Recherches sur le prétendu rôle de Jacques Coeur*, in *Mémoires de la société archéologique de Montpellier* (1900).—H. Pirenne, *Les étapes de l'histoire sociale du capitalisme*, p. 133, n. 19.—J. Strieder, *Studien zur Geschichte kapitalistischer Organisationsformen. Monopole, Kartelle und Aktiengesellschaften im Mittelalter und zum Beginn der Neuzeit*, 2nd ed. (Munich, 1925).

in supplying the local market to raise, or at least to sta-
bilise, prices. Their vision was bounded by the town walls,
and all were convinced that their prosperity could be
secured by the simple expedient of shutting out all competition from outside. Their particularism became more
and more rabid; never has the conception that each profession is the exclusive possession of a privileged body been
pressed to such extremes as it was in these medieval crafts.
In their eyes there were no rights save those which had
been acquired, and for each group the notion of the common good gave way before that of its own interests.

Evidences of this outlook are to be found on all sides.
Perhaps the most significant are the restrictions on the
acquisition of citizenship, which were everywhere imposed. Each town naturally wished to reserve for its own
citizens the advantages which it was able to secure for
them, and the greater those privileges, the less willing
were the citizens to share them with others. This accounts
for the constant increase in the fees payable for entry into
the franchise and the multiplication of the qualifications
required, such as legitimate birth, certificates of origin,
or of good character, and so on. Hence, too, the policy
pursued by each craft in excluding "foreigners" and the
increasingly marked tendency to create, so to speak, an
industrial vacuum round the walls of the town, so as to
ensure its economic preponderance. Under the pretext
of a privilege, or in virtue of one extorted from the ruler
by a revolt or a bribe, it was forbidden to open a shop or
a workroom outside the town boundaries, or to sell in the
town (except during fair time) a commodity which had
not been manufactured there. The severity of these measures increased with the growth of "democratic" government. At Ghent in 1297 the introduction of cloth woven
outside the town was still permitted, provided that it had
been fulled inside; but in 1302 this concession was withdrawn and from 1314 the manufacture of cloth within a
radius of three miles of the walls was prohibited. Nor was
this a vain threat. All through the fourteenth century reg-

ular armed expeditions were sent out against all the villages in the neighbourhood, and looms or fulling-vats were broken or carried away.[16] On the other hand, every great manufacturing city employed the women of the country-side in spinning woollen yarn and reserved their labour exclusively for its own use. At Florence, as in Flanders, the peasant women were thus employed in the service of the town workshops and obliged to bring their thread to depôts established for the purpose. The precept that might is right prevailed everywhere. The great towns took upon themselves the right to forbid their neighbours to manufacture the stuffs which were in greatest demand, and an accusation of counterfeiting this or that speciality was often enough to get rid of their competition. Ypres, Ghent and Bruges brought the industry of all the secondary centres of the County under their control, by virtue of pretended "privileges," which no one had ever seen, but whose existence it was quite enough for them to declare. The lawsuit brought by Poperinghe against Ypres in 1373 throws a lurid light on the situation. When the drapers of that town invoked in their favour "the natural right of each man to gain his livelihood," Ypres relied upon the "urban right" which justified their privilege.[17]

The attitude of the crafts towards the capitalist *entrepreneurs* was naturally one of the greatest distrust and suspicion. The great merchants who organised the cloth industry were obliged to enrol themselves in the weavers' gild and to submit to regulations which reduced them to the position of mere heads of workshops. Of course the nature of "the great industry" inevitably kept this regulation within limits which could not be transgressed without bringing about immediate ruin. It was impossible to

[16] G. Espinas and H. Pirenne, *Recueil de documents relatifs à l'histoire de l'industrie drapière en Flandre*, t. II, p. 606 *et seq.*

[17] G. Espinas and H. Pirenne, *Recueil de documents relatifs à l'histoire de l'industrie drapière en Flandre*, t. III, p. 168 *et seq.*

prevent these rich masters from entering into business relations with the Italian companies or the Hanseatic merchants, who took their place in all the Flemish towns both as wool importers and as cloth exporters. The fact that they were foreigners protected them from legislation to which only the citizens were subject. Nevertheless, the industry gradually declined, as a result of the constant rise of wages, the growing claims of the workers, the permanent hostility of weavers and fullers, and the obstinate maintenance of technical processes which could not be altered without a breach of privilege. Round about 1350 workers began to migrate to Florence, tempted, no doubt, by the promises of Italian factors, or in even greater numbers to England, whose kings adroitly took advantage of the situation to promote the native cloth manufacture.[18] The island which had for so many centuries provided Flanders with its raw material, now began to compete with it and by the beginning of the fifteenth century the competition was already irresistible. In Brabant, too, like causes produced like effects. When at last some notice was taken of what was happening, it was already too late and in 1435 Brussels in vain freed her wholesale clothiers from the obligation to join the weavers' gild.[19]

Urban particularism led the towns to hamper large-scale commerce in exactly the same way that they hampered large-scale industry. The decline of fairs in the course of the fourteenth century is not unconnected with

[18] For the emigration of Flemish and Brabantine workmen to Florence, see A. Doren, *Deutsche Handwerker und Handwerkbrüderschaften im mittelalterlichen Italien* (Berlin, 1903). M. Battistini, *La confrérie de Sainte-Barbe des Flamands à Florence* (Brussels, 1931). A. Grunzweig, *Les soi-disant statuts de la confrérie de Sainte-Barbe de Florence*, in *Bulletin de la Commission royale d'histoire*, t. XCVI (1932), p. 333 *et seq.* For their emigration to England: E. Lipson, *English Economic History*, t. I, pp. 309, 399. H. de Sagher, *L'immigration des tisserands flamands et brabançons en Angleterre sous Edouard III.*, in *Mélanges . . . Pirenne* (Brussels, 1926).

[19] G. des Marez, *L'organisation du travail à Bruxelles*, p. 484.

the dislike of the artisans for an institution so incompatible with their violent protectionism. Moreover, the "staple right," in virtue of which many towns obliged merchants passing through them to unpack and offer their wares for sale to the burgesses before going on, was a serious hindrance to interlocal transport. Elsewhere the boatmen's craft claimed the exclusive right of towing all boats passing up and down the watercourses in the neighbourhood of the town and sometimes even of unlading the cargoes in order to carry them on their own boats.[20]

There were, of course, exceptions to the rule. The development of towns was not everywhere equally rapid, nor was the domination of the crafts everywhere exercised with equal intensity, and there were therefore nuances in the degree of urban protectionism. For instance, it was much less marked in the South of Germany, where large-scale industry and commerce were only just beginning to flourish in the course of the fourteenth century, than it was in the Low Countries or the Rhineland, with their long economic history. In France and England, the royal authority prevented its results from developing to the full.[21] Moreover, in Italy the power of capital had always been sufficiently great to impose limits upon it. All that can be said without exaggeration is that, in the fourteenth, as compared with the thirteenth century, urban industry pushed to the extreme limit that spirit of local exclusiveness which had always been inherent in it.

But it was in vain that the towns pursued their policy of taxing and exploiting large-scale commerce; they could not escape it, nor indeed did they desire to do so, for the richer, the more active and the more populous a city

[20] G. Bigwood, *Gand et la circulation des grains en Flandre du XIVe au XVIIIe siècles*, in *Vierteljahrschrift für Social-und Wirtschaftsgeschichte*, t. IV (1906), p. 397 *et seq.*

[21] See above, pp. 199–200. The ordinance of 1351 in France, for the suppression of the gilds, aimed at diminishing their restrictions on the liberty to work with a view to lowering prices.

was, the more commerce was indispensable to it. After all, it provided the townspeople with a great part of their food supply and the crafts with almost all their raw materials. It was by means of trade that the taverners got their wine, the fishmongers their dried fish and herrings, the spicers their sugar, pepper, cinnamon and ginger, the apothecaries their drugs, the cordwainers their leather, the potters their lead and tin, the weavers their wool, the fullers their soap, the dyers their woad, alum, and Brazil-wood. It was by trade that the products of urban industry were exported to outside markets. All that the towns could do was to regulate the forms which this multifarious and essential activity assumed within their walls. They were quite unable to exercise any control over its expansion and circulation, the sources from which it was fed, or the credit which it employed; indeed the whole economic organisation which was dependent on wholesale commerce eluded it. Over this enormous field the power of capital reigned supreme, dominating both large-scale navigation and land transport, both the import and the export trade. It spread over the whole of Europe and the towns were borne upon its bosom, as islands are borne upon the circumambient ocean.

One of the most striking phenomena of the fourteenth and fifteenth centuries is the rapid growth of great commercial companies, each with its affiliations, correspondents and factors in different parts of the Continent. The example of the powerful Italian companies in the thirteenth century had now found followers north of the Alps. They had taught men the management of capital, bookkeeping and the various forms of credit, and though they continued to dominate the trade in money, they found themselves faced by a growing number of rivals in the trade in merchandise. It is enough to call attention to the existence in Germany of commercial firms such as that of Hildebrand Vickinchusen of Lübeck, whose dealings stretched from Bruges to Venice and to the far ends of the Baltic, or such as the *Grosse Ravensburger Gesell-*

schaft, which had correspondents all over Central Europe, and in Italy and Spain. France and England, the former ruined and the latter absorbed by the Hundred Years' War, displayed less energy in the expansion of capital.

Nevertheless, Italy still held the first place by reason of its extraordinary vitality. New firms sprang up to succeed those whose bankruptcy had shaken the mid-fourteenth century, and the greatest of all, that of the Medici, was to rise in the fifteenth century to a position of financial power such as the world had never before seen.

The rise and vigour of capitalism in the later Middle Ages made itself apparent in a number of directions. From the outset of the fifteenth century, the rate of interest, which had generally maintained itself in the neighbourhood of 12 to 14 per cent, fell to 10 to 5 per cent. The functioning of credit was perfected by new devices such as the technique of acceptances and of protests of bills of exchange. At Genoa the *casa di S. Georgio,* founded in 1407, may be regarded as the first modern bank, and the speculation in its shares has been compared in importance and in influence upon the financial situation to that of the English consols in the seventeenth and eighteenth centuries.[22] Other banks, such as those of the Centurioni at Genoa, the Soranzo at Venice and the Medici at Florence, which carried on both a trade in money and a trade in merchandise, were not far behind it in the size of their capital and the scope of their operations.[23] The whole of this movement was set on foot by a class of new men, who appeared just at the moment

[22] J. Kulischer, *op. cit.,* t. I, p. 347.

[23] The archives of the merchant, Francesco Datini (d. 1410), which are preserved in the hospice of Prato, near Florence, and comprise more than 100,000 letters, representing his correspondence with his "factors" or clients in Italy, Spain, Africa, France and England, bear witness, by their mass, to the wide range of the Italian business houses of the age. G. Livi, *Dall' Archivio di Francesco Datini* (Florence, 1910). Enrico Bensa, *Francesco di Marco da Prato* (Milan, 1928).

when urban economy was being transformed under the influence of the crafts. This was certainly no chance coincidence. The old town patricians, driven from power and thrown out of gear by the new conditions which were henceforth to dominate economic life, became, with few exceptions, a class of rentiers, living on the house and land rents, in which they had always invested a part of their profits. In their place parvenus formed a new group of capitalists, who were hampered by no traditions and able to accept without any difficulty the changes which took place in the old order. For the most part they were "factors," commercial agents, or sometimes well-to-do artisans, for whom the progress of credit, speculation and exchange had opened a career;[24] but many who had grown rich in the service of princes also ventured their fortunes in business.

Indeed, the advance of administration and the increasing expense of maintaining armies of mercenaries and arming them with artillery, had obliged kings and great territorial lords alike to surround themselves with a personnel of counsellors and agents of all sorts, who undertook the task which the nobility either disdained or was unable to perform. Their chief occupation was the management of finance, and as long as they procured the

---

[24] See G. Yver, *De Guadagnis, mercatoribus florentinis Lugduni commorantibus* (Paris, 1902); M. Jansen, *Studien zur Fuggergeschichte. I. Die Anfänge der Fugger* (Leipzig, 1907); A. H. Johnson, *English Nouveaux-riches in the XIV Century*, in *Transactions of the Royal Historical Society*, new series, XV, 63.—E. Coornaert, *La Draperie-Sayetterie d'Hondschoote*, pp. 362, 411, 445, points out that "from the fifteenth to the sixteenth century drapers and merchants, who were in the first rank of the *sayette* manufacture, came from 'poor' or 'very poor' families." From the fourteenth century, nobles began to engage in commercial affairs in the Low Countries. A. de Chestret, *Renaud de Schoenau*, in *Mémoires de l'Académie royale de Belgique* (Brussels, 1892). At the beginning of the fifteenth century, Henri de Borsselen, sire de Veere, caused several ships to be built and traded with them. Z. W. Sneller. *Walcheren in de XVe eeuw* (Utrecht, 1916).

money of which their masters were always short. there was every disposition not to enquire too closely into the profits which went into their own pockets, as a result of the coinage or of the contracts with army contractors, bankers and moneylenders of all kinds which passed through their hands. Jacques Coeur is only the most brilliant representative of this class of *nouveaux riches*. There were many others round him, such as Guillaume de Duvenvoorde, the confidential adviser of the Duke of Brabant, whose riches founded the fortune of the house of Nassau, or Nicolas Rolin and Pierre Bladelin, who owed their wealth to offices performed in the service of Philip the Good, Duke of Burgundy, or the Semblançays and the d'Orgements at the court of the King of France.[25] The provisioning of royal courts, whose luxury grew with their power, and the business of contracting for the armies, were both the source of vast profits. In 1388 a Parisian merchant, Nicolas Boullard, contracted for the provision of the troops levied by Charles VI for the Guelders expedition, for a sum of 100,000 *écus d'or*.[26] Dino Rapondi of Lucca became the chief moneylender of the court of Burgundy.[27] Everywhere the great financiers grew in importance in the entourage of the government and were welcomed by the highest aristocracy, who gave them social prestige in return for their services.

Indeed, however various their origins, the capitalists of the fourteenth and fifteenth centuries were all obliged to enter into relations with princes and a complete solidarity of interests was established between the two. On the one

[25] J. Cuvelier, *Les origines de la fortune de la maison d'Orange-Nassau,* in *Mémoires de l'Académie royale de Belgique* (1921); L. Mirot, *Une grande famille parlementaire au XIV° et au XV° siècle. Les d'Orgemont, leur origine, leur fortune, etc.* (Paris, 1913); A. Spont, *Semblançay. La bourgeoisie financière au début du XVI° siècle* (Paris, 1895).

[26] *Chronique du Religieux de Saint-Denys,* ed. Bellaguet, t. I, p. 533. In 1383 he had already supplied the wheat necessary for the royal troops, *ibid.,* p. 265.

[27] L. Mirot, *Études lucquoises* (Paris, 1930).

side the princes could not meet either their public or their private expenses without recourse to the financiers, but on the other the great merchants, bankers and ship-owners looked to the princes to protect them against excessive municipal particularism, to put down urban revolts, and to secure the circulation of their money and merchandise. The more "those who had something to lose" were alarmed by social upheavals or communistic movements, the further they were driven into the arms of the royal power as their sole refuge. Even the artisans, when it came to their turn to be threatened by the journeymen, turned to it for protection, because it was the protector of order.

Urban particularism, which was disliked by the princes for political reasons, was equally disliked for economic reasons by all whose business and interests were hampered by it. In Flanders the small towns appealed to the Count against the tyranny of the great cities. Even more characteristic was his intervention on behalf of the rural industry which the cities had so relentlessly persecuted. From the reign of Louis de Mâle (1346–84), more and more villages and lordships were granted the right to manufacture cloth. Side by side with the privileged manufacture, which was falling into decline in the great cloth-making cities, there now appeared "the new drapery," which differed from the old both in its technique and in the conditions under which it was carried on. In it Spanish wool took the place of the English wool, which was becoming increasingly scarce as the demand for it grew at home, and light and low-priced cloths took the place of the old "fine cloth." But above all, liberty now replaced privilege in the sphere of manufacture; this young rural industry was quite clearly a capitalist industry, and in it the rigid municipal regulation was replaced by a more elastic system, in which the employee enjoyed complete freedom to enter into a contract and to fix his wages with an employer. Hardly anything was left of the urban economy. The capital which it had sought to fetter was already showing signs, in this rural industry, of the power which it was to wield in the sixteenth century.[28] The same process may be observed in all the new industries which appeared in the fourteenth century, such as tapestry-making and linen-weaving and the first paper manufactures, which were springing up in many parts of Europe at the same time.[29]

In the favour which they showed to the progress of capitalism the kings and princes were not actuated solely by financial considerations. The conception of the State which began to emerge as their power increased, led them to consider themselves as protectors of the "common good." The same fourteenth century which saw urban particularism at its height, also saw the advent of the royal power in the sphere of economic history. Hitherto it had intervened there only indirectly, or rather in pursuance of its judicial, financial and military prerogatives. Though in its capacity as guardian of the public peace it had protected merchants, laid tolls upon commerce, and in case of war placed embargoes on enemy ships and promulgated stoppages of trade, it had left the economic activities of its subjects to themselves. Only the towns made laws and regulations for them. But the competence of the towns was limited by their municipal boundaries, and their particularism caused them to be continually in opposition to each other and made it manifestly impossible for them to take measures to secure the general good, at the possible expense of their individual interests. The princes alone were capable of conceiving a territorial

[28] H. Pirenne, *Une crise économique au XVI⁰ siècle. La draperie urbaine et la nouvelle draperie en Flandre*, in *Bull. de la Classe des Lettres de l'Acad. royale de Belgique* (1905). E. Coornaert, *La Draperie-Sayetterie d'Hondschoote*. Cf. the control exercised by the English clothiers over the cloth industry from the end of the fourteenth century. E. Lipson, *op. cit.*, p. 714 *et seq.*

[29] A. Blum, *Les premières fabriques de papier en Occident*, in *Comptes rendus des séances de l'Académie des Inscriptions*, 1932.

economy, which would comprise and control the urban economies. At the close of the Middle Ages men were, of course, still far from a decided movement, or a conscious policy, directed towards this end. As a rule only intermittent tendencies are to be observed, but they are such as to make it evident that, wherever it had the power, the State was moving in the direction of mercantilism. Obviously the word can only be used within strict limitations, but, alien as the conception of a national economy still was to the governments of the late fourteenth and early fifteenth centuries, it is plain from their conduct that they desired to protect the industry and commerce of their subjects against foreign competition, and even, here and there, to introduce new forms of activity into their countries. In this they were inspired by the example of the towns, and their policy was really no more than the urban policy writ large. It still retained the chief characteristic of that policy, to wit, its protectionism. It was the beginning of a process which in the long run was destined to throw aside medieval internationalism, and to imbue the relations of states with each other with a particularism every whit as exclusive as that of the towns had been for centuries.

The first signs of this evolution showed themselves in England, the country which enjoyed a more powerful and united government than any other. In the first half of the fourteenth century Edward II tried to prohibit the import of foreign cloth, except such as was destined for the use of the nobility. In 1331 Edward III invited Flemish weavers to settle in England. Most significant of all, an Act was passed in 1381 reserving the trade of the country for English ships, an early forerunner of Cromwell's Navigation Act, which it was of course impossible to carry out. The movement became still more active in the fifteenth century. In 1455 the import of silken goods was forbidden in order to protect the native manufacture; in 1463 foreigners were forbidden to export wool; and in 1464 the prohibition of Continental cloth foreshadowed the resolutely protectionist and mercantilist policy of Henry VII (1485–1509), the first modern King of England, which had now become a country in which industry was gaining steadily upon agriculture.[30]

These measures naturally provoked reprisals in the Low Countries, whose most important manufacture suffered from them. Philip the Good, Duke of Burgundy (1419–67), who had united the different territories under his rule, replied by prohibiting the entry of English cloth. But he ruled over a land through which too much trade passed to allow him to content himself with a policy of pure protectionism. He set to work to promote the rising mercantile marine of Holland and to encourage it in a competition with the Teutonic Hanse, which was to be completely successful in the following century.[31] Not only did he encourage the Dutch carrying trade and fishing industry (the latter being favoured by the invention of the herring cask in 1380), but he assisted the rise of the port of Antwerp, which henceforth ousted Bruges from its position of supremacy, and was to become, a century later, the greatest commercial entrepôt in the world.

France was ruined by the Hundred Years' War, and it was not until Louis XI came to the throne that measures were taken to bring about its economic revival. The energy and ability with which he pursued his policy are well known. He ensured the pre-eminence of the fair of Lyons over that of Geneva, tried to acclimatise the silkworm in the kingdom and to introduce the mining industry in Dauphiné, and even thought of organising a kind of exhibition at the French embassy in London, in order that the English "cognussent par effect que les

[30] E. Lipson, *op. cit.*, p. 502. On the protectionist policy of Edward IV (1461–83), see F. R. Salter, *The Hanse, Cologne and the Crisis of 1468*, in *The Economic History Review* (1931), p. 93 *et seq.*

[31] E. Vollbehr, *Die Holländer und die deutsche Hanse* (Lübeck, 1930).

marchands de France estoient puissans pour les fournir comme les autres nations." [32]

The political anarchy which reigned in Germany prevented it, in the absence of central government, from imitating its western neighbours. The capitalist movement which grew at this period in the South German towns, notably in Nuremberg and Augsburg, and to which the prosperity of the mines of Bohemia and the Tyrol is due, owed nothing to the influence of the State. Italy, torn between princes and republics all struggling for supremacy, continued to fall into independent economic areas, two at least of which, Venice and Genoa, were, by reason of their establishments on the Levant, great economic powers. Indeed, the supremacy of Italy in banking and luxury industries was still so marked that it was successfully maintained over the rest of Europe, in spite of her political disunion, until the discovery of new routes to the Indies turned the main current of navigation and commerce from the Mediterranean to the Atlantic.

[32] De Maulde, *Un essai d'exposition internationale en 1470,* in *Comptes rendus des séances de l'Académie des Inscriptions* (1889). For the economic policy of Louis XI, see De la Roncière, *Première guerre entre le protectionnisme et le libre-échange,* in *Revue des questions historiques,* t. LVIII (1895). P. Boissonnade, *Le socialisme d'État. L'industrie et les classes industrielles en France pendant les deux premiers siècles de l'ère moderne* (1453–1551) (Paris, 1927).

GENERAL BIBLIOGRAPHY

There exists no collection of sources specially devoted to economic and social history. But documents of all kinds relating to the latter: polyptycha, terriers, *urbaren,* records, *weistümer,* industrial regulations, accounts of administrative bodies both public and private, correspondence, etc., have been published in every country, and continue to be published in increasing numbers. It would serve no useful purpose to mention them here. The reader will find references to these and other sources for the different countries and periods in the works cited in the course of the following pages.

Moreover, in addition to documents directly concerned with social and economic development, the historian who deals with this subject must necessarily be familiar also with the sources for the general history of the period with which he is dealing. This is particularly true of the Middle Ages, for which a great part of his material is derived as much from annals, chronicles and memoirs as from public and private acts, cartularies, registers, custumals, etc. Thus a complete bibliography of social and economic history would resolve itself into a bibliography of all the sources for the history of the Middle Ages.

The writer has, therefore, been content to set down modern works dealing with economic and social development throughout the Middle Ages, or for a great part of the period, either in general or in a particular country, together with those which trace the general history of a particular aspect of that development. Bibliographies relating to special questions have been added to each chapter.

GENERAL SURVEYS

K. Bücher, *Die Entstehung der Volkswirtschaft* (1893), Tübingen, 7th ed., 1910.

W. Cunningham, *An Essay on Western Civilisation in Its Economic Aspects,* Cambridge, 1898–1900, 2 vols.

M. Kowalewsky, *Die ökonomische Entwickelung Europas bis*

zum Beginn der kapitalistischen Wirtschaftsform (German trans.), Berlin, 1901–14, 7 vols.

A. Dopsch, *Wirtschaftliche und soziale Grundlagen der Euro-*
päischen Kulturentwickelung aus der Zeit von Caesar bis
auf Karl den Grossen, Vienna, 2nd ed., 1923–4, 2 vols.

R. Kötzschke, *Allgemeine Wirtschaftsgeschichte des Mittelalters,*
Jena, 1924.

J. Kulischer, *Allgemeine Wirtschaftsgeschichte des Mittelalters*
und der Neuzeit, Munich-Berlin, 1928–9, 2 vols.

J. W. Thompson, *An Economic and Social History of the*
Middle Ages, New York-London, 1928–31, 2 vols.

M. Knight, *Economic History of Europe to the End of the*
Middle Ages, Cambridge (Mass.), 1926.

WORKS DEALING WITH PARTICULAR COUNTRIES

GERMANY

K. T. von Inama-Sternegg, *Deutsche Wirtschaftsgeschichte,*
Leipzig, 1879–1901, 4 vols. New edition of t. I, 1909.

K. Lamprecht, *Deutsches Wirtschaftsleben im Mittelalter.*
Untersuchungen über die Entwickelung der materiellen
Kultur des platten Landes . . . zunächst des Mosellands,
Leipzig, 1886, 4 vols.

Th. von der Goltz, *Geschichte der deutschen Landwirtschaft,*
Stuttgart, 1902–3, 2 vols.

ENGLAND

W. J. Ashley, *An Introduction to English Economic History*
and Theory, London, 1888–93, 2 vols.

W. Cunningham, *The Growth of English Industry and Com-*
merce, vol. I, Middle Ages, Cambridge, 5th ed., 1910.

E. Lipson, *Economic History of England,* London, vol. I, 5th
ed., 1929.

J. E. T. Rogers, *History of Agriculture and Prices in England,*
vols. I–III, Oxford, 1866–92.

L. F. Salzman, *English Industries of the Middle Ages,* Oxford,
2nd ed., 1923.

BELGIUM

L. Dechesne, *Histoire économique et sociale de la Belgique,*
Paris-Liége, 1932.

FRANCE

H. Pigeonneau, *Histoire du commerce de la France,* Paris,
1885–9, 2 vols.

E. Lavasseur, *Histoire du commerce de la France*, t. I, Paris, 1911.

Id., *Histoire des classes ouvrières et de l'industrie en France avant 1789*, Paris, 2nd ed., 1901.

H. Sée, *Esquisse d'une histoire économique et sociale de la France, des origines jusqu'à la guerre mondiale*, Paris, 1929.

Id., *Les classes rurale et le régime domanial en France au Moyen Age*, Paris, 1901.

Id., *Französische Wirtschaftsgeschichte*, Jena, 1930–36, 2 vols.

G. d'Avenel, *Histoire économique de la propriété, du salaire et des prix* (in France), Paris, 1894–8, 4 vols.

M. Bloch, *Les caractères originaux de l'histoire rurale française*, Paris, 1931.

ITALY

G. Arias, *Il sistema della constituzione economica e sociale italiana nell'età dei communi*, Turin-Rome, 1905.

G. Yver, *Le commerce et les marchands dans l'Italie méridionale au XIIIe et au XIVe siècle*, Paris, 1903.

A. Doren, *Italienische Wirtschaftsgeschichte*, I, Jena, 1934.

SURVEYS OF PARTICULAR SUBJECTS

W. Heyd, *Histoire du commerce du Levant au Moyen Age*, ed. Furcy-Raynaud, Leipzig, 1885–6, 2 vols. (new impression, 1923).

A. Schaube, *Handelsgeschichte der romanischen Völker des Mittelmeergebiets bis zum Ende der Kreuzzüge*, Munich-Berlin, 1906.

L. Goldschmidt, *Universalgeschichte des Handelsrechts*, t. I, Stuttgart, 1891.

P. Huvelin, *Essaie historique sur le droit des marchés et des foires*, Paris, 1897.

P. Boissonnade, *Le travail dans l'Europe chrétienne au Moyen Age*, Paris, 1921.

A. Schulte, *Geschichte des mittelalterlichen Handels und Verkehrs zwischen Westdeutschland und Italien*, Leipzig, 1900, 2 vols.

W. Sombart, *Der Moderne Kapitalismus*, Leipzig, 2nd ed., 1916–27, 4 vols.

PERIODICALS

Vierteljahrschrift für Social-und Wirtschaftsgeschichte, herzg. von L. Aubin, Leipzig (1893–1900, under the title: *Zeitschrift für Social-und Wirtschaftsgeschichte*).

Revue d'histoire économique et sociale, Paris, first published in 1903.

Economic History. A Supplement of the Economic Journal, ed. by J. M. Keynes and D. H. Macgregor, London, first published in 1926.

The Economic History Review, ed. by E. Lipson and R. H. Tawney, 1927–34, and by M. M. Postan from 1934, London, first published in 1927.

Journal of Economic and Business History, ed. by E. F. Gay and N. S. B. Gras, Harvard University, 1928–32.

Annales d'histoire économique et sociale, ed. by M. Bloch and L. Febvre, Paris, first published in 1929.

It is unnecessary to add that economic history occupies an increasingly large place in all historical periodicals.

INDEX OF AUTHORS

GENERAL INDEX